European Yearbook of International Economic Law

Special Issue

The European Yearbook of International Economic Law (EYIEL) is an annual publication in International Economic Law, a field increasingly emancipating itself from Public International Law scholarship and evolving into a fully-fledged academic discipline in its own right. With the yearbook, the editors and publisher intend to make a significant contribution to the development of this "new" discipline and provide an international reference source of the highest possible quality. The EYIEL covers all areas of IEL, in particular WTO Law, External Trade Law for major trading countries, important Regional Economic Integration agreements, International Competition Law, International Investment Regulation, International Monetary Law, International Intellectual Property Protection and International Tax Law. In addition to the regular annual volumes, EYIEL Special Issues routinely address specific current topics in International Economic Law.

Marc Bungenberg • August Reinisch
Editors

New Frontiers for EU Investment Policy

External and Internal Dimensions

Springer

Editors
Marc Bungenberg
Europa-Institut
Saarland University
Saarbrücken, Germany

August Reinisch
University of Vienna
Vienna, Austria

ISSN 2364-8392 ISSN 2364-8406 (electronic)
European Yearbook of International Economic Law
ISSN 2510-6880 ISSN 2510-6899 (electronic)
Special Issue
ISBN 978-3-031-41976-8 ISBN 978-3-031-41977-5 (eBook)
https://doi.org/10.1007/978-3-031-41977-5

This Springer imprint is published by the registered company Springer Nature Switzerland AG
The registered company address is: Gewerbestrasse 11, 6330 Cham, Switzerland

Paper in this product is recyclable.

Preface

This EYIEL Special Issue collects the contributions to a conference that took place at the University of Vienna on 19 and 20 September 2022. It was not the first time that leading experts in the field met in Vienna to discuss the latest developments in EU investment law and policy. Previous conferences on such topics were held in 2012 (Marc Bungenberg, August Reinisch and Christian Tietje (eds.), EU and Investment Agreements. Open Questions and Remaining Challenges, Nomos, 2013), 2013 (Marc Bungenberg and August Reinisch (eds.), Special Issue: The Anatomy of the (Invisible) EU Model BIT, Journal of World Investment & Trade, 2014, Vol. 14(3–4), pp. 375 et seq.) and 2016 (Marc Bungenberg and August Reinisch (eds.), Special Issue: Legal Problems of Intra-EU BITs, Journal of World Investment & Trade, 2016, Vol. 17(6), pp. 871 et seq.) and then again after a longer break (mostly due to the global pandemic) in 2022. We are glad to be able to add a new conference volume to this series, mirroring the gradual developments that can be observed in EU investment law and policy since the entry-into-force of the Lisbon Treaty.

The focus of this conference volume lies on the "internal" and "external" dimensions of EU investment policy that have gradually developed over time. Christoph Schreuer's keynote address provides a general introduction. In his chapter on the "Challenges resulting from the EU's Participation in International Dispute Settlement", he gives an overview of the different roles of the EU institutions in international investment arbitration. He criticises *inter alia* the appearance of the EU Commission as *amicus curiae*, often not really acting as a "friend" of the arbitral tribunal.

In the following four chapters, different aspects of the external dimension of EU investment policy are addressed. August Reinisch advocates for the "Reform of Substantive Standards in a Multilateral Instrument" as the only viable means to create more consistency and predictability in the outcomes of investor-State dispute settlement (ISDS). He argues that even though much attention has been devoted to the topics of consistency and predictability in UNCITRAL Working Group III, a discussion on a single multilateral investment treaty to further this goal has been remarkably absent from the discussion.

The chapter of Marc Bungenberg, Bianca Böhme and Lars Ruf discusses a new development in the relationship between the EU and its Member States. The authors observe that even though EU investment policy is shaped at the central level, its implementation is increasingly carried out at the decentral level by means of the Member States' own investment agreements. After comparing the agreements at the central and decentral levels, the chapter argues that there is a high degree of convergence between EU investment agreements and those concluded by its Member States, but also some limited room for divergence and an "EU-plus approach" in investment law.

Nikos Lavranos defends in his chapter the position that the proposed Multilateral Investment Court fails to address the real concerns of ISDS. He argues that the reform process should focus on the harmonisation of substantive protection standards rather than procedural issues. Moreover, he expresses the view that many of the criticisms raised against ISDS are rather misconceptions than real concerns.

The chapter of Yuriy Pochtovyk and Lukas Stifter deals with the controversial modernisation of the Energy Charter Treaty. The authors describe the modernisation process that resulted in an agreement in principle in June 2022, and the main innovations reflected therein. Despite the uncertain political destiny of the Energy Charter Treaty and its modernisation efforts, the chapter provides valuable thoughts on the question how the threat of climate change may be reconciled with foreign investment in the energy sector.

The last five chapters then turn to the internal dimension of EU investment law and policy. Christina Binder and Philipp Janig analyse the question whether EU investors are provided with sufficient protection under EU law in the face of the dismantling of the system of intra-EU investment arbitration. The authors highlight that the answer to this question will depend on the specific comparator chosen on the side of international investment law. They conclude that potentially lower standards of protection under EU law may not necessarily be undesirable for policy reasons.

After this analysis of substantive investment standards, Christoph Herrmann and Tim Ellemann turn to the topic of how these standards can be enforced under EU law. They point out that the stringent requirements for State liability as established in *Francovich* create greater barriers for claiming monetary compensation before national courts compared to international tribunals. Moreover, the *Francovich* conditions are often not consistently applied by Member State courts, thus further hampering enforcement under EU law.

Nicolaj Kuplewatzky deals in his chapter with the question whether an intra-EU investment court could be a workable post-*Achmea* dispute settlement system for the internal dimension. To that purpose, he analyses the legal feasibility of different policy options: a specialised chamber at the Court of Justice of the European Union, a specialised investment tribunal attached to that institution, the establishment of a self-standing tribunal modelled on the Unified Patent Court or a third body outside the system of judicial remedies of the EU legal order. He concludes that a self-standing intra-EU investment court appears as a legally feasible option.

The chapter of Patricia Nacimiento discusses another milestone in the jurisprudence of the Court of Justice of the European Union when it comes to intra-EU investment arbitration: the decision in *Republic of Poland v. PL Holdings*. This case dealt with a new angle within the intra-EU debate: the validity of arbitration clauses in intra-EU investor-State contracts. The author analyses the decision and argues that it will have considerable implications for investment law practice within the EU.

The final chapter is dedicated to the question whether intra-EU investment mediation could constitute an alternative to intra-EU arbitration. Catherine Kessedjian answers this question in the negative. She argues that mediation is an *additional* means of dispute resolution, but no alternative or substitute. However, if certain barriers are overcome, mediation could become the preferred dispute settlement mechanism in investment matters.

Taken together, all these chapters analysing the internal and external dimensions demonstrate that the EU follows a multi-layered approach towards investment protection, which might be controversial or even contradictory at times. Moreover, the book shows that the shift of competences is no longer at the core of the discussions. Today, the discussions focus on how EU law and policy influence international investment law, *inter alia*, by burying intra-EU investment arbitration, by imposing standards for Member States' BITs and by guiding the multilateral reform efforts.

Saarbrücken, Germany — Marc Bungenberg
Vienna, Austria — August Reinisch

Contents

Challenges Resulting from the EU's Participation in International Dispute Settlement

Christoph Schreuer

Abstract The EU Commission has moved from a supportive attitude towards investment arbitration to outright hostility. The CJEU has developed a practice to the effect that intra-EU investment arbitration is impermissible under EU law. The EU Commission routinely submits *amicus curiae* submissions in intra-EU investment arbitrations. Often these interventions ignore applicable procedural rules and go beyond the role of an *amicus curiae*. Substantively, the EU Commission has argued that EU law takes precedence over other legal obligations and that conflicting treaties must be disapplied. Arguments based on the law of treaties developed by the EU Commission to the effect that investment treaties had become inapplicable have been almost universally rejected by investment tribunals. The Commission, with the support of the CJEU, has also argued that compliance with awards stemming from intra-EU arbitration would be contrary to EU law. In doing so, it has ignored the multilateral nature of obligations under the ICSID Convention.

The EU's attitude towards investor-State dispute settlement has undergone considerable changes. In the 1990s the EU took a decidedly supportive attitude towards investment arbitration within the Community. During the accession process of formerly communist States as new Members, the EU actually prompted the candidates for membership to enter into bilateral investment treaties with existing members. For instance, the Europe Agreement of 1993 between the European Community and Romania[1] in its Article 74(2) specifically foresaw "the conclusion by the Member States and Romania of Agreements for the promotion and protection of investment". The declared aim was to "establish a favourable climate for private investment, both domestic and foreign, which is essential to economic and industrial reconstruction". This led to a series of new BITs of Romania and other accession candidates with existing EU Members which foresaw investor-State arbitration.

[1] In force: 1 February 1995. Romania presented its application for EU membership on 22 June 1995.

C. Schreuer (✉)
Zeiler Floyd Zadkovich, Vienna, Austria
e-mail: christoph.schreuer@investmentlaw.at

M. Bungenberg, A. Reinisch (eds.), *New Frontiers for EU Investment Policy*, Special Issue, https://doi.org/10.1007/978-3-031-41977-5_1

Over the years, the EU, led by the Commission, has changed its attitude towards investor-State arbitration dramatically. Its exact legal position was often unclear. It has oscillated between arguing that the relevant BITs, or at any rate their arbitration provisions, were void, or had become inapplicable, or that the BITs had been terminated through the new States' accession to the EU or that Member States were under an obligation to terminate them.

These various statements are difficult to reconcile but the common denominator of the numerous pronouncements is an increasing hostility towards investment arbitration, especially intra-EU, and a desire to get rid of it by whatever means possible. The clearest expression of this sentiment was a statement by Commissioner Malmström in 2015 when she said that "ISDS is now the most toxic acronym in Europe".

The Commission went further than just arguing against the availability of investor-State arbitration in intra-EU relations. In *Micula* it prohibited payments under an award resulting from an ICSID arbitration. It also started infringement proceedings against EU Member States that had failed to terminate their intra-EU BITs.

The position of the CJEU towards investment arbitration has also shown evolving legal interpretations. In its famous *Achmea* Judgment of March 2018,[2] the Court found that EU law precluded a provision in a bilateral investment treaty between EU Member States under which an investor could bring investment arbitration under the UNCITRAL Rules against a Member State. The relevant provisions of European Law were Article 267 TFEU dealing with preliminary rulings to be requested of the CJEU by courts and tribunals of Member States and Article 344 TFEU under which the Member States undertake to submit disputes concerning the interpretation and application of the European Treaties only to the methods of settlement foreseen in the Treaties.

In *Komstroy*,[3] in September 2021, the European Court extended its rejection of intra-EU investment arbitration to cases pursuant to a multilateral treaty, the ECT. It found that for reasons analogous to those expressed in *Achmea*, Article 26 of the ECT, which provides for investor State arbitration, "must be interpreted as not being applicable to disputes between a Member State and an investor of another Member State".[4] The Court's anxiousness to extend its position on intra-EU arbitration beyond BITs to disputes under the multilateral ECT is best illustrated by the fact that its extensive discussion of the matter was entirely *obiter*. The case concerned Moldova and was hence not intra-EU.

In *PL Holdings*,[5] decided in October 2021, the European Court realized that its condemnation of arbitration clauses in treaties did not fully dispose of intra-EU investment arbitration. In that case the arbitration agreement had come about by the

[2] Case C-284/16, *Slovak Republic v. Achmea BV*, ECLI:EU:C:2018:158.

[3] Case C-741/19, *Republic of Moldova v. Komstroy LLC*, ECLI:EU:C:2021:655.

[4] Ibid., at para 66.

[5] Case C-109/20, *Poland v. PL Holdings Sàrl*, ECLI:EU:C:2021:875.

tacit acceptance of the Tribunal's jurisdiction by the respondent State. The Court found that an *ad hoc* agreement between a Member State and a national of another Member State to settle an investment dispute by arbitration would have the same effect as a treaty-based arbitration clause and was therefore impermissible and invalid. The clear implication is that, in the eyes of the European Court, European Law prohibits not only treaty-based arbitration but also contract based arbitration to settle investment disputes.

Against this background let me say a few words about the participation of the EU Commission as *amicus curiae* in investment arbitration cases. In October 2017, at a conference held in Vienna, an enthusiastic representative of the EU Commission declared that the Commission was intervening in all investment arbitration cases of which it was aware, that these interventions were well-received by tribunals and that tribunals were happy to adopt their conclusions. This announcement made before an expert audience caused surprise and consternation. It is true that the Commission tries to intervene in investment cases whenever possible. Whether these interventions are well-received depends on what you understand by that term. They are certainly treated with politeness. But the assertion that tribunals routinely accept the Commission's position is clearly wrong. In fact, the opposite is true. With one recent exception,[6] tribunals have always rejected the Commission's arguments. The reasons for this dismal record are procedural as well as substantive.

On the procedural side, the challenges arising from the EU Commission's participation as *amicus curiae* in investment arbitration stems from a certain over eagerness in pushing its point. I remember a case, in which the tribunal had not yet been constituted, when the Commission addressed its wish to intervene to the only arbitrator already appointed who curiously was addressed as the '*ad hoc* committee'.

Not infrequently, the Commission raises jurisdictional points before the Respondent has had a chance to make jurisdictional objections. Under the ICSID Arbitration Rules (37(2)) of 2006, however, a non-disputing party may file a submission regarding "a matter within the scope of the dispute". In other words, an *amicus*, if admitted, may comment on matters that are contested between the parties. It may not raise jurisdictional objections and other points on its own initiative.

In an ICSID annulment proceeding, the Commission unsuccessfully sought to make its own application for annulment on grounds that had not been put forward by the party seeking annulment. Nor had the Commission's arguments been before the original tribunal. Apart from the impermissibility of a non-party to the original proceedings to apply for annulment, the Commission also ignored the Convention's deadline for annulment applications.

Generally, the Commission seeks to act in arbitration proceedings in a manner that goes beyond the role of an *amicus curiae*. Not infrequently, the Commission seeks access to documents and attendance at hearings in order to present oral argument. It seeks the full procedural rights of a party to present written and oral arguments, developing its own independent reasoning in the process, and making its

[6] *Green Power Partners v Kingdom of Spain*, SCC Award, 16 June 2022.

own submissions to tribunals and *ad hoc* committees. This, however, is outside the role of an *amicus curiae*.

The ICSID Arbitration Rules require that an *amicus* submission "assist the Tribunal to determine a factual or legal issue related to the proceeding by bringing a perspective, particular knowledge or insight that is different from that of the parties;" The Commission has on numerous occasions stated its position concerning intra-EU investment arbitration. That position is well known to the Parties who are free to adopt it and to present it to the Tribunal. Therefore, it is doubtful whether the Commission can offer knowledge or insights that would be different from those of the Parties.

Under the ICSID Arbitration Rules (67(4)) "[t]he Tribunal shall ensure that the non-disputing party submission does not disrupt the proceeding or unduly burden or unfairly prejudice either party". In actual fact, the Commission is not playing the role of a friend of the court but of an additional party doing advocacy in pursuit of its own agenda. This creates a considerable extra burden in terms of workload and cost. The Tribunal in *Electrabel* v. *Hungary*,[7] after dismissing the EU Commission's submission, pointed to the extra burden that the Commission's intervention had caused:

> the Commission's submissions to the Tribunal (as a "non-disputing party") raised important and extensive issues of jurisdiction and applicable law. These were not issues, particularly as to jurisdiction, raised by Hungary. However, Electrabel had to expend much time and cost to deal with the Commission's submissions. In effect, far from exercising the traditional role of an "amicus curiae", the Commission became a second respondent more hostile to Electrabel than Hungary itself. ... Overall, the Commission's participation in this arbitration was a hugely complicating factor,[8]

It is unclear in what role the EU Commission sees itself when it intervenes in arbitration proceedings. In one case the Commission stated that the Tribunal should have solicited the views of the European Union before making a decision on its jurisdiction. Failure to do so, the Commission argued, would be a serious departure from a fundamental rule of procedure. This suggests that the Commission perceives its position as going beyond that of an *amicus curiae* or even that of a party approximating that of a higher authority.

It is not clear whether the EU Commission's failure to follow procedural rules when intervening in arbitration cases is more the result of ignorance or disdain. A statement by the Commission before a domestic court to the effect that "the ICSID Convention must be ignored in light of the EU primacy principle"[9] suggests contempt rather than unfamiliarity.

Tribunals have reacted politely but firmly to the Commission's attempts to intervene in proceedings. In some cases, they required an undertaking from the Commission that it would bear the resulting additional costs. The Commission's

---

[7] *Electrabel S.A. v Republic of Hungary*, Award, 25 November 2015.

[8] Ibid., at para 234.

[9] Observations of the European Commission to the Bucharest Tribunal of 7 May 2014.

refusal to do so resulted in its exclusion from *amicus curiae* status.[10] In other cases, the Commission's participation was reduced to a written submission of limited length. This did not stop the Commission from making additional submissions.

Substantively, the EU Commission when intervening in investment arbitration adamantly and relentlessly argues that investor-State arbitration is not available in intra-EU relations. To this end it has developed a certain repertoire of arguments that it presents to tribunals. An overarching theme in these arguments is the primacy of EU law which means that the EU treaties take precedence over other legal obligations including those stemming from treaties. If there is a conflict, treaties like the ICSID Convention must be "disapplied".

The most relevant provisions in European Law are said to be Article 267 TFEU dealing with preliminary rulings to be requested of the CJEU by courts and tribunals of Member States and Article 344 TFEU under which the Member States undertake to submit disputes concerning the interpretation and application of the European Treaties only to the methods of settlement foreseen in the Treaties.

The Commission also seeks to rely on arguments derived from international law, notably the Vienna Convention on the Law of Treaties. To give a flavour of the EU Commission's arguments and the reaction of tribunals thereto let me focus on the Commission's recurrent argument that the relevant rules of European law prevail because they are later in time—*lex posterior*. The Treaty of Lisbon of 2007 (in force 2009), which codified the relevant principles of EU law would be later in time and would hence prevail over treaties providing for investment arbitration. This would follow from Article 59 of the VCLT which provides for the termination or suspension of a treaty through the conclusion of a later treaty and from Article 30 of the VCLT dealing with the application of successive treaties relating to the same subject-matter.

Tribunals have uniformly rejected these arguments as unsound. In relation to the ECT, which entered into force in 1998, they have held that the critical provisions of EU law Articles 267 and 344, although they were repeated and renumbered through the Treaty of Lisbon in the TFEU in 2009, have existed in substantially similar form since the 1957 Treaty of Rome. Therefore, it could not be said that the relevant provisions of European Law were later in time in relation to the ECT.[11] The fact that a preexisting treaty provision is recast and renumbered in a newly named treaty does not make it a 'later treaty' for purposes of the provisions on successive treaties in the VCLT.

In addition, the ECT contains a specific provision in its Article 16 governing its relation to other agreements. It provides that, irrespective of timing, the provisions more favourable to the investor is to prevail. Although the EU Commission contends that EU law offers "complete, strong and effective protection of their investments",

---

[10] *Watkins v Spain*, Award, 21 January 2020, paras 30–40.

[11] *Vattenfall v Germany*, Decision on the Achmea Issue, 31 August 2018, para 218; *Renergy v Spain*, Award, 6 May 2022, para 389.

tribunals have found that direct access to international arbitration was more favourable to investors.

Even in relation to BITs that had entered into force before one of the parties had become a Member of the EU, the Commission's reliance on the principle of *lex posterior*, as expressed on Articles 30 and 59 of the VCLT, was not successful. The operation of Articles 30 and 59 require that the successive treaties relate to the same subject-matter and that they are incompatible.

Tribunals have rejected the argument that treaties between EU Member States providing for investment arbitration had become inapplicable by virtue of subsequent provisions of EU law. They have held that the provisions of EU law and the arbitration provisions in the BITs and the ECT did not address the same subject-matter.[12] They also held that the two sets of provisions were not incompatible.[13] Rather, there was a situation of complementarity of the substantive norms.[14]

The Tribunal in *UP and C.D v Hungary*, said:

> The BIT and the TFEU do not relate to the same subject matter, and this renders Art. 59(1)(b) of the VCLT (implicit termination of an earlier treaty by a subsequent one) and Art. 30(3) of the VCLT (inapplicability of incompatible provisions in the earlier treaty) inapplicable. The *lex posterior* rule of Art. 30 of the VCLT does not apply because neither requirement – (1) the existence of a fundamental incompatibility between provisions of two successively ratified treaties, or (2) that the two rules in conflict have the same subject matter – is fulfilled. Respondent has failed to demonstrate that a fundamental or material incompatibility exists between Art. 9(2) of the BIT and the TFEU.[15]

With respect to the ECT, the EU Commission has argued the existence of an implicit disconnection clause. It argued that a tacit understanding would have to be read into the ECT that its investor-State dispute settlement clause did not apply as between EU Members and nationals of other EU Members. During the ECT's drafting, the EU had proposed the explicit insertion of such a disconnection clause, but the clause was ultimately dropped from the draft treaty.[16] Tribunals have decided that neither the ECT's ordinary meaning nor the systematic analysis of its provisions allowed the

---

[12] *Eastern Sugar* v. *Czech Republic*, Partial Award, 27 March 2007, para. 180; *Oostergetel* v. *Slovakia*, Decision on Jurisdiction, 30 April 2010, para. 104; *Marfin v Cyprus*, Award, 26 July 2018, paras 583–595; *NextEra v Spain*, Decision on Jurisdiction, Liability and Quantum Principles, 12 March 2019, para 352; *Eskosol v Italy*, Decision on Italy's Request for Immediate Termination, 7 May 2019, paras 127–147; *OperaFund v Spain*, Award, 6 September 2019, para 383; *BayWa v Spain*, Decision on Jurisdiction and Liability, 2 December 2019, paras 272–273; *Micula v Romania II*, Award, 5 March 2020, paras 273–281.

[13] *Electrabel v Hungary*, Decision on Jurisdiction, Applicable Law and Liability, 30 November 2012, para 4.191; *Blusun v Italy*, Award, 12 December 2016, paras 229–303; *United Utilities v Estonia*, Award, 21 June 2019, paras 544–566; *Belenergia v Italy*, Award, 6 August 2019, paras 320–321.

[14] *Eureko* v. *Slovakia*, Award on Jurisdiction, Arbitrability and Suspension, 26 October 2010, paras. 268–277.

[15] *UP and C.D v Hungary*, Award, 9 October 2018, para 218.

[16] *Vattenfall et al v Germany*, Decision on the *Achmea* Issue, 31 August 2018, para 205; *Renergy v Spain*, Award, 6 May 2022, para 368.

conclusion that intra-EU claims were removed from ECT dispute settlement. Tribunals have declared unanimously that such a disconnection clause with regard to intra-EU claims could not be implicit but would have to be express and clear.[17]

The EU Commission has not just denied the permissibility of intra-EU arbitration proceedings but has argued that compliance with awards resulting from such arbitrations may constitute unlawful State aid and would be contrary to EU law.[18]

The Commission's rejection of intra-EU investment arbitration received support from the CJEU in a Judgement of January 2022. The Court underpinned its position by describing consent to investment arbitration in the following terms:

> Such consent, unlike that which would have been given in commercial arbitration proceedings, does not originate in a specific agreement reflecting the freely expressed wishes of the parties concerned, but derives from a treaty concluded between two States in the context of which they have, generally and in advance, agreed to exclude from the jurisdiction of their own courts disputes which may concern the interpretation or application of EU law in favour of arbitration proceedings.[19]

I have serious doubts whether this is an accurate description of consent pursuant to an arbitration clause in a treaty. Consent to arbitration under a treaty does originate from a specific agreement between the parties to the arbitration. It is given through the acceptance by the investor of the offer to arbitrate contained in the treaty. This leads to a specific agreement between the host State and the investor. Also, the offer of arbitration contained in the treaty does not exclude disputes from the jurisdiction of the host State's courts. It merely adds an additional option for dispute settlement that is open to the investor.

More important are the consequences of a prohibition to comply with awards under the ICSID Convention. Can it be said that the obligation to abide by and comply with an award does not apply as between Member States of the EU? At first sight Article 41 of the VCLT would open the possibility to modify a multilateral treaty as between certain of its parties only. But that possibility only exists if the modification "does not affect the enjoyment by the other parties of their rights under the treaty or the performance of their obligations".

The Commission has argued that the ICSID Convention merely creates a bundle of bilateral international obligations between the investor's home State and the host

---

[17] *Renergy v Spain*, Award, 6 May 2022, paras 367–370, 410 with references to earlier decisions.

[18] *Masdar v Spain*, Award, 16 May 2018, paras 296–341; *Vattenfall v Germany II*, Decision on the *Achmea* Issue, 31 August 2018, paras 48–59; *Adamakopoulos v Cyprus*, Decision on Jurisdiction, 7 February 2020, paras 50–63; *Addiko Bank v Croatia*, Decision on Croatia's Jurisdictional Objection Related to the Alleged Incompatibility of the BIT with the *EU Acquis*, 12 June 2020, paras 62–65, 125–131, 136–143. See also Declaration of EU Member States of 15 January 2019 on the Legal Consequences of the *Achmea* Judgment and on Investment Protection (and Declaration of 5 EU Member States on 16 January 2019 as well as the separate Declaration of Hungary on 16 January 2019).

[19] Judgment of 25 January 2022 in Case C-638/19P, para 144. The Court refers back to its judgments in *Achmea* and *Komstroy*.

State. Since these rights can be bilateralised, the Commission argues, rights of third countries are not at stake.

A multilateral treaty like the ICSID Convention, however, cannot be broken down into discrete bilateral relationships. It is more than a bundle of bilateral rights and obligations. The International Court of Justice has recognized that under certain multilateral treaties the "common interest implies that the obligations in question are owed by any State party to all the other States parties to the Convention." It speaks of "obligations *erga omnes partes*".[20]

The ICSID Convention contains several obligations that are owed to all parties. First and foremost is the exclusive remedies rule of Article 26: unless otherwise stated, consent to ICSID arbitration excludes other remedies in all member States. Article 53 of the ICSID Convention provides that each party shall abide by and comply with the terms of an award. All States parties to the ICSID Convention have an interest in the compliance with awards and every State party to the Convention may demand that other States parties meet their obligations under the Convention including compliance with awards.[21]

Most importantly, Article 54 of the ICSID Convention imposes a general duty on all participating States to recognize and enforce ICSID awards. That duty applies not only to the State party to the proceedings and to the State who's national was a party to the proceedings. Recognition and enforcement of an award may be sought in any State party to the ICSID Convention. Therefore, all States parties to the ICSID Convention, whether they are home States of investors or not, have not merely a right to demand compliance with an award but also a duty to cooperate in its enforcement.

The duty to comply with an award and the duty to recognize and enforce an award are obligations that operate vis-à-vis the entire membership of the ICSID Convention. Non-compliance with an award and failure to enforce an award have legal consequences not only in relation to the award creditor and its State of nationality.

Non-compliance with an award triggers the obligation of all other States parties to the ICSID Convention to participate in its recognition and enforcement. Therefore, the duty of all States parties to the ICSID Convention to enforce these obligations also means that they are affected by any non-compliance with an award.

In the same manner, any failure of a Party to the ICSID Convention to live up to its obligation to enforce an award has repercussions on other States parties to the Convention. Non-enforcement by a Party means that the duty to enforce will devolve upon other States parties to the Convention. Failure of a State party to the Convention to recognize and enforce an award affects all other States parties and would be a breach of a treaty obligation.

The Supreme Court of the United Kingdom in a Judgment of 19 February 2020 has aptly described the multilateral nature of the obligation under Article 54 of the

---

[20] *Questions relating to the Obligation to Prosecute or Extradite (Belgium v Senegal)*, Judgment, 20 July 2012, I.C.J. Reports (2012), p 422, paras 68, 69.

[21] Schreuer et al. (2009), Article 53, para 46; Schill et al. (2022), Article 53, para 57.

ICSID Convention to enforce an award. It found that the ICSID Convention creates a network of mutual enforcement obligations and that a Contracting State which has obligations under the Convention in relation to an award owes those obligations to all other States party to the Convention.[22]

Interestingly, European Law recognizes that rights and obligations vis-à-vis non-EU States arising from treaties concluded by EU Member States before their accession to the EU, remain unaffected by the EU Treaties (Article 351(1) of the TFEU).

This result is confirmed also by customary international law. The *Articles on Responsibility of States for Internationally Wrongful Acts* adopted by the International Law Commission in 2001 ('ILC Articles on State Responsibility')[23] contain a provision that specifically addresses this situation. It deals with the rights of States not immediately affected by the breach of a duty towards a group of States, or the international community as a whole.

Article 48 of the ILC Articles on State Responsibility entitled *Invocation of responsibility by a State other than an injured State* states that

> 1. Any State other than an injured State is entitled to invoke the responsibility of another State [in accordance with paragraph 2] if:
>
> (*a*) the obligation breached is owed to a group of States including that State, and is established for the protection of a collective interest of the group

As the ILC points out in its Commentary, a State acting under this rule is acting to protect the collective interest of the group of States that transcends the sphere of bilateral relations of the States parties. The collective interest of States participating in the ICSID Convention requires the effective compliance with and enforcement of awards rendered under the auspices of ICSID and the payment of debts under these awards.

Let me make some concluding remarks:

Despite its poor rate of success in investment arbitrations, ultimately the Commission's standpoint will prevail. Sooner or later Member States will terminate intra-EU BITs despite reluctance from some of them. The process to revise or to 'modernize' the ECT will most likely result in an explicit exclusion of intra-EU investment arbitration. These developments are not driven by legal considerations but are part of a political agenda.

The EU, including the Commission, has rightly expressed concern about the erosion of the rule of law in some Member States and has taken action against these States. It should not be allowed to apply double standards by simultaneously abolishing indispensable procedural and substantive protections on the international level. The argument that existing European Law and domestic courts offer an equivalent or even superior level of protection to investors is based on a fiction. In

[22] United Kingdom Supreme Court, *Micula and others v Romania*, [2020] UKSC 5, Judgment, 19 February 2020, paras 104–108.

[23] Crawford (2002).

investment disputes, the principles of mutual trust and sincere cooperation sound hollow to investors who seek protection.

Recently, there has been much discussion about the need to promote renewable energy production especially through the creation and expansion of wind parks and solar power. These efforts require massive investments by private investors. Numerous cases, especially against Spain and Italy, have shown that these investments are vulnerable to the vagaries of changing political trends and the *ex post facto* abolition of incentives that motivated the investments in renewable energy. The withdrawal of even the basic protection offered by BITs and the ECT will send a disastrous signal to potential investors. These investors will find that they cannot assume an incalculable risk without the safety net of international standards enforceable by international tribunals. The abolition of these standards and protections so fervently pursued by the Commission will be a serious obstacle to the transition to renewable sources of energy.

The promotion of investments by way of treaties like BITs or the ECT is not the only way to create the necessary safeguards. An effective system of protection of investments through a mechanism within the EU is clearly an alternative.

The construction of a new edifice may require the demolition of old structures. So far, however, the Commission has focussed on dismantling the existing methods to protect and promote investments. It is time that we start planning the construction of a new system of protection. I hope that this conference will point the way towards a more constructive approach in this endeavour.

References

Crawford J (2002) The international law commission's articles on state responsibility. CUP
Schill S et al (2022) Schreuer's commentary on the ICSID convention, 3rd edn. CUP
Schreuer C et al (2009) The ICSID convention: a commentary, 2d edn, CUP

Reform of Substantive Standards in a Multilateral Instrument and the Rule of Law

August Reinisch

Contents

Abstract The consistency and predictability of outcomes is a core rule of law-requirement for any form of dispute setlement. The fairly rapid development of investor-state dispute settlement (ISDS), with mostly *ad hoc* arbitral tribunals deciding on the basis of differently formulated investment agreements, has led to sometimes inconsistent outcomes. So far, attempts to foster predictable outcomes have focused on procedural measures, such as creating an appellate mechanisms or an investment court or giving the parties to investment agreements more control by providing them with authentic treaty interpretation powers. It seeem though that, ultimately, consistency can only be reached by harmonizing the applicable investment standards.

I am grateful for the research assistance of Nina Öllinger and Johannes Tropper.

A. Reinisch (✉)
University of Vienna, Vienna, Austria
e-mail: august.reinisch@univie.ac.at

M. Bungenberg, A. Reinisch (eds.), *New Frontiers for EU Investment Policy*, Special Issue, https://doi.org/10.1007/978-3-031-41977-5_2

1 Introduction

This chapter looks at a core rule of law requirement that has impacted the ongoing debate about investor-state dispute settlement (ISDS) for quite some time, the quest for consistency and predictability in the outcomes of ISDS. That the law is sufficiently clear and precise and will be applied by adjudicators in a manner that is coherent and predictable are essential rule of law requirements.

The rapidly developing investment arbitration practice of the last two to three decades has often demonstrated that similar, but also similarly vague standards of protection contained in a myriad of mostly bilateral, and sometimes multilateral, international investment agreements (IIAs) can be applied and interpreted in divergent ways. Almost inevitably, decisions and awards have not been fully consistent and left the users of the system at a loss when it came to predict the possible outcomes of future disputes.

Such concerns have contributed to calls for a reform of the ISDS system. Especially, UNCITRAL Working Group III has devoted much attention to the topic of consistency and proposed various solutions, such as making IIAs more clear and precise, increasing the role of contracting parties in "authentic" treaty interpretation, improving the existing review and annulment mechanisms, and enhancing the role of domestic courts. What is remarkably absent is a call for a coherent, single, multilateral investment treaty with clear and precise protection standards to ensure consistency and predictability of outcomes.

Given the successful example of the reform of the international trade law system from a GATT *à la carte* to the single undertaking approach of the WTO this is surprising. But it seems that since the aborted OECD attempt to negotiate a Multilateral Agreement on Investment (MAI) in the 1990s the issue of a multilateral investment agreement has been the elephant in the room for those discussing reforms of the ISDS system with a view to creating more consistent and predictable outcomes. No one wants to see it and to recognize that in respect of a number of the actual and perceived inconsistency issues a multilateral agreement would be a real cure, albeit not a panacea for all reform issues.

2 Consistency as a Rule of Law Requirement

It is undisputed that a certain level of consistency and predictability of dispute settlement outcomes is part of any concept of the rule of law.[1] However, as has been rightly pointed out the concept of the rule of law is a contested one.[2] It is contested as a Western concept imposing a Washington consensus-dominated, free

[1] See, e.g., Raz (1979), pp. 214–215; Waldron (2016).

[2] Chesterman (2008), pp. 331, 340.

market-ideology on countries adhering to other value systems.[3] It is thus important to ascertain elements of the rule of law in order to determine to what extent they form part of a universal or at least broadly shared concept.

It is submitted that the most promising avenue for identifying a rule of law concept that is accepted on a broad basis by all or at least virtually all states is to be guided by the rule of law notion used in the United Nations (UN).[4] The UN's General Assembly annually adopts rule of law resolutions by consensus.[5] In the UN context, debates focus on the existence and relevance of the rule of law on the international level. In this context, implementation of judgments of the International Court of Justice (ICJ)[6] as well as acceptance of its contentious jurisdiction are central.[7] However, and more important for the rule of law in ISDS, the UN has also addressed the rule of law at the national level.

An already fairly precise and important definition of the rule of law is contained in the UN Secretary-General 2004 Report on the Rule of Law and Transitional Justice in Conflict and Post-Conflict Societies.[8] As the name suggests, this Report focuses on the rule of law not on the international level, but rather on the national level. The Report refers, inter alia, to

> [...] the demands of equal enforcement and independent adjudication of legal rules and principles as well as fairness in the application of the law, legal certainty, the avoidance of arbitrariness and procedural and legal transparency.[9]

---

[3]Waldron (2007), pp. 91, 118; Cejie (2022), pp. 287, 293.

[4]See also ILA Committee on the Rule of Law and International Investment Law (2018), p. 380.

[5]See, e.g., United Nations General Assembly, The Rule of Law at the National and International Levels, A/RES/69/123, 18 December 2014; United Nation General Assembly, The Rule of Law at the National and International Levels, A/RES/76/117, 9 December 2021.

[6]See, e.g., United Nations General Assembly, Millennium Declaration, A/RES/55/2, 18 September 2000, para. 9 (UN Member States resolving to 'strengthen respect for the rule of law in international as in national affairs and, in particular, to ensure compliance by Member States with the decisions of the International Court of Justice, in compliance with the Charter of the United Nations, in cases to which they are parties.').

[7]United Nations General Assembly, Declaration of the High-level Meeting of the General Assembly on the Rule of Law at the National and International Levels, A/RES/67/1, 30 November 2012, para. 32 ('We recognize the positive contribution of the International Court of Justice, the principal judicial organ of the United Nations, including in adjudicating disputes among States, and the value of its work for the promotion of the rule of law; we reaffirm the obligation of all States to comply with the decisions of the International Court of Justice in cases to which they are parties; and we call upon States that have not yet done so to consider accepting the jurisdiction of the International Court of Justice in accordance with its Statute.').

[8]*See* United Nations Security Council, *Report of the Secretary-General on the Rule of Law and Transitional Justice in Conflict and Post-Conflict Societies,* S/2004/616, 23 August 2004.

[9]United Nations Security Council, *Report of the Secretary-General on the Rule of Law and Transitional Justice in Conflict and Post-Conflict Societies,* S/2004/616, 23 August 2004, para. 6 ('The "rule of law" is a concept at the very heart of the Organization's mission. It refers to a principle of governance in which all persons, institutions and entities, public and private, including the State itself, are accountable to laws that are publicly promulgated, equally enforced and independently adjudicated, and which are consistent with international human rights norms and

While there is often an emphasis on the fair trial aspects of adjudication inherent in ISDS, also the rule of law requirement addressed at the quality of the applicable law itself is important. Legal certainty, consistency and predictability of the law are inherently necessary in order to speak of a law that is equally applied to those that are subject to it. It was quite correctly summarized in the 2018 UNCITRAL Secretariat note "that consistency and coherence would support the rule of law, enhance confidence in the stability of the investment environment and further bring legitimacy to the regime."[10] It is thus not surprising to find repeated calls for consistency in the efforts of Working Group III on ISDS Reform.[11]

A survey by the Subcommittee on Investment Treaty Arbitration of the International Bar Association published in 2016 also found that 'substantive inconsistency was a concern'[12] but noted that survey participants[13] 'indicated that an appellate mechanism or increased state participation in multilateral treaties might address that concern.'[14]

The link between the need for consistency, legal certainty and rule of law has also been explicitly acknowledged by some arbitral tribunals. The ICSID tribunal in *Saipem v. Bangladesh* pointed out that

> [. . .] it must pay due consideration to earlier decisions of international tribunals. Specifically, it deems that, subject to compelling contrary grounds, it has a *duty to adopt solutions established in a series of consistent cases*. It further deems that, subject to the specific provisions of a given treaty and of the circumstances of the actual case, it *has a duty to contribute to the harmonious development of investment* law, with a view to meeting the

standards. It requires, as well, measures to ensure adherence to the principles of supremacy of law, equality before the law, accountability to the law, fairness in the application of the law, separation of powers, participation in decision-making, legal certainty, avoidance of arbitrariness and procedural and legal transparency.').

[10] Possible reform of investor-State dispute settlement (ISDS): Consistency and related matters, Note by the Secretariat, dated 28 August 2018, A/CN.9/WG.III/WP.150, para. 5. See also ibid., para. 28.

[11] See, e.g., Possible reform of investor-state dispute settlement (ISDS): Multilateral instrument on ISDS reform, Note by the Secretariat, dated 16 January 2020, A/CN.9/WG.III/WP.194, para. 12 ("The Working Group may wish to consider that the multilateral instrument could be conceived so as to contribute to more consistency and coherence in respect of those norms that are shared."); see also Report of Working Group III (Investor-State Dispute Settlement Reform) on the work of its forty-third session (Vienna, 5-16 September 2022), dated 7 October 2022, A/CN.9/1124, para. 100 ("Considering the support expressed to continue work on the assessment of damages and compensation, the Working Group requested the Secretariat to draft text comprised of draft provisions and guidelines that could address concerns about correctness and consistency, as well as cost and duration, that damages and compensation presented.").

[12] IBA Subcommittee on Investment Treaty Arbitration, 'Report on the Subcommittee's Investment Treaty Arbitration survey' (May 2016) https://www.arbitragem.pt/xms/files/Estudos_da_APA/report-subcommittee-investment-treaty-arbitration-survey-may-2016.pdf, 2.

[13] Ibid., 1 (109 individuals with experience in investment arbitration in one capacity or another provided responses).

[14] Ibid., 2.

> legitimate expectations of the community of States and investors towards *certainty of the rule of law*.[15]

The tribunal in *Kruck v. Spain* emphasized that

> [...] the consistency and predictability of legal decisions is a goal of the most fundamental importance. No tribunal is an island entire of itself. It is one element of a much more extensive, evolving system for the protection of parties' rights; and individual tribunals are, rightly, slow to depart from principles and analyses that are generally accepted and established within the system. This axiomatic point has a particular poignancy in investment arbitration, given the roles placed by the principles of non-discrimination and of fair and equitable treatment within the applicable substantive law.[16]

3 Lack of Consistency and Predictability of ISDS Outcomes as Major Point of Criticism

Turning to the present state of investment law, it becomes quickly evident that predictability and consistency of the law are sometimes problematic on two levels.

On the one hand, there is not one single body of investment law to be applied.[17] Rather, tribunals have to apply numerous bilateral investment treaties, sometimes multilateral agreements and often national investment protection legislation. Currently, there are roughly 2200 BITs and numerous multilateral investment agreements in force.[18] When looking at statistical surveys it appears that over the last decade roughly 350 BITs and almost 10 multilateral investment agreements[19]

---

[15] *Saipem S.p.A. v. The People's Republic of Bangladesh*, ICSID Case No. ARB/05/07, Decision on Jurisdiction and Recommendation on Provisional Measures, 21 March 2007, para. 67; *Planet Mining Pty Ltd v. Republic of Indonesia*, ICSID Case No. ARB/12/14 and 12/40, Decision on Jurisdiction, 24 February 2014, para. 85 (emphasis added). See also *Renée Rose Levy and Gremcitel S.A. v. Republic of Peru*, ICSID Case No. ARB/11/17, Award, 9 January 2015, para. 76; *Horthel Systems BV, Poland Gaming Holding BV and Tesa Beheer BV v. Republic of Poland*, PCA Case No. 2014-31, Final Award, 16 February 2017, para. 92.

[16] *Mathias Kruck and others v. Kingdom of Spain*, ICSID Case No. ARB/15/23, Decision on Jurisdiction and Admissibility, 19 April 2021, para. 115.

[17] See e.g. De Brabandere (2012), pp. 245, 272 ('Since every dispute needs to be solved according to the specific rules applicable to that particular dispute –mainly the contract and the bilateral investment treaty- it is indeed not surprising, in principle, to have divergent case law.' [footnote omitted]). See also Report of Working Group III (Investor-State Dispute Settlement Reform) on the work of its thirty-fourth session (Vienna, 27 November–1 December 2017), dated 26 February 2018, A//CN.9/930/Add.1/Rev.1, para. 13 ('The fragmented nature of the underlying investment treaties, as well as the ad hoc nature of arbitration, in which individual tribunals were tasked with interpreting investment treaties, were mentioned as contributing to a lack of consistency and predictability in outcomes.').

[18] International Investment Agreement Navigator, available at https://investmentpolicy.unctad.org/international-investment-agreements.

[19] In particular, ECT; NAFTA; OIC Agreement; USMCA; CIS Investor Rights Convention; Treaty of the Eurasian Economic Union; Eurasian Investment Agreement; Arab Investment Agreement; CAFTA-DR.

have been, sometimes repeatedly, invoked as bases for investment claims in ISDS.[20]

Although these separate treaties often contain relatively similarly phrased protection standards, there are also often significant differences in their wording. To provide just a few examples: some IIAs protect "investments made in accordance with host state law",[21] others do not;[22] some IIAs oblige parties to offer national and most favoured national treatment "in their territory,"[23] others do not;[24] some provide for FET or FPS pursuant to the international minimum standard[25] others conceive them as autonomous standards;[26] some umbrella clauses expressly speak of commitments made by host states to investors,[27] others do not contain such a limitation;[28] some MFN clauses refer to all matters regulated in an IIA,[29] others are more limited.[30] As will be seen in a moment, differences in wording entail different outcomes.

---

[20] Investment Dispute Settlement Navigator, available at https://investmentpolicy.unctad.org/investment-dispute-settlement.

[21] Art 1(b) Türkiye-Romania BIT (2010) ('"Investment" means in conformity with the national laws and regulations of the hosting Contracting Party every kind of asset and includes but not inclusively: [. . .]').

[22] Art 1 Rwanda-United States of America BIT (2008) ('"investment" means every asset that an investor owns or controls, directly or indirectly, that has the characteristics of an investment, including such characteristics of an investment, including such characteristics as the commitment of capital or other resources, the expectation of gain or profit, or the assumption of risk.').

[23] Article 4(2) Australia-India BIT (1999) ('A Contracting Party shall at all times treat investments in its own territory on a basis no less favourable than that accorded to investments or investors of any third country.').

[24] Article 3(1) Austria-Ukraine BIT (1996) ('Each Contracting Party shall accord to investors of the other Contracting Party and their investments treatment no less favourable than that which it accords to its own investors and their investments or to investors in third States and their investments.').

[25] Article 1105 North American Free Trade Agreement (1992) ('Each Party shall accord to investments of investors of another Party treatment in accordance with international law, including fair and equitable treatment and full protection and security.').

[26] Article 2(2) German Model BIT (2004) ('Each Contracting State shall in its territory in any case accord investments by investors of the other Contracting State fair and equitable treatment as well as full protection under the Treaty.').

[27] Article 10(1) Energy Charter Treaty (1994) ('Each Contracting Party shall observe any obligations it has entered into with an Investor or an Investment of an Investor of any other Contracting Party.').

[28] Article II(2)(c) Argentina-US BIT (1991) ('Each Party shall observe any obligation it may have entered into with regard to investments.').

[29] Article IV (2) Argentina-Spain BIT (1991) ('In all matters governed by this Agreement, such treatment shall be not less favourable than that accorded by each Party to investments made in its territory by investors of a third country.').

[30] Article 4(1) Canadian Model FIPA (2004) ('Each Party shall accord to investors of the other Party treatment no less favourable than that it accords, in like circumstances, to investors of a non-Party with respect to the establishment, acquisition, expansion, management, conduct, operation, and sale or other disposition of investments in its territory.').

On the other hand, the law to be applied is not applied by a single adjudicator in the currently prevailing system of ISDS. Usually, there are three different arbitrators for each single dispute in investment arbitration, rendering awards that cannot be appealed and that do not have any precedential value for subsequent arbitration proceedings.

It was thus no surprise that with the growing 'case-law' of investment tribunals their interpretations of standards started to diverge. In fact, the problem of inconsistent outcomes has been one of the 'oldest' points of criticism voiced against ISDS.[31] With a rather high number of investment decisions in a relatively short period of time, the risk of divergent interpretations of similar and, even worse, of sometimes even identical treaty provisions started to materialize, first in regard to the scope of MFN clauses,[32] then as to the content of the inherent notion of 'investment' pursuant to Article 25 of the ICSID Convention,[33] the requirements for a respondent state to invoke state of necessity,[34] the reach of umbrella clauses,[35] and other issues, many of which have the potential to be decisive for the outcome of ISA.

In some situations, the inconsistency was even aggravated in situations where different investment tribunals came to diverging conclusions in regard to the same facts, as in the well-known *CME/Lauder* cases.[36]

4 Lessons from Trade Law

The problem of inconsistent outcomes was well known in pre-WTO trade law.

The GATT 1947 was an improvised rescue package for the unsuccessful attempt to create an International Trade Organization.[37] In a remarkable development the provisionally applied GATT 1947[38] provided the framework and the main

[31] *See* Arato et al. (2020), p. 336; De Luca et al. (2020), p. 374.

[32] *Emilio Agustín Maffezini* v. *The Kingdom of Spain*, ICSID Case No. ARB/97/7, Decision on Jurisdiction, 25 January 2000; Gaillard (2005), p. 105; Douglas (2011), p. 97; Maupin (2011), p. 157; Paparinskis (2011), pp. 14–58; Schill (2011), p. 353.

[33] *See* Manciaux (2008), p. 443; Schreuer et al. (2009), p. 128 et seq.; Reinisch (2010), p. 749; Dupont (2011), p. 245; Dolzer and Schreuer (2012), p. 44 *et seq.*

[34] *See* Burke-White and von Staden (2007), p. 307; Reinisch (2007), p. 191; Schill (2007), p. 265; Waibel (2007), p. 637; Bjorklund (2008a), p. 495; Alvarez and Khamsi (2009), p. 379; Binder (2009), p. 608; Bjorklund (2009), p. 479; see also Reinisch and Tropper (2022), p. 119.

[35] *See* Alexandrov (2004), p. 555; Schreuer (2004), p. 231; Sinclair (2004), p. 411; Wälde (2005), p. 183.

[36] *Ronald S. Lauder* v. *The Czech Republic*, UNCITRAL, Final Award, 3 September 2001; *CME Czech Republic B.V.* v. *The Czech Republic*, UNCITRAL, Partial Award, 13 September 2001. *See* Brower and Sharpe (2003), p. 211; Reinisch (2004), p. 37.

[37] *See* Van den Bossche and Zdouc (2022), p. 88 *et seq.*

[38] Protocol of Provisional Application of the GATT 1947, 55 UNTS 308 ("1. The Governments of [...] undertake, provided that this Protocol shall have been signed on behalf of all the foregoing Governments not later than 15 November 1947, to apply provisionally on and after 1 January 1948:

substantive rules governing relations among states. Over decades though, additional side agreements were entered into which bound only a limited number of GATT contracting parties.[39] This phenomenon led to what is also known as GATT *à la carte*,[40] a situation where it became increasingly difficult to ascertain which precise rules governed trade relations between specific parties.

One of the major goals of reforming the international trade system during the Uruguay Round was to increase predictability and security. The approach was to eliminate GATT *à la carte* as far as possible and to create a uniform body of rules. This was referred to as the WTO's 'single undertaking approach.'[41] The resulting GATT 1994 plus its side agreements which had to be accepted as a whole—thus 'single undertaking' approach—achieved a remarkably high degree of consistency in regard to the applicable law. Only few so-called plurilateral agreements were not part of this package and could thus be selectively adhered to by WTO Members.[42]

The unification of the applicable rules was complemented by a dispute settlement reform. Instead of merely *ad hoc* panels as under the previous GATT system, the WTO introduced a two-tiered dispute settlement system with panels as—still *ad hoc*—first instance adjudicatory bodies and an Appellate Body consisting of only seven members who sit in chambers of three to decide on appeals. This latter body was introduced with the express aim of dispute settlement to guarantee consistency and predictability of outcomes.[43] While it is undeniable that the WTO dispute settlement system has been subject to sharp criticism, being accused adjudicatory activism,[44] the first two decades of the WTO dispute settlement clearly brought about an increase in consistency, stemming from the parallel approach of unifying the applicable law and the adjudicatory system.[45]

(a) Parts I and III of the General Agreement on Tariffs and Trade, and (b) Part II of that Agreement to the fullest extent not inconsistent with existing legislation. [. . .] DONE at Geneva, in a single copy, in the English and the French languages, both texts authentic, this thirtieth day of October one thousand nine hundred and forty-seven.").

[39] These side agreements are often referred to as 'codes' *see* Kennedy (1997), p. 421 f. Topics were government procurement, subsidies and dumping, product standards, customs valuation and import licensing *see* Zeiler (2012), p. 114 f.

[40] Mavroidis (2008), p. 24; Hoekman and Mavroidis (2015).

[41] WTO, 'Ministerial Declaration' (World Trade Organization, Ministerial Conference, Fourth Session, Doha, 9–14 November 2001: WT/MIN(01)/DEC/W/1, 14 November 2001) at para 47; Mendoza and Wilke (2011), p. 486 *et seq*; Hoekman (2012), p. 746 f.

[42] Annex 4 used to include four plurilateral agreements. The International Dairy Agreement and the International Bovine Meat Agreement were terminated at the end of 1997. *See* Van den Bossche and Zdouc (2022), p. 55. The other two are the Agreement on Trade in Civil Aircraft (1979) and the Agreement on Government Procurement as revised in 2014.

[43] See Article 3.2 DSU 1869 UNTS 401("The dispute settlement system of the WTO is a central element in providing security and predictability to the multilateral trading system. [. . .].").

[44] See e.g. Kelly (2022), p. 353; Bartels (2004), pp. 861–862.

[45] *See* Van den Bossche and Zdouc (2022), p. 193 *et seq*; McRae (2010), p. 372.

5 Ways to Achieve Consistency Discussed so Far

Reverting to ISDS, inconsistent outcomes in the interpretation and application of IIAs have been deplored for some time and the discussion about how to remedy this development has started with intra-systemic answers.

The first response was to consider whether and to what extent ISDS itself may react by adopting a system of quasi-precedent. Second came the external system reformers. In parallel with those who wanted to abolish ISDS as a whole, major reform ideas have been discussed within UNCITRAL and other fora aimed at replacing the current system either piecemeal or in total by a multilateral investment court. In addition, other methods aimed giving back control over investment law to states have been introduced. These approaches will be briefly outlined in the following subsections.

5.1 Promoting **Stare Decisis** *in the Existing System*

It is trite to state that international dispute settlement systems, in general,[46] and investment arbitration, in particular, do not adhere to a 'rule of *stare decisis*.' [47]

To some extent, international courts and tribunals have developed a *de facto* case law.[48] More cautious labels also frequently used in this regard are the notion of persuasive authority and *jurisprudence constante*.[49] Investment tribunals have actually also consolidated the law in quite a remarkable fashion and contributed to the specification of the meaning of often vague treatment standards contained in IIAs.[50]

---

[46] See, e.g., Article 59 Statute of the International Court of Justice, Charter of the United Nations, Annex, 26 June 1945, 33 UTS 993; 3 Bevans 1153 ('The decision of the Court has no binding force except between the parties and in respect of that particular case').

[47] *Amco* v. *Indonesia*, ICSID Case no. ARB/81/1, Decision on Annulment, 16 May 1986, para. 44. Article 53(1) ICSID Convention, stating that an 'award shall be binding on the parties,' has been generally interpreted to exclude a system of binding precedent in ICSID arbitration. *See* Schreuer *et al. (*2009*)*, p. 1101; more specifically Article 1136 (1) NAFTA ('An award made by a Tribunal shall have no binding force except between the disputing parties and in respect of the particular case'). See also *AES Corporation* v. *The Argentine Republic,* ICSID Case no. ARB/02/17, Decision on Jurisdiction, 26 April 2005, para. 23(d) ('There is so far no rule of precedent in general international law; nor is there any within the specific ICSID system for the settlement of disputes between one State party to the Convention and the National of another State Party.').

[48] *See* Shahabuddeen (1996); Kaufmann-Kohler (2007), p. 357; Reinisch (2008), p. 495; Reed (2010), p. 95.

[49] *See* in general Glenn (1987), p. 261; Bjorklund (2008b), p. 265.

[50] With regard to the fair and equitable treatment standard, *see Suez, Sociedad General de Aguas de Barcelona S.A., and InterAgua Servicios Integrales del Agua S.A.* v. *The Argentine Republic*, ICSID Case no. ARB/03/17, Decision on Liability, 30 July 2010, para. 189 ('In interpreting this vague, flexible, basic, and widely used treaty term, this Tribunal has the benefit of decisions by prior tribunals that have struggled strenuously, knowledgeably, and sometimes painfully, to interpret the

They have done so by paying respect to earlier investment awards, taking their reasoning into account without adhering to a system of actual precedent. Tribunals tend to treat preceding interpretations as more or less persuasive evidence of the interpretation and specification of the law,[51] which they will adhere to in order to build a *jurisprudence constante*.[52] In this softened version of an emerging 'case-law', investment arbitration contributes to core aspects of the rule of law, *i.e.*, that like cases should be decided in a like way and that a consistent interpretation of the same treaty standards enhances certainty and predictability of adjudicatory outcomes.[53]

These are informal developments in the jurisprudence of arbitral tribunals that are clearly not bound by precedent. It appears though that some of the current reform proposals intend to go further and aim at "introducing or implementing a system of precedents."[54] Such proposals mentioned in UNCITRAL WG III

words "fair and equitable" in a wide variety of factual situations and investment relationships. Many of these cases arose out of Argentina's economic crisis of 2001-2003. Although this tribunal is not bound by such prior decisions, they do constitute "a subsidiary means for the determination of the rules of [international] law."').

[51] *See, e.g., ADC Affiliate Limited and ADC & ADMC Management Limited* v. *Republic of Hungary*, ICSID Case no. ARB/03/16, Award, 2 October 2006, para. 293 ('It is true that arbitral awards do not constitute binding precedent. It is also true that a number of cases are fact-driven and that the findings in those cases cannot be transposed in and of themselves to other cases. It is further true that a number of cases are based on treaties that differ from the present BIT in certain respects. However, cautious reliance on certain principles developed in a number of those cases, as persuasive authority, may advance the body of law, which in turn may serve predictability in the interest of both investors and host States.').

[52] *See, e.g., Société Générale de Surveillance S.A.* v. *Republic of the Philippines*, ICSID Case no. ARB/02/6, Decision on Jurisdiction, 29 January 2004, para. 97 ('In the Tribunal's view, although different tribunals constituted under the ICSID system should in general seek to act consistently with each other, in the end it must be for each tribunal to exercise its competence in accordance with the applicable law, which will by definition be different for each BIT and each Respondent State. Moreover there is no doctrine of precedent in international law, if by precedent is meant a rule of the binding effect of a single decision. There is no hierarchy of international tribunals, and even if there were, there is no good reason for allowing the first tribunal in time to resolve issues for all later tribunals. It must be initially for the control mechanisms provided for under the BIT and the ICSID Convention, and in the longer term for the development of a common legal opinion or *jurisprudence constante*, to resolve the difficult legal questions discussed by the SGS v. Pakistan Tribunal and also in the present decision.'); *AES Corporation* v. *The Argentine Republic,* ICSID Case no. ARB/02/17, Decision on Jurisdiction, 26 April 2005, para. 33 ('From a more general point of view, one can hardly deny that the institutional dimension of the control mechanisms provided for under the ICSID Convention might well be a factor, in the longer term, for contributing to the development of a common legal opinion or *jurisprudence constante*, to resolve some difficult legal issues discussed in many cases, inasmuch as these issues share the same substantial features').

[53] *See Saipem S.p.A.* v. *The People's Republic of Bangladesh*, ICSID Case no. ARB/05/07, Decision on Jurisdiction, 21 March 2007, para. 67, footnote 15 above.

[54] Possible reform of investor-State dispute settlement (ISDS): Consistency and related matters, Note by the Secretariat, dated 28 August 2018, A/CN.9/WG.III/WP.150, para. 32.

circles would indeed be difficult to implement, as acknowledged by some delegations.[55]

To introduce a true system of precedent in ISDS would be a challenging task from a technical perspective. At a minimum it would require an adaptation of existing procedural rules and/or IIAs that are currently excluding any precedential effect of awards. Most likely, the creation of a multilateral investment court or an appellate mechanism in itself would not be sufficient.

5.2 *Authentic Treaty Interpretation*

Another method to counter inconsistent outcomes is the idea of authentic treaty interpretation by the treaty parties. It is often advanced as a means to "correct" so-called "incorrect" outcomes and it is rightly also seen as tool for treaty parties to "regain control" through the power of interpreting IIAs.[56]

A 2020 UNCITRAL Secretariat note on the 'Interpretation of investment treaties by treaty Parties' outlined the different stages when and mechanisms through which state parties could determine or influence how investment treaties are interpreted.[57] The note discussed authentic interpretation in the form of 'binding interpretation' by state parties through *ad-hoc* mechanisms or institutionalized mechanisms such as commissions specifically tasked with adopting binding interpretations.[58] Against this backdrop the Secretariat proposed adopting model treaty provisions for both existing and future treaties allowing for joint interpretations binding on tribunals.[59]

---

[55] Report of Working Group III (Investor-State Dispute Settlement Reform) on the work of its resumed thirty-eighth session, dated 28 January 2020, A/CN.9/1004/Add.1 para. 44 ("Some doubts were expressed about establishing a system of precedent (doctrine of *stare decisis*) and it was said that a decision rendered by an appellate tribunal should bind only the disputing parties and in case of remand, the first-tier tribunal. Another view was that the appellate body decision should have a broader effect to ensure consistency, particularly in cases where the tribunals would be interpreting the same provisions of an investment treaty or similar text. It was further noted that the design and features of an appellate body as well as the nature of the first-tier tribunals would have an impact on the effect of the decision.").

[56] Possible reform of investor-state dispute settlement (ISDS): Interpretation of investment treaties by treaty Parties, Note by the Secretariat, dated 17 January 2020, A/CN.9/WG.III/WP.191, para. 6 ('The Working Group may wish to note that the proposals for reform submitted by Governments in preparation for the deliberations on the third phase of the mandate ("Submissions") also address this matter, underlying that it may serve to ensure a better control by treaty Parties over the interpretation of their treaties and to address concerns of lack of consistency, coherence, predictability and correctness of decisions by ISDS tribunals."). See also Kulick (2016).

[57] Possible reform of investor-State dispute settlement (ISDS): Interpretation of investment treaties by treaty Parties, Note by the Secretariat, dated 17 January 2020, A/CN.9/WG.III/WP.191, paras. 23 et seq.

[58] Ibid., paras. 36-40.

[59] Ibid., para. 47.

In fact, such a technique is not new and has also found its way into IIAs, usually in the form of authoritative interpretations by the contracting parties to IIAs.[60] The most prominent example is the power of the NAFTA Free Trade Commission ('FTC') to interpret the meaning of its investment chapter, which was first asserted in the 2001 interpretation of the FET clause.[61]

All these methods do not address the underlying problem that different standards in different IIAs can be consistently interpreted only to a certain degree. True consistency can be reached only through identically worded texts or one single standard to be applied by all arbitral tribunals.

5.3 *An Appellate Mechanism or Investment Court*

The focus of attention within UNCITRAL working group III seems to be on the creation of an appellate mechanism or a multilateral court in order to ensure consistency and predictability. When consensus was reached in 2019 to enter the third stage of the UNCITRAL reform process, based on the assessment that reform was desirable to develop relevant solutions to be recommended to the Commission,[62] the option of an institutionalised and even multilateralized ISDS has received heightened attention.[63]

Within UNCITRAL, the UN-based and thus potentially global forum to discuss ISDS reform, views have not always been in harmony and one has to recognise that some delegations are more in favour of institutional reform than others.

Within this forum, the European Union (EU) has for quite some time most vocally advocated the establishment of a multilateral investment court instead of the current system of *ad hoc* arbitration. This may have been partly motivated by broader consistency and predictability aims. It seems, however, that it derives primarily from the European Court of Justice's reluctance to accept any competing

[60] *See, e.g.,* Article 31 of the 2012 US Model BIT; Comprehensive Economic and Trade Agreement between Canada and the European Union, 30 October 2016 (CETA).

[61] NAFTA Free Trade Commission Clarifications Related to NAFTA chapter 11, Decisions of 31 July 2001, available at www.worldtradelaw.net/nafta/chap11interp.pdf ('B.1. Article 1105-(1) prescribes the customary international law minimum standard of treatment of aliens as the minimum standard of treatment to be afforded to investments of investors of another Party. 2. The concepts of "fair and equitable treatment" and "full protection and security" do not require treatment in addition to or beyond that which is required by the customary international law minimum standard of treatment of aliens.').

[62] Possible reform of investor-State dispute settlement (ISDS), Note by the Secretariat, dated 30 July 2019, A/CN.9/WG.III/WP.166, para. 4; Report of the Working Group III (Investor-State Dispute Settlement Reform) on the work of its thirty-seventh session (New York, 1-5 April 2019), dated 9 April 2019, A/CN.9/970, para. 71.

[63] Report of the Working Group III (Investor-State Dispute Settlement Reform) on the work of its forty-fourth session (Vienna, 23-27 January 2023), dated 7 February 2023, A/CN.9/ 1130, paras. 119 et seq.

dispute settlement institutions.[64] Especially, the EU's sceptical attitude towards arbitration in general and investment arbitration in particular may have motivated the chief negotiator of the EU concerning Transatlantic Trade and Investment Partnership (TTIP) and Comprehensive Economic and Trade Agreement between Canada and the European Union (CETA) during the 2010s, Commissioner Malmström, to propose the establishment of a multilateral court in 2015.[65]

Over time, it became clear that the EU's hostility towards investment arbitration focuses on intra-EU investor-state arbitration, as is most evident in the Court's *Achmea* decision,[66] but also in the follow-ups of *Komstroy*[67] and *PL Holding*,[68] and did not extend towards external trade agreements with an investment chapter as evident in the *Singapore* opinion[69] as well as subsequently in the Court's opinion concerning *CETA*.[70] At that stage, the negotiators could fully support a multilateral investment court. Investment agreements or chapters within free trade agreements concluded by the European Union with third parties started to provide initially for an investment court system (ICS) as in CETA and subsequently inserted clauses aimed at the eventual setting up of a multilateral investment court.[71]

It is clear that the creation of a body composed of a smaller number of individual adjudicators that may sit in review of lower tier decisions is likely to produce a body of more coherent outcomes. Nevertheless, the basic shortcoming of a system that comprises a centralised court, but continues to apply different investment agreements with differently formulated substantive protection standards will remain. Such a single appellate court or mechanism will have to apply different treaties and will sometimes have to arrive at different outcomes. This may then not be unpredictable, but it means that its judgments or awards will not be fully consistent. This implies that the aim of full consistency and predictability cannot be reached.

[64] Howse (2017), p. 209.

[65] European Commission, European Union's proposal for Investment Protection and Resolution of Investment Disputes in the Transatlantic Trade and Investment Partnership (TTIP), EU-US TTIP Negotiations, 12 November 2015, 21.

[66] C-284/16, *Slovak Republic v. Achmea BV*, CJEU, 6 March 2018, ECLI:EU:C:2018:158.

[67] C-741/19, *Republic of Moldova v. Komstroy LLC*, CJEU, 2 September 2021, ECLI:EU:C:2021:655.

[68] C-109/20, *Republiken Polen v. PL Holding Sàrl*, CJEU, 26 October 2021, ECLI:EU:C:2021:875.

[69] CJEU, Opinion 2/15, 16 May 2017, ECLI:EU:C:2017:376.

[70] CJEU, Opinion 1/17, 30 April 2019, ECLI:EU:C:2019:341.

[71] Art 3.41 EU-Viet Nam Investment Protection Agreement (2019) ('The Parties shall enter into negotiations for an international agreement providing for a multilateral investment tribunal in combination with, or separate from, a multilateral appellate mechanism applicable to disputes under this Agreement.'); Art 3.12 EU-Singapore Investment Protection Agreement (2018) ('The Parties shall pursue with each other and other interested trading partners, the establishment of a multilateral investment tribunal and appellate mechanism for the resolution of international investment disputes').

6 Reforming at the Level of the Applicable Law: Reforming the Substantive Standards

All the above considerations have shown that procedural reform may support the aim of creating more consistency and predictability, but cannot guarantee it as long as the applicable legal provisions differ substantially.

In investment law, the relevant applicable legal provisions are in first line the protection standards contained in IIAs. Major factors contributing to their sometimes inconsistent interpretation and application are their generally high level of abstraction as well as their sometimes markedly different wording. Correcting these developments can be achieved by two approaches: (1) making the applicable rules more precise and (2) making them more uniform.

To a certain degree the first approach is already gradually taking place. A peculiar feature of new generations of IIAs has been a far higher level of determination and precision than the classic BITs of the 1960s, 1970s and 1980s. Most recent investment agreements contain fairly precise standards often analogous to the old formulations, but coupled with language defining far more clearly, for instance the notion of what constitutes an expropriation[72] or what amounts to a breach of fair and equitable treatment.[73] Typically such more precise language is added in an annex sometimes it is contained in the main part of IIAs.

However, making treaty texts more detailed and specific in itself will not address all inconsistency problems. Such problems can be achieved either by increased harmonization, or more radically by unification of the applicable law.

The first approach (A.) resembles what the EU does internally under the heading of 'approximation of the laws' when it adopts directives which set a certain level of harmonized goals to be implemented by the member states in achieving such a goal. This will be described below under the heading of EU Model BITs.

The second approach (B.) resembles what the EU does internally under the heading of unification when it adopts regulations which become uniformly binding law within all the member states. This will be addressed below under the heading of a multilateral instrument.

[72] Art 7(2) Hungary-United Arab Emirates BIT (2021) ('[. . .] the determination of whether a measure or series of measures by a Contracting Party, in a given specific situation, constitutes an indirect expropriation requires a case-by-case, fact-based inquiry that considers, among other factors [. . .]'); Canada-Moldova BIT (2028) Annex B.10.

[73] Art 5(2a) Hong Kong, China SAR-Mexico BIT (2020) ('"fair and equitable treatment" include the obligation not to deny justice in criminal, civil, or administrative adjudicatory proceedings in accordance with the principle of due process'); Art 4(2a) Australia-Uruguay BIT (2019) ('"fair and equitable treatment" includes the obligation not to deny justice in criminal, civil or administrative adjudicatory proceedings in accordance with the principle of due process embodied in the principal legal systems of the world.').

6.1 EU Model BITs

As already mentioned, another avenue on the road to consistency and predictability is the development of new generations of IIAs which should not only contain more clear and precise rules, but also more similar formulations ensuring that in cases of disputes these provisions are applied in a way that prevents inconsistent outcomes.

While the EU has not adopted a model IIA, it has adopted a relatively uniform approach to negotiating IIA standards. For the EU as participant in investment treaty making, CETA has been a blueprint so far. Subsequent treaties negotiated by the Commission have very closely followed the formulations of the substantive standards contained in CETA. Thus, in practice the text of CETA could be viewed as the invisible model BIT of the EU.[74] And this model seems to influence also the negotiating template which is used by EU member states which according to the grandfathering regulation[75] are authorised to continue negotiating investment treaties with third parties as long as the EU does not exercise its power to do so.[76] Unfortunately, though the precise text of what members may use in their negotiations with third parties has not been made publicly available by the EU.[77]

From a broader perspective such a harmonisation approach may create quite a substantive level of harmonisation and thus contribute to the predictability and consistency of outcomes with substantive standards being fairly similar. If coupled with an adjudication system that relies on appellate review a separate procedural layer of safeguarding consistency has been established. However, it seems clear that for ensuring consistency and predictability the unification model (B.) would be preferable.

6.2 The Multilateral Instrument as Taboo

Already in the 1960s[78] and 1990s[79] when ideas for a multilateral convention on investment protection have been discussed the goal of securing more coherence was obvious.[80]

---

[74] See Hoffmeister and Alexandru (2014), p. 379.

[75] Regulation (EU) No 1219/2012 of the European Parliament and of the Council of 12 December 2012 establishing transitional arrangements for bilateral investment agreements between Member States and third countries, OJEU L 351/40, 20 December 2012.

[76] Art 9(1b) Regulation (EU) No 1219/2012.

[77] See M. Bungenberg in this volume.

[78] OECD Draft Convention on the Protection of Foreign Property (1963) 2 ILM 241.

[79] OECD, Draft Multilateral Agreement on Investment (Draft MAI), DAFFE/MAI(98)7/REV1, draft consolidated text of 22 April 1998, available at http://www1.oecd.org/daf/mai/pdf/ng/ng987/r1e.pdf.

[80] Cremades (2004), p. 89.

While the dramatic demise of the OECD plans to draft a multilateral investment agreement in the 1990s may have been a traumatic experience for negotiators,[81] it still remains difficult to understand why the most obvious answer to the problem of inconsistency and unpredictability in ISDS does not receive more attention.

It is particularly surprising that it does not figure prominently in current ISDS reform discussions of UNCITRAL Working Group III. Of course, the mandate of this body is limited to procedural reform.[82] But that has not prevented it from discussing, for instance, IIA reform.

That a single multilateral instrument as the most obvious solution to divergent outcomes is indeed the 'unspeakable' solution is evident from the discussion at UNCITRAL. In the 2018 secretariat note on consistency possible solutions were discussed, ranging from

> [. . .] amending investment treaties that contained vague wording; providing solutions to give greater control by State parties to investment treaties, such as joint interpretative statements and guidelines on interpretation of standards, non-disputing party submissions to allow other member States to provide their views about the interpretation of a standard, a mechanism through which tribunals could direct questions to the treaty partners prior to the issuance of awards; adopting a systemic approach through institutional solutions (appeal mechanisms or permanent adjudicatory bodies); considering reforming the domestic framework on investment, including substantive standards of protection contained in domestic laws; introducing or implementing a system of precedents; encouraging consolidation where possible, as well as coordination among tribunals; improving the existing review mechanisms and annulment procedures; and enhancing the role of domestic courts.[83]

The usual procedural suspects are all listed, even some reform ideas affecting the applicable rules are stated, such as making IIAs more precise or reforming substantive standards in national legislation. However, establishing a multilateral instrument containing single versions of substantive standards to be applied by an ISDS mechanism was not even mentioned. This is all the more surprising since the same note recognizes that under different scenarios tribunals may sometimes apply different IIAs and sometimes the same IIA when arriving at inconsistent results.[84] That such inconsistencies are much more likely and sometimes even required as a matter of treaty interpretation (of different formulations of substantive standards) would appear obvious.

In the Secretariat note, however, the importance of a literal interpretation given to IIAs seems to receive reduced attention. Rather than stressing that different outcomes may result from differently worded treaty texts, the note emphasizes that

[81] Muchlinski (2000), p. 1033.

[82] United Nations General Assembly, Report of the United Nations Commission on International Trade Law, Fiftieth session, dated 3-21 July 2017, A/72/17, paras. 263, 264; Report of Working Group III (Investor-State Dispute Settlement Reform) on the work of its thirty-fourth session (Vienna, 27 November – 1 December 2017) Part I, dated 19 December 2017, A/CN.9/930/Rev.1, paras. 6, 19, 20.

[83] Possible reform of investor-State dispute settlement (ISDS): Consistency and related matters, Note by the Secretariat, dated 28 August 2018, A/CN.9/WG.III/WP.150, para. 32.

[84] Ibid, paras. 11–13.

treaty interpretation rules may "require a decision maker to consider more than the plain language of a treaty provision when interpreting it" and that the arguments of the parties may "inevitably" affect the outcome of dispute settlement.[85]

While it is certainly true that these are also factors impacting upon the outcome of ISDS, it appears curious that the most important factor, the wording of different IIAs, is not even mentioned in the Secretariat paper. It is submitted though that when taking consistency and predictability of ISDS outcomes seriously it will be necessary to discuss a multilateral investment agreement. Only where a single uniform body of substantive protection standards forms the applicable law we will have achieved the necessary groundwork for consistent and predictable outcomes.

7 Conclusion

A multilateral investment agreement is likely to be the most important tool to achieve one of the most important rule of law criteria, consistency/predictability of outcomes, stemming from the requirement that like case have to be decided alike.

Consistency of outcomes can only be reached by a single undertaking approach as we know from WTO law. Where investment protection *à la carte* prevails, divergent outcomes will necessarily be produced also under a reformed system with appellate structures or other innovative features, such as a single multilateral investment court.

When taking consistency and predictability of ISDS outcomes seriously it will thus be necessary to seriously discuss a multilateral investment agreement.

References

Alexandrov S (2004) Breaches of contract and breaches of treaty – the jurisdiction of treaty-based arbitration tribunals to decide breach of contract claims in SGS v Pakistan and SGS v Philippines. J World Invest Trade 5

Alvarez J, Khamsi K (2009) The Argentine crisis and foreign investors: a glimpse into the heart of the investment regime. In: Sauvant KP (ed) Yearbook on international investment law and policy 2008–2009. Oxford University Press

[85] Possible reform of investor-State dispute settlement (ISDS): Consistency and related matters, Note by the Secretariat, dated 28 August 2018, A/CN.9/WG.III/WP.150, para. 6 ("It may be noted that different factors may justify differences between arbitral decisions or awards. For example, differences may emerge because the fundamental rules of treaty interpretation (codified in Articles 31–33 of the Vienna Convention on the Law of Treaties) require a decision maker to consider more than the plain language of a treaty provision when interpreting it. Further, differences in reasoning and outcome may inevitably flow from differences in the manner and extent to which relevant evidence was presented, and positions were argued.").

Arato J, Brown C, Ortino F (2020) Parsing and managing inconsistency in investor-state dispute settlement. J World Investment Trade 21
Bartels L (2004) The separation of powers in the WTO: how to avoid judicial activism. ICLQ 53: 861
Binder C (2009) Changed circumstances in international investment law: interfaces between the law of treaties and the law of state responsibility with a special focus on the Argentine crisis. In: Binder C et al (eds) International investment law for the 21st century. OUP
Bjorklund AK (2009) Economic security defenses in international investment law. In: Sauvant KP (ed) Yearbook on international investment law and policy 2008-2009. OUP
Bjorklund AK (2008a) Emergency exceptions: state of necessity and force majeure. In: Muchlinski P et al (eds) Oxford handbook of international investment law. OUP
Bjorklund AK (2008b) Investment treaty arbitral decisions as Jurisprudence Constante. In: Picker C et al (eds) International economic law: the state and future of the discipline. Hart
Brower CN, Sharpe JK (2003) Multiple and conflicting international arbitral awards. J World Invest Trade 4
Burke-White W, von Staden A (2007) Investment protection in extraordinary times: interpreting non-precluded measures provisions. Virginia J Int Law 48
Cejie K (2022) Rule of law: a fundamental concept without a coherent meaning, analysis of the Swedish and Chinese understandings. Eur J Comp Law Gov
Chesterman S (2008) An international rule of law. Am J Comp Law 56
Cremades BM (2004) Has the proliferation of BITs gone too far: is it now time for a multilateral investment treaty. J World Invest Trade 5
De Brabandere E (2012) Arbitral decisions as a source of international investment law. In: Gazzini T, De Brabandere E (eds) International investment law: the sources of rights and obligations. Brill Nijhoff
De Luca A, Feldman M, Paparinskis M, Titi C (2020) Responding to incorrect decision-making in investor-state dispute settlement: policy options. J World Investment Trade 21
Dolzer R, Schreuer C (2012) Principles of international investment law. Oxford University Press
Douglas Z (2011) The MFN clause in investment arbitration: treaty interpretation off the rails. J Int Disp Settlement 2(1)
Dupont P-E (2011) The notion of ICSID investment: ongoing confusion or emerging synthesis. J World Investment Trade 12(2)
Gaillard E (2005) Establishing jurisdiction through a most-favoured-nation clause. New York Law J 233
Glenn M (1987) Persuasive authority. McGill Law J 32
Hoekman B (2012) Proposals for WTO reform: a synthesis and assessment. In: Narlikar A, Daunton M, Stern RM (eds) The Oxford handbook on the World Trade Organization. Oxford University Press
Hoekman B, Mavroidis P (2015) WTO 'à la carte' or 'menu du jour'? Assessing the case for more plurilateral agreements. Eur J Int Law 26
Hoffmeister F, Alexandru G (2014) A first glimpse of light on the emerging invisible EU model BIT. In: Bungenberg M, Reinisch A (Guest eds) The anatomy of the (Invisible) EU model BIT. JWIT, p 15
Howse R (2017) Designing a multilateral investment court: issues and options. Yearb Eur Law 36(1)
ILA Committee on the Rule of Law and International Investment Law (2018) Report 2018. Int Law Ass'n Rep Conf 78:380
Kaufmann-Kohler G (2007) Arbitral precedent: dream, necessity, or excuse. Arbitr Int 23(4)
Kelly JP (2022) Judicial activism at the World Trade Organizational: development principles of self-restraint. Northwest J Int Law Bus 22:353
Kennedy K (1997) The GATT-WO System at fifty. Wisconsin Int Law J 16
Kulick A (ed) (2016) Reassertion of control over the investment treaty regime. Cambridge University Press, Cambridge

Manciaux S (2008) The notion of investment: new controversies. J World Investment Trade 9(6)
Maupin J (2011) MFN-based jurisdiction in investor-state arbitration: is there any hope for a consistent approach? J Int Econ Law 14(1)
Mavroidis P (2008) Trade in goods: the GATT and the other agreements regulating trade in goods. Oxford University Press)
McRae D (2010) The WTO appellate body: a model for an ICSID appeals facility?. J Int Disp Settlement 2
Mendoza MR, Wilke M (2011) Revisiting the single undertaking: towards a more balanced approach to WTO negotiations. In: Birkbeck D (ed) Making global trade governance work for development: perspectives and priorities from developing countries. Cambridge University Press
Muchlinski PT (2000) The rise and fall of the multilateral agreement on investment: where now. Int Lawyer 34
Paparinskis M (2011) MFN clauses and international dispute settlement: moving beyond Maffezini and Plama. ICSID Rev Foreign Invest Law J 26
Raz J (1979) The authority of law: essays on law and morality. Clarendon Press
Reed L (2010) The de facto precedent regime in investment arbitration: a case for proactive case management. ICSID Rev 25(1)
Reinisch A (2004) The use and limits of *Res Judicata* and *Lis Pendens* as procedural tools to avoid conflicting dispute settlement outcomes. Law Pract Int Courts Trib 3
Reinisch A (2008) The role of precedent in ICSID arbitration. In: C. Klausegger et al (eds) Austrian arbitration yearbook. Beck, Stämpfli & Manz
Reinisch A (2010) From the Perennial Issue of the Notion of Investment Pursuant to Article 25 ICSID Convention and Narrow Dispute Settlement Provisions to Further Clarifications of Substantive Standards of Protection – ICSID Arbitration in 2009. Global Community Yearbook of International Law and Jurisprudence 10
Reinisch A, Tropper J (2022) The Argentinian crisis arbitrations. In: Ruiz Fabri H, Stoppioni E (eds) International investment law an analysis of the major decisions. Hart
Reinisch A (2007) Necessity in international investment arbitration – an unnecessary split of opinions in recent ICSID Cases? J World Invest Trade 8
Schill S (2007) International investment law and the Host State's power to handle economic crises. J Int Arbitr 24(3)
Schill S (2011) Allocating adjudicatory authority: most-favoured-nation clauses as a basis of jurisdiction – a reply to Zachary Douglas. J Int Disp Settlement 2(2)
Schreuer C et al (2009) ICSID Convention Commentary
Schreuer C (2004) Travelling the BIT route: of waiting periods, umbrella clauses and forks in the road. J World Invest Trade 5
Shahabuddeen M (1996) Precedent in the World Court. Cambridge University Press
Sinclair A (2004) The origins of the umbrella clause in the international law of investment protection. Arbitr Int 20
Van den Bossche P, Zdouc W (2022) The law and policy of the World Trade Organization. Cambridge University Press
Waibel M (2007) Two worlds of necessity in ICSID arbitration: CMS and LG&E. Leiden J Int Law 20
Wälde T (2005) The "Umbrella" clause on investment arbitration – a comment on original intentions and recent cases. J World Invest Trade 6
Waldron J (2007) Legislation and the Rule of Law. Legisprudence 1
Waldron J (2016) The Rule of Law. (22 June 2016) <https://plato.stanford.edu/entries/rule-of-law/ > Accessed 8 Mar 2023
Zeiler T (2012) The expanding mandate of the GATT: the first seven rounds. In: Narlikar A, Daunton M, Stern RM (eds) The Oxford handbook on the World Trade Organization. Oxford University Press

Decentral Implementation of EU Investment Policy: Convergence, Divergence and EU-Plus

Marc Bungenberg, Bianca Böhme, and Lars Ruf

Contents

Abstract The legal protection of investments around the globe is mainly influenced by a broad variety of international agreements, such as Free Trade Agreements (FTAs) with investment chapters, specific Investment Protection Agreements (IPAs) as well as Bilateral Investment Treaties (BITs). Within the EU, the past decades have shown fundamental changes in the way that negotiations and the conclusion of such agreements are carried out. The central approach with negotiations on an EU level has faced several problems, especially in light of the need for ratification by the Member States. Therefore, more room is given to a new decentral approach with negotiations of BITs by individual Member States being authorised by the European Commission. This calls for a comparison of EU agreements and Member States' BITs with regard to procedural and substantive investment protection standards. As this comparative exercise will show, new Member States' BITs are largely convergent with the EU's international investment policy, but also leave limited room for divergence (following the old European gold standard) and an EU-plus approach.

M. Bungenberg · B. Böhme (✉) · L. Ruf
Europa-Institut, Saarland University, Saarbrucken, Germany
e-mail: bungenberg@europainstitut.de; boehme@europainstitut.de; ruf@europainstitut.de

M. Bungenberg, A. Reinisch (eds.), *New Frontiers for EU Investment Policy*, Special Issue, https://doi.org/10.1007/978-3-031-41977-5_3

1 Introduction

In recent years, numerous Member States of the European Union (EU) are increasingly concluding new Bilateral Investment Treaties (BITs) and reforming existing ones. Even though Foreign Direct Investment (FDI) became an EU-exclusive competence with the entry into force of the Treaty of Lisbon in 2009, Regulation 1219/2012 permits Member States to continue concluding new BITs and to amend existing ones.[1] As its title suggests ("*transitional* arrangements for bilateral investment agreements between Member States and third countries"), Regulation 1219/2012 was intended to regulate Member States' treaty-making practices until the EU developed its proper international investment policy exercising its exclusive competence over Foreign Direct Investment (FDI). In fact, the European Commission (Commission) stated in 2010 that "[i]n the long run, we should achieve a situation where investors from the EU and from third countries will not need to rely on BITs entered into by one or the other Member State for an effective protection of its investment".[2] Accordingly, it appears that the original idea after the shift of competences was that most investment negotiations take place at the EU level, relegating the Member States' national investment policies to a subordinated position (central approach).

Thirteen years later, the picture looks quite different. The EU's central approach has been complemented by a new decentral approach, meaning that the EU's international investment policy is directly implemented through Member States' BITs. This new approach has not been laid down or explained by the Commission by means of any formal communication but can be regarded as the natural result of the EU's own struggle implementing the central approach. So far, the EU has negotiated investment protection standards with Canada, Mexico, Singapore and Vietnam, and has at least discussed this topic with the US, China, Japan and the UK. These negotiations have *inter alia* resulted in the conclusion of the EU-Canada Comprehensive and Economic Trade Agreement (CETA),[3] and the EU-Singapore[4] and EU-Vietnam[5] Investment Protection Agreements. However, at the time of writing none of these agreements have entered into force and there is no prospect of a sudden

[1] Regulation (EU) No 1219/2012 of the European Parliament and of the Council of 12 December 2012 establishing transitional arrangements for bilateral investment agreements between Member States and third countries, OJ L 251/40.

[2] European Commission (2010), p. 11.

[3] See Council Decision (EU) 2017/38 of 28 October 2016 on the provisional application of the Comprehensive Economic and Trade Agreement (CETA) between Canada, of the one part, and the European Union and its Member States, of the other part, OJ L 11/1080.

[4] See Council Decision (EU) 2018/1676 of 15 October 2018 on the signing on behalf of the EU of the Investment Protection Agreement between the EU and its Member States, of the one part, and the Republic of Singapore, of the other part, OJ L 279/1.

[5] See Council Decision (EU) 2019/1096 of 25 June 2018 on the signing on behalf of the EU of the Investment Protection Agreement between the EU and its Member States, of the one part, and the Socialist Republic of Vietnam, of the other part, OJ L 175/1.

revival of the stagnated EU international investment policy any time soon. As a result, the central approach finds itself at a dead end due to the stalled ratification process of the EU's investment agreements in a number of Member States.[6]

While the central approach has stagnated, numerous Member States have actively pursued their own extra-EU investment negotiations recently. In 2020, the Commission published a report that provided notable information on Member States' treaty practice in the field of extra-EU investment protection between 2013 and 2019.[7] According to that report, the Commission received a total of 442 requests to authorise the opening of negotiations or the conclusion of Member States' BITs in accordance with the authorization mechanism provided under Regulation 1219/2012.[8] In addition, the Commission recently published a list of the implementing decisions issued to authorise the negotiation or conclusion of Member States' BITs.[9] The list indicates that more than 100 implementing decisions authorizing the conclusion of new Member States' BITs have been issued since March 2019. Those implementing decisions often allow a Member State to open negotiations with numerous third countries at the same time. By way of example, the Commission issued an implementing decision in October 2022 authorizing Hungary to open formal negotiations to conclude a BIT with the Principality of Andorra, the Republic of Maldives, the Federal Republic of Nigeria, the Republic of Ghana, the Republic of Cote d'Ivoire, the Republic of Peru, the Republic of Senegal, the Republic of Seychelles, the Republic of Sierra Leone, the United Republic of Tanzania, and the Republic of Uganda.[10]

The implementing decisions are not only notable in that they show the high activity of EU Member States engaging in extra-EU investment negotiations, they also illustrate how the Commission promotes but also conditions those negotiations by imposing a number of requirements emanating from the EU's international investment policy, which the Member States must implement in their new BITs. In other words, the EU's international investment policy is shaped at a central level and then implemented at a decentral level through the Member States.[11]

This way of shaping Member States' international investment policy even led the Commission to elaborate a set of "Model Clauses for Negotiation or Re-negotiation of Member States' Bilateral Investment Agreements with Third Countries" (Model Clauses). These Model Clauses, which are largely based on the provisions included in EU investment agreements, are contained in an informal document that is sent to

[6] On this, see Bungenberg (2022), pp. 907–976; Rosas (2021), pp. 27–46; Stifter (2022), Art. 8.44, paras. 24 ff.; Griller (2020), pp. 41 ff.; Cremona (2018), pp. 235 ff.

[7] See European Commission (2020).

[8] Ibid, p. 5. More details on the numbers provided in the Commission's Report can be found in Bungenberg and Böhme (2022), pp. 631 f.

[9] The list can be found at: https://ec.europa.eu/transparency/documents-register/ searching for "bilateral investment agreements" (last accessed 20 February 2023).

[10] Commission Implementing Decision C(2022)7177 of 13 October 2022.

[11] Bungenberg and Böhme (2022), pp. 633 ff.

Member States for their extra-EU investment negotiations. Even though the Model Clauses are non-binding, Member States appear to follow them quite closely in their own treaty-making practice. Unfortunately, they are not (yet) publicly available.

2 The New Member States' International Investment Policy

The following sections will take a closer look at recent Member States' (Model) BITs. The sample comprises the publicly available BITs concluded and the Model BITs adopted from 2016 to 2023.[12] The analysis will show that there is a large convergence with the EU approach [Sect. 2.1] with regard to most of the contents of those (Model) BITs. At the same time, there seems to be reduced space for divergent approaches in accordance with the old European "gold standard" [Sect. 2.2]. Finally, some Member States' (Model) BITs go beyond the standards negotiated by the EU in its own investment agreements, thus indicating the potential for an EU-plus approach [Sect. 2.3] with regard to certain issues.

2.1 Convergence with the EU Approach

Most provisions on substantive investment protection contained in recent Member States' (Model) BITs closely follow the EU approach as envisaged in CETA and other EU agreements. A prominent example is the definition of the Fair and Equitable Treatment (FET) standard, where we may observe almost full convergence. Article 8.10 CETA defines the standard by enumerating a number of situations that constitute unfair and inequitable treatment, including denial of justice, a

[12] All referenced (Model) BITs can be found through the UNCTAD Investment Policy Hub's International Investment Agreements Navigator, available at: https://investmentpolicy.unctad.org/international-investment-agreements (last accessed 15 March 2023). The given analysis covers the period from 2016 to March 2023, including the following: Czech Model BIT (2016), adopted 28/12/2016; Slovak Model BIT (2019); Dutch Model BIT (2019), adopted 22/3/2019; Belgium-Luxemburg Economic Union Model BIT (2019), adopted 28/3/2019; Italian Model BIT (2022), adopted August 2022; Austria-Kyrgyzstan BIT (2016), in force since 1/10/2017; Cambodia-Hungary BIT (2016), in force since 30/8/2017; Slovakia-UAE BIT (2016), in force since 5/2/2018; Iran-Slovakia BIT (2016), in force since 30/8/2017; Hungary-Iran BIT (2018), in force since 23/3/2022; Hungary-Tajikistan BIT (2017), in force since 4/11/2018; Lithuania-Turkey BIT (2018), signed 28/8/2018 but not yet in force; Belarus-Hungary BIT (2019), in force since 28/9/2019; Côte d'Ivoire-Portugal BIT (2019), signed 13/6/2019 but not yet in force; Cabo Verde-Hungary BIT (2019), in force since 2/5/2020; Hungary-Kyrgyzstan BIT (2020), in force since 10/4/2022; Hungary-UAE BIT (2021), in force since 10/4/2022; Hungary-Oman BIT (2022), signed 2/2/2022 but not yet in force; Hungary-San Marino BIT (2022), signed 21/9/2022 but not yet in force.

fundamental breach of due process, manifest arbitrariness, targeted discrimination, or harassment.[13]

Member States' BITs concluded in early 2016 still followed the old European gold standard,[14] including an unqualified FET (and Full Protection and Security, FPS) clause without the "closed list" approach followed in EU investment agreements. By way of example, Article 3(1) of the Austria-Kyrgyzstan BIT[15] provides that

> [e]ach Contracting Party shall accord to investments by investors of the other Contracting Party fair and equitable treatment and full and constant protection and security.

A similar clause can be found in Article 2(2) of the Cambodia-Hungary BIT[16], and in Article 2(2) of the 2016 Czech Model BIT. Hungary, which has been actively concluding new BITs in recent years, changed its policy with regard to the FET (and FPS) standard as of 2017. Since then, almost all Hungarian BITs[17] follow the same "closed list" approach as the EU. One notable example is the Hungary-Kyrgyzstan BIT concluded in 2020. While Kyrgyzstan still negotiated an unqualified FET standard with Austria in 2016, it accepted the EU approach in its BIT with Hungary in 2020. All other Member States' BITs[18] concluded since late 2016, as well as their Model BITs[19] adopted after 2016, equally started to follow the EU approach in this regard. The "closed list" approach, as first adopted in CETA, has even spread further. For instance, it can also be found in the latest Indian Model BIT.[20]

The FET (and FPS) standard is not the only example of convergence. Many other substantive protection standards, such as national treatment, transfer provisions or

---

[13] See also Art. 2(4) EU-Singapore Investment Protection Agreement and Art. 2(5) EU-Vietnam Investment Protection Agreement.

[14] *Titi* defines the European gold standard as synonymous with the "highest levels of investment protection". See Titi (2015), p. 649.

[15] Signed on 22 April 2016 and entered into force on 1 October 2017, available at: https://investmentpolicy.unctad.org/international-investment-agreements/treaty-files/5500/download.

[16] Signed on 14 January 2016 and entered into force on 30 August 2017, available at: https://investmentpolicy.unctad.org/international-investment-agreements/treaty-files/5988/download.

[17] See Art. 2(3) the Hungary-Iran BIT (2017); Art. 2(3) Belarus-Hungary BIT (2019); Art. 2(3) Cabo Verde-Hungary BIT (2019); Art. 2(3) Hungary-Kyrgyzstan BIT (2020); Art. 2-(3) Hungary-United Arab Emirates BIT (2022); and Art. 2(3) Hungary-Oman BIT (2022). The Hungary-Tajikistan BIT (2017) constitutes an exception to this trend. Art. 2(2) thereof follows the old gold standard by including an unqualified FET and FPS standard.

[18] See Art. 3(2) Iran-Slovakia BIT (2016); Art. 5(2) Lithuania-Turkey BIT (2018); Art. 5(2) Côte d'Ivoire-Portugal BIT (2019).

[19] Art. 5(2) Slovak Model BIT (2019); Art. 9(2) Dutch Model BIT (2019); Art. 4(3) Belgium-Luxembourg Economic Union Model BIT (2019); Art. 4(2) Italian Model BIT (2022).

[20] As noted by *Dumberry*, Art. 3.1 of the 2016 Indian Model BIT is particularly notable for dispensing with the term "fair and equitable", simply referring to a "violation of customary international law", which is then linked to a similar closed list as in the CETA. See Dumberry (2022), p. 260.

the prohibition of unlawful expropriation[21] are regulated in a very similar manner in EU investment agreements, recent Member States' (Model) BITs and the Commission's Model Clauses. In addition, a largely convergent approach within all of these instruments can be seen with regard to a number of general provisions, which may appear in the form of streamlined objectives, definitions or the agreements' scope of application.[22] Finally, many examples contain the clarification that the provisions of the agreement cannot be construed as preventing the Member States from discontinuing the granting of State aid or requesting its reimbursement where such action stems from an administrative or judicial decision.[23]

The Most Favoured Nation (MFN) standard is an example for almost full convergence. CETA clearly limits the scope of the MFN clause vis-à-vis the old gold standard. Member States' BITs used to include an unqualified MFN clause, which required host States to extend to foreign investors treatment no less favourable than that given to any third country. Some arbitral tribunals interpreted these provisions quite broadly, allowing the substantive and procedural standards contained in other BITs concluded by the host State with third countries to be imported to an agreement with less favourable standards.[24] Article 8.7 CETA clarifies the intended scope of the MFN clause by explicitly excluding the importation of substantive and procedural standards contained in other agreements.

This exclusion is now also expected of the Member States in their own agreements. Accordingly, the Commission's implementing decisions explicitly require Member States to provide in their BITs for

> most-favoured nation treatment that would prevent the importation of standards of treatment and procedural rights from other investment agreements, and that would not require [the

[21] On the CETA standard for expropriation, see Kriebaum (2022a), pp. 297 ff.; on the interplay between expropriation and the rule of law, see Bungenberg (2023), pp. 61 ff.

[22] Art. 8.1 and 8.2 CETA; Ch. 1 EU-Viet Nam Investment Protection Agreement; Ch. 1 EU-Singapore Investment Protection Agreement; Art. 1 Czech Model BIT (2016); Art. 1 and 2 Slovakia Model BIT (2019); Art. 1 and 2 Dutch Model BIT (2019); Art. 1–3 Belgium-Luxemburg Economic Union Model BIT (2019); Art. 1–3 Italian Model BIT (2022); Art. 1 Austria-Kyrgyzstan BIT (2016); Art. 1 Cambodia-Hungary BIT (2016); Art. 1 and 2 Slovakia-UAE BIT (2016); Art. 1 and 2 Iran-Slovakia BIT (2016); Art. 1 Hungary-Iran BIT (2018); Art. 1 Hungary-Tajikistan BIT (2017); Art. 1 and 2 Lithuania-Turkey BIT (2018); Art. 1 Belarus-Hungary BIT (2019); Art. 1–3 Côte d'Ivoire-Portugal BIT (2019); Art. 1 Cabo Verde-Hungary BIT (2019); Art. 1 Hungary-Kyrgyzstan BIT (2020); Art. 1 Hungary-UAE BIT (2021); Art. 1 Hungary-Oman BIT (2022). Notable exceptions are some of the Member States' earlier (Model) BITs, such as: Czech Model BIT (2016); Belgium-Luxemburg Economic Union Model BIT (2019); Austria-Kyrgyzstan BIT (2016); Cambodia-Hungary BIT (2016); Slovakia-UAE BIT (2016); Iran-Slovakia BIT (2016); Hungary-Tajikistan BIT (2017).

[23] Art. 8.9(4) CETA; Art. 2.2 EU-Singapore Investment Protection Agreement; Art. 4(4) Slovak Model BIT (2019); Art. 2(4) Dutch Model BIT (2019); Art. 6(4) Italian Model BIT (2022); Art. 4(4) Hungary-Iran BIT (2018); Art. 3(4) Lithuania-Turkey BIT (2018); Art. 3(3) Belarus-Hungary BIT (2019); Art. 6(5) Côte d'Ivoire-Portugal BIT (2019); Art. 3(3) Cabo Verde-Hungary BIT (2019); Art. 3(3) Hungary-Kyrgyzstan BIT (2020); Art. 3(2) Hungary-UAE BIT (2021); Art. 3(4) Hungary-Oman BIT (2022).

[24] Bungenberg and Reinisch (2021), pp. 464 f.

Member State] to extend to investors of the other Party the benefit of the treatment resulting from a process of economic integration.[25]

Recent Member States' BITs closely follow this instruction given by the Commission. By way of example, the 2016 Iran-Slovakia BIT still used the old gold standard, including an unqualified MFN provision in Article 4(1) thereof. Treaty practice started to change shortly thereafter—most BITs concluded after 2016 (and all BITs concluded since 2019) follow the EU approach by clarifying "for greater certainty" that "procedures for the resolution of investment disputes" and "substantive obligations" in other international investment treaties do not in themselves constitute "treatment" under the MFN provision.[26]

With regard to the exceptions from the MFN standard, there are minor differences between the central and decentral approach. CETA contains an exception for the recognition, accreditation and certification of services and the respective suppliers, which can also be found in the Model Clauses but not yet in many Member States' (Model) BITs.[27] The latter contain, however, additional exceptions for beneficial treatment granted from a process of economic integration or from an international agreement relating to (double) taxation.[28] CETA used to mention these exceptions in Article X.8(3)(a) and (b) of the 2013 Draft, but they did not make it into the final treaty text.[29] Instead, they can now be found somewhere else within the agreement. The exception for taxation treaties migrated to the general CETA Chapter on Exceptions (Article 28.7(6) CETA) and an "obscure" version of the exception for economic integration processes moved to an annex as envisaged by Article 8.15 CETA.[30]

Investor-State Dispute Settlement (ISDS) is a special case. The EU follows a rather atypical approach in its own investment agreements by providing for a

---

[25] See Commission Implementing Decision of 13 October 2022 authorising Hungary to open formal negotiations to amend its bilateral investment agreement with, respectively, the Republic of Albania, the Argentine Republic, the Republic of Cuba, the Republic of Moldova, the Republic of Paraguay, the Swiss Confederation, the Eastern Republic of Uruguay, the Republic of Turkey, and the Republic of Uzbekistan.

[26] See Art. 3(3) Hungary-Iran BIT (2017); Art. 4(3) Belarus-Hungary BIT (2019); Art. 8(2) Cote d'Ivoire-Portugal BIT (2019); Art. 4(3) Cabo Verde-Hungary BIT (2019); Art. 4(3) Hungary Kyrgyzstan BIT (2020); Art. 4(3) Hungary-United Arab Emirates BIT (2021); Art. 4(4) Hungary-Oman BIT (2022).

[27] Art. 8.7(3) CETA; At the decentral level, this exception can only be found in Art. 5(3) lit. c Italian Model BIT (2022).

[28] Art. 3(5) and (6) Czech Model BIT (2016); Art. 3(5) and (6) Belgium-Luxemburg Economic Union Model BIT (2019); Art. 5(3) Italian Model BIT (2022); Art. 3(4) Austria-Kyrgyzstan BIT (2016); Art. 3(5) Cambodia-Hungary BIT (2016); Art. 3(5) Hungary-Iran BIT (2018); Art. 3(3) and (5) Hungary-Tajikistan BIT (2017); Art. 5(8) lit. b Lithuania-Turkey BIT (2018); Art. 4(4) and (6) Belarus-Hungary BIT (2019); Art. 9 Côte d'Ivoire-Portugal BIT (2019); Art. 4(4) and (6) Cabo Verde-Hungary BIT (2019); Art. 4(4) and (6) Hungary-Kyrgyzstan BIT (2020); Art. 4(4) and (6) Hungary-UAE BIT (2021); Art. 4(5) and (7) Hungary-Oman BIT (2022).

[29] Reinisch (2022), mn. 34.

[30] Reinisch (2022), mn. 37 f.

permanent investment court structure (the so-called Investment Court System, ICS). Member States do not negotiate an ICS in their respective BITs, but continue to provide for traditional arbitration for the resolution of investor-State disputes. In fact, it is questionable whether this approach of establishing a permanent court structure would be even eligible to be copied by Member States in their own BITs, as long as they negotiate individually instead of collectively with third countries.[31] In any case, even though the central and decentral approaches are clearly divergent in this regard, certain elements of procedural modernization can be found in both EU and Member States' agreements (and in the Model Clauses).[32] Examples of procedural convergence are:

- the reference to the UNCITRAL Rules on Transparency (or a comparable level of transparency);[33]
- the commitment to make investment disputes subject to a future appellate mechanism;[34]

[31] On the idea of a plurilateral re-negotiation, see Bungenberg and Böhme (2022), p. 639; Griebel (2010), p. 213.

[32] The existence of procedural convergence becomes apparent when analysing certain similarities between CETA, the EU-Singapore IPA and almost all of the Member States' (Model) BITs. It is noteworthy, however, that those similarities do not exist with regard to the EU-Viet Nam IPA. This could simply be reflective of the nature of bipolar negotiations, highlighting that the EU can only streamline its investment policy to the extent that international partners are willing to agree to.

[33] Art. 8.36 CETA; Art. 3.16 and Annex 8 EU-Singapore IPA; Art. 8.5 Czech Model BIT (2016); Art. 15.7 Slovak Model BIT (2019); Art. 20(13) Dutch Model BIT (2019); Art. 19(O.1) Belgium-Luxemburg Economic Union Model BIT (2019); Art. 25(1) Italian Model BIT (2022); Art. 14-(3) Austria-Kyrgyzstan BIT (2016); Art. 22(2) Slovakia-UAE BIT (2016); Art. 14(4) Iran-Slovakia BIT (2016); Art. 14(13) Hungary-Iran BIT (2018); Art. 12(15) Lithuania-Turkey BIT (2018); Art. 11(2) Belarus-Hungary BIT (2019); Art. 20(12) Côte d'Ivoire-Portugal BIT (2019); Art. 11 Cabo Verde-Hungary BIT (2019); Art. 11 Hungary-Kyrgyzstan BIT (2020); Art. 18 Hungary-UAE BIT (2021); Art. 12 Hungary-Oman BIT (2022).

[34] Art. 8.29 CETA; Art. 3.12 EU-Singapore IPA; Art. 8(17) Czech Model BIT (2016); Art. 28(4) Slovak Model BIT (2019); Art. 15(1) Dutch Model BIT (2019); Art. 21(2) Belgium-Luxemburg Economic Union Model BIT (2019); Art. 24(6) Italian Model BIT (2022); Art. 24(4) Iran-Slovakia BIT (2016); Art. 14(14) Hungary-Iran BIT (2018); Art. 19(5) Lithuania-Turkey BIT (2018); Art. 9(11) Belarus-Hungary BIT (2019); Art. 25(1) Côte d'Ivoire-Portugal BIT (2019); Art. 9(11) Cabo Verde-Hungary BIT (2019); Art. 9(11) Hungary-Kyrgyzstan BIT (2020); Art. 24-(6) Hungary-UAE BIT (2021); Art. 10(11) Hungary-Oman BIT (2022).

- the clarification that the domestic law of the EU or the national law of the Member States can be used to interpret the consistency of measures with investment agreements but is not part of the applicable law;[35] and
- the reference to arbitrators' ethics, sometimes to a specific Code of Conduct.[36]

In sum, it is possible to identify a high degree of convergence between the central and decentral approach with regard to both substantive and procedural elements. Admittedly, (Member States') BITs have always developed a surprisingly uniform structure with similar wordings and guiding principles despite their bilateral nature.[37] In fact, the old European gold standard describes a largely uniform European approach to international investment law.[38] What is new is that this common approach is now coordinated at the central level, but mainly implemented at the decentral level. In the past, EU Member States pursued similar investment policies by their own will, without any coordination among them. Today, the Commission—influenced *inter alia* by the European Parliament—is controlling as well as ordering the EU international investment policy at both the central and decentral level, thus limiting Member States' own negotiation leeway.

In addition to these examples of (almost full) convergence, there is reduced room for Member States' own national investment policies, either diverging from the EU approach by staying in line with the old European gold standard [Sect. 2.2] or by enhancing modern EU standards even further [Sect. 2.3].

2.2 *Divergence from the EU Approach*

One clear divergence between the central and decentral approach was already mentioned in the previous section: whereas the EU includes a permanent court

[35] Art. 8.31 CETA; Art. 3.13(2) EU-Singapore IPA; Art. 8(14) Czech Model BIT (2016); Art. 19(2) Slovak Model BIT (2019); Art. 20(12) Dutch Model BIT (2019); Art. 26 Italian Model BIT (2022); Art. 18(2) Slovakia-UAE BIT (2016); Art. 14(10) Hungary-Iran BIT (2018); Art. 12-(13) Lithuania-Turkey BIT (2018); Art. 9(8) Belarus-Hungary BIT (2019); Art. 18(2) Côte d'Ivoire-Portugal BIT (2019); Art. 9(8) Cabo Verde-Hungary BIT (2019); Art. 9(8) Hungary-Kyrgyzstan BIT (2020); Art. 11(2) Hungary-UAE BIT (2021); Art. 10(8) Hungary-Oman BIT (2022).

[36] Art. 8.30 CETA; Art. 3.11 EU-Singapore IPA; Art. 8(2) lit. c Czech Model BIT (2016); Art. 18(4) Slovak Model BIT (2019); Art. 20(6) Dutch Model BIT (2019); Art. 19(G.5) Belgium-Luxemburg Economic Union Model BIT (2019); Art. 27 Italian Model BIT (2022); Art. 14(1) lit. c (iii) Austria-Kyrgyzstan BIT (2016); Art. 8(3) lit. c Cambodia-Hungary BIT (2016); Art. 19-(8) Slovakia-UAE BIT (2016); Art. 18(5) Iran-Slovakia BIT (2016); Art. 14(7) Hungary-Iran BIT (2018); Art. 8(2) lit. c Hungary-Tajikistan BIT (2017); Art. 12(8) Lithuania-Turkey BIT (2018); Art. 9(9) Belarus-Hungary BIT (2019); Art. 23 Côte d'Ivoire-Portugal BIT (2019); Art. 9(9) Cabo Verde-Hungary BIT (2019); Art. 9(9) Hungary-Kyrgyzstan BIT (2020); Art. 14 Hungary-UAE BIT (2021); Art. 10(9) Hungary-Oman BIT (2022).

[37] Schill (2009), p. 65.

[38] On this, see Gaffney and Akçay (2015), pp. 186 ff.

structure in its own investment agreements, Member States' BITs continue to rely on traditional investor-State arbitration, thus following the old (European) gold standard. Hence, the EU appears to follow a twofold approach when it comes to ISDS. Within the United Nations Commission on International Trade Law (UNCITRAL) Working Group III, the Commission argues for a full and incremental reform of ISDS with a view of establishing a Multilateral Investment Court (MIC) in the long run. This long-term goal is also reflected in recent Member States' BITs. An example is Article 9(1) of the Hungary-San Marino BIT (2022), providing that

> [t]he Contracting Parties shall pursue with each other and other trading partners the establishment of a multilateral investment tribunal and appellate mechanism for the resolution of investment disputes. Upon entry into force between the Contracting Parties of an international agreement providing for a multilateral investment tribunal and/or a multilateral appellate mechanism applicable to disputes under this Agreement, the relevant parts of this Agreement shall cease to apply.

Similar clauses can be found in other recent Member States' (Model) BITs[39] and the Commission's Model Clauses. Contemporaneously, these instruments continue to refer to traditional investor-State arbitration combined with elements of procedural modernisation.[40] In other words, the decentral approach allows for old-fashioned arbitration "wearing new clothes".

Another clear example of divergence between the central and decentral approach is market access. Recent Member States' BITs unequivocally deviate from the EU approach in this regard. Traditionally, International Investment Agreements (IIAs) have only provided for investment protection once the operation has been established in the host State (Controlled Market Access Model).[41] In addition, many IIAs provide that foreign investment is subject to the laws and regulations of the host State, thus heavily regulating what can and cannot enter the domestic market and under what conditions.[42] Some IIAs are slightly less restrictive with regard to market access, extending the non-discrimination principle to the pre-establishment phase (MFN and National Treatment-Based Entry Model).[43] Under these IIAs, the entry of foreign investment may only be regulated on a non-discriminatory basis.

CETA contains a unique market access clause in Article 8.4, which goes a step further with additional commitments by the Contracting Parties for the

[39] Art. 8(17) Czech Model BIT (2016); Art. 28(4) Slovak Model BIT (2019); Art. 15(1) Dutch Model BIT (2019); Art. 21(2) Belgium-Luxemburg Economic Union Model BIT (2019); Art. 24(6) Italian Model BIT (2022); Art. 24(4) Iran-Slovakia BIT (2016); Art. 14(14) Hungary-Iran BIT (2018); Art. 19(5) Lithuania-Turkey BIT (2018); Art. 9(11) Belarus-Hungary BIT (2019); Art. 25(1) Côte d'Ivoire-Portugal BIT (2019); Art. 9(11) Cabo Verde-Hungary BIT (2019); Art. 9-(11) Hungary-Kyrgyzstan BIT (2020); Art. 24(6) Hungary-UAE BIT (2021); Art. 10(11) Hungary-Oman BIT (2022).

[40] See *supra* Sect. 2.1.

[41] Shan and Zhang (2014), pp. 439 f.; de Mestral and Vanhonnaeker (2022), p. 169; Bungenberg and Blandfort (2020), p. 161.

[42] De Mestral and Vanhonnaeker (2022), pp. 162, 169.

[43] Ibid., pp. 169 f.

pre-establishment phase.[44] The first paragraph of Article 8.4 CETA lists a series of measures which are prohibited with regard to the pre-establishment phase, including limitations on

- the number of enterprises that may carry out a specific economic activity;
- the total value of transactions or assets;
- the total number of operations or the total quantity of output;
- the participation of foreign capital in terms of maximum percentage limit on foreign shareholding;
- the total number of natural persons that may be employed in a particular sector.

These prohibited measures come *inter alia* in the form of numerical quotas, monopolies, or the requirement of an economic needs test, and constitute an obstacle to the overall goal of international trade and investment law to achieve a broad level of liberalization.[45] CETA's broad market access obligations even go further than the level of liberalization currently provided under the General Agreement on Trade in Services (GATS) as part of the law of the World Trade Organization (WTO). The GATS provides for a positive-list approach, creating the right to establishment only for those sectors, where express commitments are made by the Contracting Parties. CETA opts for a negative-list approach instead. Accordingly, the measures prohibited under Art. 8.4 CETA extend to all sectors except those carved out in the Contracting Parties' schedules under Annex II.[46]

At the same time, this progressive liberalization under CETA is limited through the second paragraph of Article 8.4, which lists a series of measures potentially impeding market access, which are deemed consistent with the first paragraph.[47] The regulatory practices mentioned in paragraph 2 aim *inter alia* at ensuring fair competition in sensitive sectors, such as energy, transport and telecommunications or the conservation and protection of natural resources and the environment. Moreover, a Contracting Party's decision to deny market access to an investor is not subject to ISDS, whereas State-to-State dispute settlement remains available. In sum, CETA's market access clause under the investment chapter may be deemed the most progressive of its kind but still remains subject to certain limitations that preserve States' sovereign regulatory autonomy.[48]

In conformity with the development described in the previous section, one could have expected that the Member States would equally be required to adapt their market access policy under investment agreements convergent to the EU approach, thus making express commitments for the pre-establishment phase in their BITs. However, the topic of market access is not dealt with at all at the decentral level. To the contrary, the Commission's Model Clauses merely clarify that Member States'

---

[44] Bungenberg and Reinisch (2021), p. 461.

[45] See Gómez Palacio and Muchlinski (2008), pp. 228 f.

[46] De Mestral and Vanhonnaeker (2022), p. 172.

[47] Ibid.

[48] Bungenberg and Reinisch (2021), p. 461.

BITs should not cover the pre-establishment phase or matters of market access. In a uniform manner, *none* of the Member States' BITs concluded or the Model BITs adopted since 2016 follow the EU approach. By contrast, all of them stick to the old European gold standard, thus subjecting the admission of foreign investment to domestic laws. By way of example, Article 2(1) of the Austria-Kyrgyzstan BIT (2016) merely provides that

> [e]ach Contracting Party shall, according to its laws and regulations, promote and admit investments by investors of the other Contracting Party.

A similar clause is included in recent Hungarian BITs, for instance Article 2(1) of the Hungary-Oman BIT (2022), whereby

> [e]ach Contracting Party shall encourage and create favourable conditions for Investors of the other Contracting Party to make Investments in its Territory and shall admit such Investments in accordance with its laws and regulations.[49]

The Italian Model BIT (2022) is even more definite when it comes to market access.[50] Article 3 thereof clarifies "for greater certainty" that the agreement "provides only post-establishment protection and does not cover the pre-establishment phase or matters of market access", thus following the same wording as the Model Clauses. These examples show that Member States' (Model) BITs do not provide for international commitments with regard to market access, subjecting the pre-establishment phase entirely to domestic law and thus significantly deviating from the EU approach.

This disparity between negotiations at the central and decentral level is, however, in line with the EU's investment policy. Naturally, the commitments made in EU investment agreements, which are concluded by both the EU and its Member States, extend to the entire EU territory, and thus, also to the territory of the Member States. However, they are only made with regard to selected third countries, such as Canada, which the EU trusts enough to make such a commitment. Notably, no provisions on market access were included in the EU-Singapore or EU-Vietnam IPAs either—CETA remains an exception so far. The Commission's implementing decisions for Member States' BITs equally do not mention market access, and the Model Clauses limit investment protection to the post-establishment phase. In other words, Member States are not expected to include a similarly broad market access clause as followed by the EU in CETA.

---

[49] See also other Member States' BITs: Art. 2(1) Austria-Kyrgyzstan BIT (2016); Art. 2-(1) Cambodia-Hungary BIT (2016); Art. 2(1) and (2) Slovakia-United Arab Emirates BIT (2016); Art. 2(5) Iran-Slovakia BIT (2016); Art. 12(2) Hungary-Iran BIT (2017); Art. 2-(1) Hungary-Tajikistan BIT (2017); Art. 2(4) Lithuania-Turkey BIT (2018); Art. 2(1) Belarus-Hungary BIT (2019); Art. 4(1) Côte d'Ivoire-Portugal BIT (2019); Art. 2(1) Cabo Verde-Hungary BIT; Art. 2(1) Hungary-Kyrgyzstan BIT (2020); Art. 2(1) Hungary-United Arab Emirates BIT (2021); and Art. 2(1) Hungary-Oman BIT (2022).

[50] See also other Model BITs: Art. 2(1) of the Czech Model BIT (2016); Art. 3(1) of the Slovak Model BIT (2019); Art. 3(1) and (2) Dutch Model BIT (2019); Art. 4(1) Belgium-Luxembourg Economic Union Model BIT (2019); and Art. 3 Italian Model BIT (2022).

Since provisions on market access of foreign direct investments unequivocally fall under the Common Commercial Policy (CCP),[51] the EU could have demanded its Member States to adopt a more progressive stance in their BITs. However, the decision to carve out market access of the harmonised EU approach is consistent with other EU instruments, in particular its cooperative screening mechanism established under Regulation 2019/452[52] (EU Screening Regulation). The purpose of the EU Screening Regulation is stated in Article 2(4) thereof, according to which the Regulation sets out the terms to "assess, investigate, authorise, condition, prohibit or unwind foreign direct investments on grounds of security or public order". In accordance with Article 3(1) of the EU Screening Regulation, "Member States may maintain, amend or adopt mechanisms to screen foreign direct investments in their territory on the grounds of security or public order". Hence, the general responsibility for the screening of foreign investment lies not with the EU but with the Member States, who may decide whether they want to establish a respective administrative procedure within their national laws.[53] In light of this screening regime, the decision to allow Member States to keep their respective standard with regard to market access under investment agreements appears to be a consistent approach. Member States may decide for themselves which foreign direct investments are able to access their markets, and which investments pose a threat to their national security or public order. Similarly, they may decide for themselves whether they want to establish a national screening mechanism in accordance with the EU Screening Regulation.

As this section has shown, despite the general trend towards a harmonised EU approach, there is still room for divergent approaches at the decentral level. In addition, there is room for an EU-plus approach for those Member States that want to go beyond EU standards, as will be shown in the ensuing section.

2.3 EU-Plus Approach

Several of the recent Member States' (Model) BITs contain provisions on the protection of non-investment policy interests that go beyond the standards embodied in EU investment agreements. These non-investment policy interests mostly reflect the areas of sustainable environmental and social development, which have become more and more important in international investment law throughout the last decade.[54] Recent IIAs reflect this trend by safeguarding the host State's regulatory

---

[51] Shan and Zhang (2010), pp. 1049 ff.; Herrmann and Müller-Ibold (2016), pp. 646 f.; Bungenberg (2010), p. 143.

[52] Regulation (EU) 2019/452 of the European Parliament and of the Council of 19 March 2019 establishing a framework for the screening of foreign direct investments into the Union.

[53] Bungenberg and Blandfort (2020), p. 171.

[54] See amongst others Nowrot (2014), pp. 612–644; Chi (2017).

space with regard to the protection of the environment, labour standards and human rights, among others. The EU's international investment policy is in line with this overall trend by reaffirming the Contracting Parties' right to regulate in Article 8.9 CETA to achieve legitimate policy objectives, such as "the protection of public health, safety, the environment or public morals, social or consumer protection or the promotion and protection of cultural diversity".[55] This list entails a two-fold guarantee for CETA's Contracting Parties to be able to use regulation to strengthen public policy objectives and to protect public welfare from negative aspects of inbound investments.[56]

CETA's preamble specifically highlights the Contracting Parties' right to regulate in the sense of Article 8.9[57] and demands the implementation of the agreement to be consistent with the enforcement and enhancement of the Contracting Parties' levels of labour and environmental protection.[58] In addition to this, the Contracting Parties reaffirm their "commitment to promote sustainable development",[59] explicitly recognise their "strong attachment to democracy and to fundamental rights",[60] and encourage enterprises operating within their territory "to respect internationally recognized guidelines and principles of corporate social responsibilities".[61]

Furthermore, CETA Chapters 23 ("Trade and Labour") and 24 ("Trade and Environment") reaffirm the Contracting Parties' right to regulate with regard to labour and environmental standards. The fact that the titles of these chapters do not specifically refer to investment should not deceive their relevance in this regard. Both chapters include specific provisions regarding the right to regulate, seeking to "ensure that [. . .] laws and policies provide for and encourage high levels of [. . .] protection"[62], and recognizing "that it is inappropriate to encourage trade or investment by weakening or reducing the levels of protection afforded in their [. . .] law"[63]. Hence, the chapters on labour and environment do not only reaffirm the right to regulate but oblige the Contracting Parties to abstain from lowering their level of protection in order to attract foreign investment.[64] Despite the fact that CETA does not include specific investor obligations regarding the protection of labour and the environment, the given legal construction is viewed as significant and "beyond minimum standards"[65]. Furthermore, Chapter 22 indicates that

[55] Art. 8.9 CETA, para. 1.

[56] Schacherer (2022), p. 243.

[57] CETA Preamble, Recitals 6 and 8.

[58] CETA Preamble, Recital 11.

[59] CETA Preamble, Recital 9.

[60] CETA Preamble, Recital 4.

[61] CETA Preamble, Recital 10.

[62] Art. 23.2 and Art. 24.3 CETA.

[63] Art. 23.3 and Art. 24.5 CETA.

[64] Titi (2019), p. 162; Schacherer (2022), p. 240.

[65] Bartels (2017), p. 4.

> the Parties agree that the rights and obligations under Chapters Twenty-Three (Trade and Labour) and Twenty-Four (Trade and Environment) are to be considered in the context of this Agreement.[66]

Hence, even though there is no explicit reference to sustainable development in CETA's Investment Chapter, the presence of these policy objectives in the Preamble and Chapters 22–24 indicate that they "will most likely have an impact on the interpretation of the investment protection standards under CETA".[67] CETA's direct reference to the right to regulate and its indirect inclusion of sustainable development into the Investment Chapter constitute a "ground-breaking change" in comparison to the old European gold standard, showing the EU's attempt to safeguard host States' regulatory autonomy.[68] Traditional Member States' BITs, by contrast, barely touched upon value-based policy objectives, exclusively focusing on investment protection standards.

The EU's approach of preserving extensive policy space, limiting investment protection for the benefit of sustainable environmental and social development, has equally found its way into the current landscape of Member States' BITs. In some of those BITs, the reservation of regulatory space is implemented through "General Exceptions" clauses with a focus on financial stability and essential security interests.[69] The majority of the analysed (Model) BITs, however, go a step further by including a clause on the right to regulate that strongly resembles the wording of Article 8.9 CETA.[70] Additionally, largely all (Model) BITs contain CETA-like best endeavour positions and clauses that prohibit lowering environmental and labour standards to attract foreign investment.[71] By way of example, Article 3(2) of the Slovak Model BIT (2019) provides that

> [t]he Contracting Parties recognise that it is inappropriate to weaken or reduce the level of protection provided by domestic health, safety, labour or environmental laws, regulations or standards with the sole intention to encourage investment. (...).

---

[66] Art. 22.2 CETA.

[67] Schacherer (2019), p. 236.

[68] Overduin (2021), para. 15.61.

[69] Art. 13 Cambodia-Hungary BIT (2016); Art. 13 Slovakia-UAE BIT (2016); Art. 11 Iran-Slovakia BIT (2016); Art. 13 Hungary-Tajikistan BIT (2017); Art. 16 Belarus-Hungary BIT (2019); Art. 16 Hungary-San Marino BIT (2022).

[70] Art. 12 Czech Model BIT (2016); Art. 4 Slovak Model BIT (2019); Art. 2 Dutch Model BIT (2019); Art. 17 Belgium-Luxemburg Economic Union Model BIT (2019); Art. 6 Italian Model BIT (2022); Art. 4 Hungary-Iran BIT (2017); Art. 3 Lithuania-Turkey BIT; Art. 6 Côte d'Ivoire-Portugal BIT (2019); Art. 3 Cabo Verde-Hungary BIT (2019); Art. 3 Hungary-Kyrgyzstan BIT (2020); Art. 3 Hungary-UAE BIT (2021); Art. 3 Hungary-Oman BIT (2022).

[71] Art. 6 Dutch Model BIT (2019); Art. 15 Belgium-Luxemburg Economic Union Model BIT (2019); Art. 20 and 22 Italian Model BIT (2022); Art. 2(3) Cambodia-Hungary BIT (2016); Art. 12(1) and (2) Slovakia-UAE BIT (2016); Art. 10(1) and (2) Iran-Slovakia BIT (2016); Art. 2(6) Hungary-Iran BIT (2017); Art. 2(3) Hungary-Tajikistan BIT (2017); Art. 17(1) and (2) Lithuania-Turkey BIT; Art. 2(7) Belarus-Hungary BIT (2019); Art. 16 Côte d'Ivoire-Portugal BIT (2019); Art. 2 (8) Cabo Verde-Hungary BIT (2019); Art. 2(7) Hungary-Kyrgyzstan BIT (2020); Art. 2(7) Hungary-UAE BIT (2021); Art. 2(7) Hungary-Oman BIT (2022).

However, even though Member States' (Model) BITs are largely convergent with the EU approach when it comes to the right to regulate, the Commission's implementing decisions appear to require Member States to go a step further when it comes to sustainable development by including in their BITs

- Provisions on climate change and clean energy transition in line with the Paris Agreement and relevant EU agreements and EU positions in ongoing negotiations;
- Prohibition of investment enhancement by lowering or relaxing domestic environmental or labour legislation and standards, or by failing to effectively enforce such legislation and standards;
- Provisions promoting human rights and international labour standards, as well as internationally recognized standards of responsible business conduct, such as the OECD Guidelines for Multinational Enterprises, the UN Guiding Principles on Business and Human Rights and the International Labour Organisation Tripartite Declaration of Principles concerning Multinational Enterprises and Social Policy.[72]

The Commission's Model Clauses go yet another step further in this regard, suggesting precise wording for the inclusion of provisions promoting these non-investment interests. The suggested preamble is similar to the one included in CETA and other EU agreements, referring *inter alia* to "sustainable development in the economic, social and environmental dimensions", "high levels of environmental and labour protection through relevant internationally recognised standards", and international commitments under "the Charter of the United Nations and having regard to the principles articulated in the Universal Declaration of Human Rights". In addition, the Model Clauses contain provisions on "General Exceptions", "Security Exceptions" and "Temporary Safeguard Measures", which all appear to be strongly influenced by Articles XIX to XXI of the General Agreement on Tariffs and Trade (GATT). Furthermore, the Model Clauses include provisions on "Corporate Social Responsibility and Responsible Business Conduct", "Investment and Environment", "Investment and Climate Change", "Investment and Labour" as well as an obligation for the Contracting Parties to enter into dialogue and cooperate on investment-related sustainable development issues.

It is notable that the instructions given at the central level through the Commission's implementing decisions and the Model Clauses appear to go beyond the standards negotiated by the EU within its own agreements. A particular issue that arises under CETA is that it follows a rather fragmented approach that leaves room for interpretation regarding the interdependence of certain chapters and specific clauses. In fact, CETA's Investment Chapter does not explicitly refer to sustainable development in its operative part. Instead, it mostly deals with non-economic concerns in its preamble and other chapters. Even though they are relevant for the interpretation of the Investment Chapter in light of its context and purpose, no direct legal obligations are created that way.[73] At the decentral level, sustainable development is dealt with in the agreement itself, therefore leaving less interpretative

---

[72] See Commission Implementing Decision C(2022)7177 of 13 October 2022, Art. 2(1)(h).
[73] Kriebaum (2022b), pp. 8 f.; Böhme (2022), pp. 256 f.

uncertainty *inter alia* about the consideration of environmental and labour standards in relation to investment protection standards.[74]

Arguably, CETA's fragmented approach is partially owed to its overall structure as a comprehensive economic and trade agreement. However, the EU-Singapore and EU-Vietnam IPAs equally fall short of provisions on sustainable development despite their condensed legal structure. In fact, in both agreements, the term "sustainable development" can only be found in the preamble but nowhere in their operative part. Similar to CETA, there is merely a provision whereby the Contracting Parties reaffirm their right to regulate.[75] In contrast, some of the recent Member States' (Model) BITs include standards on the protection of non-investment interests that go beyond the CETA-like use of positive reinforcement, the recognition of their importance, cooperation, public awareness and dialogue. By way of example, numerous Member States' (Model) BITs use a specific clause under the heading "Environmental [and Labor] Rights and other Standards" which stands out by imposing standards of conduct on protected investors in the following terms:

> Investors and investments *should* apply national, and internationally accepted, standards of corporate governance for the sector involved, in particular for transparency and accounting practices. Investors and their investments *should* strive to make the maximum feasible contributions to the sustainable development of the Host State and local community through appropriate levels of socially responsible practices.[76] [emphasis added]

Another example is Article 7(1) of the 2019 Dutch Model BIT, which provides that

> [i]nvestors and their investment *shall* comply with domestic laws and regulations of the host state, including laws and regulations on human rights, environmental protection and labor laws. [emphasis added]

These clauses are notable because they directly impose standards of conduct on protected investors. Not even the Commission's Model Clauses suggest wording in that direction. The Model Clauses' extensive provisions on the environment, climate change, and corporate social responsibility only contain obligations for the Contracting Parties but do not directly address protected investors. EU investment agreements are even less progressive in this regard—they mostly contain language of mere positive reinforcement in their preamble and refer to the Contracting Parties' right to regulate. Certain Member States' (Model) BITs, by contrast, go beyond EU

---

[74] For a detailed analysis on how the presence of sustainable development aspects within CETA's treaty body and connected instruments impacts the interpretation of CETA, see Schacherer (2019), pp. 207–238.

[75] Art. 2.2(1) EU-Singapore IPA and Art. 2.2(1) EU-Viet Nam IPA.

[76] Art. 10(3) Iran-Slovakia BIT (2016); Art. 17(3) Lithuania-Turkey BIT (2018); Art. 12-(3) Slovakia-UAE BIT (2016) contains the first sentence of the quoted clause. Art. 17 Côte d'Ivoire-Portugal BIT (2019) contains a Corporate Social Responsibility (CSR) clause with slightly softer wording, obliging the Contracting Parties to "encourage investors [...] to voluntarily incorporate in their activities internationally recognized corporate social responsibility standards, such as the OECD [...] Guidelines for Multinational Enterprises".

standards by providing the potential for a significant step towards genuine investor obligations.

This difference is important considering that only legally binding obligations can be enforced.[77] The language used in the provisions of the Member States' (Model) BITs mentioned above could be used as legal basis for enforcement, for instance, through counter-claims by the host State or by rendering the treaty-based investment protection conditional upon the observance of these obligations.[78] Article 7(4) of the 2019 Dutch Model BIT refers to the home State's jurisdiction as another possible means of enforcement in case the investor's decisions made in relation to its investment lead to "significant damage, personal injuries or loss of life in the host state".[79] Finally, another option of enforcement is to take the investor's non-compliance into account at the quantum stage.[80] This approach is followed in Article 23 of the 2019 Dutch Model BIT, which reads:

> Without prejudice to national administrative or criminal law procedure, a Tribunal, in deciding the amount of compensation, is expected to take into account non-compliance by the investor with its commitments under the UN Guiding Principles on Business and Human Rights, and the OECD Guidelines for Multinational Enterprises.[81]

As a result, there seems to be room for an EU-plus approach for those Member States that want to go beyond the standards enshrined in EU investment agreements. Some of these standards even go beyond what is required in the Commission's implementing decisions or recommended in the Model Clauses.

3 Conclusion

The main goal of this contribution was to shed light on the way the EU is currently conducting its international investment policy. The sources thereof span an ever-more differentiated net of FTAs and IPAs, informal communications such as the Model Clauses, the Commission's Implementing Decisions as well as Member States' (Model) BITs. Since the EU has seemingly come to a dead-end with regard to the ratification of its investment agreements, the implementation of the EU's international investment policy has mostly shifted from a central to a decentral

[77] Böhme (2022), p. 259.

[78] Kriebaum (2018), p. 36.

[79] Art. 7(4) of the 2019 Dutch Model BIT reads: "[i]nvestors shall be liable in accordance with the rules concerning jurisdiction of their home State for the acts or decisions made in relation to the investment where such acts or decisions lead to significant damage, personal injuries or loss of life in the host state".

[80] Böhme (2022), p. 260.

[81] As noted by *Abel*, it is notable how Art. 23 of the Dutch Model BIT provides legally non-binding CSR norms with legal effect allowing tribunals to modify the calculation method of damages after evaluating investors' behaviour towards human rights. See Abel (2021), p. 227.

approach, with Member States being the main driver of negotiations. Hence, in order to decipher a "European" investment policy, it was deemed necessary to compare the former central approach with the current decentral approach. The analysis of the aforementioned policy instruments has resulted in three key takeaways:

(1) Member States' (Model) BITs show a large amount of *convergence* with the EU's investment agreements, indicating that the Member States are currently implementing a harmonised EU investment policy.
(2) In some aspects, the Member States' (Model) BITs, the corresponding Commission Implementing Decisions and the Model Clauses show *divergence* to the central EU approach.
(3) Lastly, there seems to be potential for an *EU-plus approach*, which has so far materialised especially with regard to the promotion of non-investment objectives through the Member States' own BITs.

The sections above have highlighted how these aspects are reflected in the different investment policy instruments of the EU and its Member States. The reasons for the described developments can be manifold. IIAs are a complex political matter by nature—a certain amount of deviance can be down to national trends within EU Member States as well as their negotiating partners. In general, there seems to be a pattern of pragmatism in the landscape of EU investment policy. Its implementation at the central level has not been the most successful in recent years. As a result, the Commission now uses the respective communications and legislative instruments to give guidance and authorisation to the Member States, which appear to be willing to "take the driver's seat". The fact that the analysis has shown some differing aspects does not mean that there is a lack of coordination between the EU's Member States and institutions. In contrast, the conclusion could be drawn that the EU's investment policy shows a certain amount of flexibility to account for the differences when negotiating at a central or decentral level. In particular, the described EU-plus approach highlights the potential for willing Member States to take further steps to establish new trends in international investment protection—paving the way for other Member States, the EU, or even third countries to follow.

References

Abel P (2021) International Investor Obligations. Towards Individual International Responsibility for the Public Interest in International Investment Law. Nomos

Bartels L (2017) Human Rights, Labour Standards and Environmental Standards in CETA. University of Cambridge Legal Studies Research Paper Series, Paper No. 13/2017

Böhme B (2022) Enhancing supply chain responsibilities through international investment agreements. ZEuS 25(2):251–264

Bungenberg M (2010) Going global? The EU common commercial policy after Lisbon. In: Herrmann C, Terhechte J (eds) European yearbook of international economic law. Springer, pp 123–151

Bungenberg M (2022) Europäische Internationale Investitionspolitik. In: von Arnauld A, Bungenberg M (eds) Enzyklopädie Europarecht, Band 12: Europäische Außenbeziehungen, 2nd edn. Nomos, pp 907–976

Bungenberg M (2023) (Direct and Indirect) expropriation and the rule of law. In: Reinisch A, Schill S (eds) Investment protection standards and the rule of law. Oxford University Press, pp 61–80

Bungenberg M, Blandfort F (2020) Investment screening – a new era of European protectionism?, Law and practice of the common commercial policy. Brill Nijhoff, pp 161–184

Bungenberg M, Böhme B (2022) Under the Radar – the Return of Member States in EU investment policy. J Int Econ Law 25(4):627–642

Bungenberg M, Reinisch A (2021) A paradigm change: the CETA investment chapter. ZEuS 24(3): 437–484

Chi M (2017) Integrating sustainable development in international investment law: normative incompatibility, system integration and governance implications. Routledge

Cremona M (2018) Shaping EU Trade Policy Post-Lisbon: Opinion 2/15 of 16 May 2017. Eur Const Law Rev 14:231–259

de Mestral A, Vanhonnaeker L (2022) Article 8.4. In: Bungenberg M, Reinisch A (eds) CETA investment law. Beck/Hart/Nomos, pp 159–174

Dumberry P (2022) Article 8.10. In: Bungenberg M, Reinisch A (eds) CETA investment law. Beck/Hart/Nomos, pp 256–276

European Commission (2010) Towards a Comprehensive European International Investment Policy, COM(2010) 343 final

European Commission (2020) Report from the Commission to the European Parliament and the Council on the Application of Regulation (EU) No 1219/2012, COM(2020) 132 final

Gaffney JP, Akçay Z (2015) European bilateral approaches. In: Bungenberg M et al (eds) International investment law. A handbook. Beck/Hart/Nomos, pp 186–201

Griebel J (2010) Die neue EU-Kompetenz für ausländische Direktinvestitionen – Chance für einen multilateralen Ansatz im internationalen Investitionsrecht. In: Bungenberg M et al (eds) Internationaler Investitionsschutz und Europarecht. Nomos, pp 211–22

Griller S (2020) Die Gemeinsame Handelspolitik unter Kontrolle (sub-)nationaler Parlamente und Referenden. In: Herrmann C (ed) Die gemeinsame Handelspolitik im Europäischen Verfassungsbund, EuR Europarecht, Beiheft 2. Nomos, pp 41–76

Herrmann C, Müller-Ibold T (2016) Die Entwicklung des europäischen Außenwirtschaftsrechts. EuZW 27(17):646–653

Kriebaum U (2018) Human rights and international investment law. In: Radi, Yannick (ed) Research handbook on human rights and investment. Cheltenham/Northhampton, pp 13–40

Kriebaum U (2022a) Article 8.12. In: Bungenberg M, Reinisch A (eds) CETA investment law. Beck/Hart/Nomos, pp 297–336

Kriebaum U (2022b) International Investment Law and Sustainable Development, forthcoming In: McInereny-Langford S, McCorquodale R (eds) The Role of International Law in Development. Available at: https://papers.ssrn.com/sol3/papers.cfm?abstract_id=4298374

Nowrot K (2014) How to include environmental protection, human rights and sustainability in international investment law. J World Investment Trade 15(3–4):612–644

Overduin D (2021) Investment chapter in CETA: groundbreaking or much ado about nothing? In: Mata Dona JR, Lavranos N (eds) . Edward Elgar, International arbitration and EU law, pp 338–359

Palacio IG, Muchlinski PT (2008) Admission and establishment. In: Muchlinski PT, Ortino F, Schreuer C (eds) . The Oxford handbook of international investment law, OUP, pp 227–258

Reinisch A (2022) Article 8.7. In: Bungenberg M, Reinisch A (eds) CETA investment law. Beck/Hart/Nomos, pp 216–230

Rosas A (2021) Mixity and the common commercial policy: the first 10 years after the treaty of Lisbon. Brill, pp 27–46

Schacherer S (2019), The CETA investment chapter and sustainable development: interpretative issues. In: Mbengue MM, Schacherer S (eds) Foreign investment under the comprehensive economic and trade agreement (CETA), pp 207–238
Schacherer S (2022) Article 8.9. In: Bungenberg M, Reinisch A (eds) CETA investment law. Beck/Hart/Nomos, pp 236–255
Schill S (2009) The multilateralization of international investment law. CUP
Shan W, Zhang S (2010) The treaty of Lisbon: half way toward a common investment policy. EJIL 21:1049–1073
Shan W, Zhang S (2014) Market access provisions in the potential EU model BIT: towards a global BIT 2.0. J World Invest Trade 15(3–4):422–453
Stifter L (2022) Art. 8.44. In: Bungenberg M, Reinisch A (eds) CETA investment law. Article-by-Article Commentary. Nomos, pp 945–954
Titi C (2015) International investment law and the European Union: towards a new generation of international investment agreements. Eur J Int Law 16(3):639–661
Titi C (2019) The right to regulate. In: Mbengue MM, Schacherer S (eds) Foreign investment under the comprehensive economic and trade agreement (CETA), pp 159–184

The Institutional Design of an MIC: Why the Proposed MIC Fails to Address the Real Concerns

Nikos Lavranos

Contents

Abstract The Multilateral Investment Court (MIC) which the EU is proposing to replace the current Investor-State Dispute Settlement (ISDS) system fails to address the real concerns, which relate to the harmonisation of the substantive protection standards rather than procedural issues. More generally, it is shown that many of the concerns raised against ISDS have already been addressed or are not real concerns but rather based on misconceptions and misrepresentations. In any event, so far the support by other States for the creation of a full two-tiered MIC has been rather limited and it remains to be seen whether this going to change.

N. Lavranos (✉)
European Federation for Investment Law and Arbitration (EFILA), Haarlem, The Netherlands
e-mail: n.lavranos@efila.org

M. Bungenberg, A. Reinisch (eds.), *New Frontiers for EU Investment Policy*, Special Issue, https://doi.org/10.1007/978-3-031-41977-5_4

1 Starting Point: The MIC Is a Political Phantasy of the EU

As I will explain, the proposed Multilateral Investment Court (MIC) is trying to solve a legal problem that does not really exist, so this is why it is a political phantasy.

In fact, the MIC is purely a political project serving the needs of particular stakeholders, such as the European Commission, the European Parliament (EP), national Parliaments of the Member States, NGOs, and the Court of Justice of the EU (CJEU).

In order to fully appreciate this, it is necessary to go back in time and recall the political context of the MIC.

It all started with the TTIP negotiations[1] in the early 2010s which thanks to the NGOs were politically hijacked by replaying the "battle of Seattle",[2] when the WTO negotiations were derailed with violent protests in Seattle in 1999.

With the Lisbon Treaty entering into force at the end of 2009, the EP became the co-legislator by obtaining the power to approve international trade and investment agreements. Accordingly, the EP was the new powerful kid on the block and having no idea about investment treaties at that time, it was educated by the NGOs, which fed their own positions into the EP.

Whereas the TTIP negotiations were essentially finished with the Obama Administration, Investor-State Dispute Settlement (ISDS) became publicly toxic in Berlin, Brussels, Amsterdam, so the negotiations were frozen and of course never came alive again after Trump came into office.[3]

While TTIP was effectively killed, CETA was still on the table, so the problem for the European Commission was how to get CETA through the EP and the Member States' parliaments after it became clear that CETA must be qualified as a mixed agreement.[4]

First, the EU slightly modified the ISDS provisions but the EP and some Member States such as Germany, the Netherlands, France, said "njet" because they considered this reform as cosmetic and not far-reaching enough.[5]

Consequently, in a second step, ISDS had to be replaced or better declared "dead" as was done by former Dutch Trade Minister Ploumen.[6]

---

[1] See for an overview of the negotiations: DG Trade (2016), The Transatlantic Trade and Investment Partnership (TTIP) – State of Play, 27 April 2016, https://trade.ec.europa.eu/doclib/docs/2016/april/tradoc_154477.pdf.

[2] See: The Washington Post, Violence Breaks Out at Seattle WTO Meeting, 30 November 1999, https://www.washingtonpost.com/wp-srv/pmextra/nov99/30/wto.htm??noredirect=on.

[3] Politico, ISDS: The most toxic acronym in Europe, 17 September 2015, https://www.politico.eu/article/isds-the-most-toxic-acronym-in-europe/.

[4] Lavranos (2017), pp. 1–34.

[5] See for a detailed historic account: Lavranos (2020), pp. 441–457.

[6] De Zeeuw, Ploumen: grootste bezwaar TTIP is al "dood en begraven", NRC, 7 Oktober 2015, https://www.nrc.nl/nieuws/2015/10/07/ploumen-neemt-110-000-handtekeningen-in-ontvangst-tegen-ttip-a1412547.

So, the terminology and the perception of ISDS was changed: from being secret, bad, and ad hoc arbitration towards a public, good, permanent court. Accordingly, ISDS was replaced by the Investment Court System (ICS).

2 ICS Has Been Dumped by the EC

After the CJEU approved ICS as being compatible with EU law,[7] none of the stakeholders could block ICS any longer. Hence, ICS was eventually included in CETA, and it was attached to the already closed EU-Singapore agreement and to the EU-Vietnam FTA.

However, the truth is that even today, almost 10 years after CETA was finalized, the investment protection part has not yet entered into force. There are still several ratifications by EU Member States outstanding.[8]

Recently, however, CETA got narrowly approved in the Netherlands[9] and in Germany after the EC had offered new technical clarifications regarding "more precise definitions of the concepts of 'indirect expropriation' and 'fair and equitable treatment' of investors". According to the EC, "the aim is to ensure that the parties can regulate in the framework of climate, energy and health policies, inter alia, to achieve legitimate public objectives, while at the same time preventing the misuse of the investor to State dispute settlement mechanism by investors."[10]

Nonetheless, this cannot hide the fact that even the ICS is for many critics not good enough and they simply do not want any investor-State dispute settlement provisions included in any trade or investment agreement.[11]

In fact, the truth is that the EC itself has actually given up on the ICS because the ICS part—falling within the competence of the 27 Member States—remains a huge obstacle for a quick ratification of EU trade agreements as the example of CETA shows. Consequently, the EC has already decided not to include ICS anymore in new EU FTAs. Thus, ICS has not been included in the EU-Japan FTA (also because

[7] CJEU, Opinion 1/17 – CETA, ECLI:EU:C:2019:341.

[8] Most prominently, the Irish Supreme Court ruled that CETA cannot be ratified by Ireland without either changing certain domestic legislation or hold a referendum, see Leonard (2022), pp. 113–126.

[9] Lavranos (2022), Dutch Senate approves CETA ratification, Borderlex, 12 July 2022, https://borderlex.net/2022/07/12/dutch-senate-approves-ceta-ratification/.

[10] EC Press release (2022), Statement from the Commission on clarifications discussed with Germany regarding investment protection in the context of the CETA agreement, 19 August 2022, https://ec.europa.eu/commission/presscorner/detail/en/STATEMENT_22_5223.

[11] See e.g. Global Justice Now (2022), 380+ civil society organisations demand world governments quit ISDS, 15 November 2022, https://www.globaljustice.org.uk/news/380-civil-society-organisations-demand-world-governments-quit-isds/; see also: the EP Resolution for a coordinated withdrawal from the ECT; Dreyer (2022), Energy Charter Treaty: MEP resolution calls for withdrawal, Borderlex, 24 November 2022, https://borderlex.net/2022/11/24/energy-charter-treaty-mep-resolution-calls-for-withdrawal/.

Japan vehemently rejects the ICS) which entered into force on 1 February 2019 nor is it part of the EU-New Zealand FTA, which was concluded in June 2022, and neither is it on the table for the FTA negotiations with Mercosur. However, ICS appears to have been included in the updated EU-Chile FTA (2022)[12] and EU-Mexico FTA (2018).[13]

3 Exporting the ICS and Multilaterizing It Into the MIC

So, with the very slow progress of getting ICS off the ground at the bilateral level, the EC has changed strategy by moving from the bilateral level to the multilateral level by exporting the MIC and it found UNCITRAL as a forum to achieve that through the creation of UNCITRAL Working Group III (WG III) on ISDS reforms.[14]

For some, the choice for UNCITRAL seemed surprising but actually UNCITRAL was already previously used by the EC to get the UNCITRAL Transparency Rules done very fast.[15]

Despite the fact that the EC has only observer status within UNCITRAL, it has been able to be the main driver of the UNCITRAL WG III negotiations, although the EC has realized that the negotiations remain difficult and that the progress has been slower than expected.

4 Lack of Transparency: Really?

Let me now turn to some of the criticisms against the current ISDS system, the first being the often-heard claim of lack of transparency.

[12] Djanic (2022), Analysis: EU-Chile Agreement implements ICS, clarifies FET and FPS and provides for mechanisms aimed at expediting proceedings, IA Reporter, 15 December 2022, https://www.iareporter.com/articles/analysis-eu-chile-agreement-implements-investment-court-system-clarifies-fet-and-fps-and-provides-for-mechanisms-aimed-at-expediting-proceedings/.

[13] See EU-Mexico FTA text 2018, https://policy.trade.ec.europa.eu/eu-trade-relationships-country-and-region/countries-and-regions/mexico/eu-mexico-agreement/agreement-principle_en.

[14] Lavranos (2017), Insight: The road to the Multilateral Investment Court, Borderlex, 14 July 2017, https://borderlex.net/2017/07/14/comment-the-road-to-multilateral-investment-court/.

[15] The negotiations started in 2010 and were concluded in 2013, and in 2014 they entered into force. The text is available here: https://uncitral.un.org/sites/uncitral.un.org/files/media-documents/uncitral/en/rules-on-transparency-e.pdf.

The truth is that nowadays, most if not all arbitral awards, are publicly available, at ITALAW,[16] or behind paywalled services such as GAR,[17] Jus Mundi,[18] and IA Reporter.[19] Indeed, recently, the Spanish legal representative published the *Green Power*[20] award himself on Linkedin before it was available anywhere else!

Moreover, we now have the UNCITRAL Transparency Rules mentioned above in place and also ICSID has further increased the transparency requirements in its new Rules adopted in 2022.[21] Indeed, the ICSID and PCA websites increasingly publish more case documents.

In addition, many hearings are open to the public or are even live streamed. For example, one can still watch all the *Vattenfall v. Germany* hearings on YouTube.[22]

In short, I have practically never encountered the problem of not getting hold of an award. Indeed, the level of transparency of ISDS proceedings awards is similar to WTO proceedings, and certainly much higher compared to commercial arbitration proceedings.

So, in my view, transparency or a lack thereof is not a real problem any more as regards ISDS proceedings.

5 Pro-Investor Biased System?

The second often heard criticism is that the system is rigged in favour of large multinationals, in other words, ISDS is presented as a pro-investor biased dispute settlement system. This has been repeated so often by NGOs and the media, that the perception has been created that the ISDS system is pro-investor biased.

However, the statistics clearly dump this perception. UNCTAD, which is certainly not a pro-investor institution, consistently records that States win more than 38% of all cases, while investors win only 28% and the rest is settled or otherwise discontinued.[23] These numbers are also confirmed by the ICSID statistics.[24]

Thus, the system is in fact pretty fair and actually more favourable to States than investors. So, the question arises: why would States want to change the system that is

[16] https://www.italaw.com/.

[17] https://globalarbitrationreview.com/.

[18] https://jusmundi.com/en/.

[19] https://www.iareporter.com/.

[20] See case-note by: Lavranos (2022), pp. 166–174.

[21] ICSID Rules 2022, https://icsid.worldbank.org/rules-regulations/2022-rules-and-regulations/resources.

[22] See *Vattenfall v. Germany*, Day 1, opening statements, 10 October 2016, https://www.youtube.com/watch?v=7Sv81ebnxAc.

[23] UNCTAD Issue Note (2022), p. 4.

[24] ICSID Case-load statistics, Issue 2022-2, https://icsid.worldbank.org/sites/default/files/publications/The_ICSID_Caseload_Statistics_2022-2_ENG.pdf.

favourable to them? May be because they want to win 80% of the cases? Or prevent any cases from being initiated in the first place?

6 Substantive Protection Standards Are the Elephant in the Room

In my view, States are not really interested in the procedural reforms, which are currently negotiated in UNCITRAL WG III. Some States may want to tweak the procedural rules here and there, such as creating an appeal possibility, which could have easily been done in ICSID by expanding the annulment grounds but apparently there was no overwhelming appetite for this.

Or by reducing the perceived conflicts of interests of arbitrators due to the so-called "double hatting", which is addressed now by a very strict Code of Conduct[25] within the UNCITRAL WG III, which has been adopted by the UNCITRAL Trade Commission in July 2023,[26] or by tightening Third Party Funding (TPF),[27] which is also addressed by the UNCITRAL WG III without too much problems. All these issues can and will be easily addressed within UNCITRAL WG III.

In fact, the truth is that States are much more concerned about the substantive protection standards and wanted to address them in the UNCITRAL WG III. However, the mandate of the WG III is limited to procedural aspects, although the chair tried to expand the mandate as much as possible.

Nonetheless, especially in the early days of the discussions within WG III, many States were complaining about the expansive interpretation of the FET and of the umbrella clause, or of the indirect expropriation and legitimate expectation standards and the in their eyes lack of respect for the right to regulate.

These are the real concerns of States, as is also proven by the revised but now abandoned draft ECT[28] text and CETA. However, all these issues are not and will not be solved by the proposed MIC.

However, the EU, its Member States and the other OECD members have recently started discussions within the OECD under a new work stream called "Broad

[25] UNCITRAL WG III (2022).

[26] Lavranos (2023), Q&A: Status of investor-state dispute settlement reforms at UNCITRAL, Borderlex, 19 April 2023, https://borderlex.net/2023/04/19/qa-status-of-investor-state-dispute-settlement-reforms-at-uncitral/.

[27] UNCITRAL WG III (2019).

[28] See the leaked revised ECT text, dated 27 June 2022, https://www.bilaterals.org/IMG/pdf/reformed_ect_text.pdf.

government work on reform of substantive investment treaty clauses and on climate change: the future of investment treaties".[29]

Several meetings have already taken place (the last one on 11 April 2023[30]) and it can be expected that the outcomes of those discussions will have significant harmonising effect on substantive protection standards for the investment treaties of the OECD members.

7 Inconsistencies and Lack of Predictability Remains Inherent Because of the Existence of 3000 BITs

As we all know, the provisions of BITs are inherently different because the 3000 BITs are spanning several decades and encompass all the different levels of economic development—ranging from least development, to transitional and developed economies.

The MIC cannot change that, but it will have to deal with these divergent provisions and legal contexts and will have to apply teleological interpretation as the CJEU does to craft provisions of the 1980s in such a way that they are fit for the twenty-first century.

However, obviously, there is a limit to the use of teleological interpretation, so inconsistencies will remain until you have one global investment treaty text, such as the good old GATT 1947/1994.

At the same time, in whatever way you craft legal provisions, there is always room for inconsistency and imprecision. Indeed, I would argue that you actually need some flexibility in order to be able to develop the law for future challenges.

So, in any event, at a maximum, the MIC could only achieve some kind of "relative consistency and predictability", and only if there were to be a global investment treaty, which is what should have been developed in the first place. However, such a global investment treaty currently remains a dream.[31]

[29] See the OECD website on the Future of Investment Treaties, https://www.oecd.org/investment/investment-policy/investment-treaties.htm.

[30] The videos of the 11 April 2023 meeting are available at: https://www.oecd-events.org/investment-treaty-conference.

[31] The OECD members attempted to develop a MIA in the early 1990s but ultimately failed to adopt it due to the resistance of France. See Muchlinski (2000), pp. 1033–1053.

8 Impartiality and Independence

On the issue of impartiality and independence, we have to see how and who will be selected for the MIC. The discussions on this are currently ongoing in WG III.[32]

The fact that I have been placed on the EU rooster as an arbitrator for the EU agreements, which was rather surprising to me, could be seen as a good sign that actually a more inclusive selection is possible, but it could also simply be seen as window dressing.

For me the fact remains that if only States select the judges of the MIC—as is currently proposed—they are inherently biased to select persons whom they consider to be least pro-investor biased if not outright pro-State biased.

In any event, it is important that MIC judges should have non-renewable tenure in order to avoid the WTO Appellate Body paralysis. Moreover, it should be avoided that the selection should focus only on judges and academics because they are perceived as neutral whereas arbitration practitioners are automatically perceived as biased and conflicted.

In general, there is an inherent risk of politicization of the whole selection process of MIC judges, which inevitably will reflect on the MIC. Therefore, it is very important to make sure the MIC is not perceived a pro-State biased.

9 Duration, Costs and Affordable Access to Justice

It is often claimed that the MIC will be much cheaper than the current ISDS system. However, that will not be the case simply because the overwhelming majority of the costs of an arbitration proceeding relate to the fees for legal counsel[33]—and this will not be different for MIC proceedings.

Indeed, due to the fact that MIC allows for appellate proceedings, claimants will probably have to bear even higher costs because if they win at the first instance, they can be sure that the State will appeal. Consequently, additional costs for the appeal round will have to be covered by the claimants as well.

While some States run all ISDS cases by in-house government lawyers (such as Spain), most States still hire expensive external law firms and that will remain so, especially, because the new MIC rules will be new and complex, including the new appeal procedure. Hence, States will not want to run any risk of making stupid mistakes and thus loose the case, which means States will also continue to bear high

[32] See UNCITRAL WG III (2021).

[33] See for a detailed analysis: BIICL & Allen Overy, 2021 Empirical Study: Costs, Damages and Duration in Investor-State Arbitration, https://www.biicl.org/documents/136_isds-costs-damages-duration.pdf; see also the book launch video by Prof. Susan Franck, Arbitration Costs: Myths and Realities in Investment Treaty Arbitration, 19 July 2019, https://icsid.worldbank.org/resources/multimedia/book-launch-arbitration-costs-myths-and-realities-investment-treaty.

(or even higher) legal costs for MIC proceedings. Maybe the MIC proceedings will be faster if the deadlines are met, which as we know from the WTO experience is usually not the case. Thus, it seems very unlikely that the establishment of MIC will reduce the overall costs for the parties.

This also raises the question whether the MIC will be more affordable for SMEs? Whenever I mentioned the interests of SMEs in UNCITRAL WG III, there was silence. I cannot recall that the EC or any EU Member State somehow pushed for the interests of the SMEs. In fact, when I proposed that the envisaged Advisory Centre[34] should also be made available for SMEs, there was very little enthusiasm for that. Thus, in short international arbitration will remain largely unavailable for SMEs, just as it is now.

10 The MIC Is Not Loved by Every State

The UNCITRAL WG III negotiations so far have shown that the MIC is not loved by every State, otherwise we would have already had a deal.

Now that we are getting into the nitty-gritty, delegations realize that creating a new International Organization is expensive and not so easy, especially, if other less radical reform measures might actually address many of the concerns, much faster and cheaper.[35]

Indeed, the EU has realized that too and has accepted that a MIC will be a long-term project and that in the short-term as an intermediate step only an Appeal Court might create sufficient traction. This means that the arbitral tribunals will remain as they are for the first instance and then one could go to the Appeal Court. The advantages for this option are clear: there is no need for a fully developed organization and the Appeal Court judges could be retained on a retainer basis. This would be much cheaper and faster to implement.

Moreover, the EU has realized that only a flexible opt-in system is viable, so that States do not feel forced to buy into the full MIC immediately. This has also been the approach used for the UNCITRAL Transparency Rules.

[34] See for a recent analysis on the Advisory Centre: Braun and Adekemi (2023), Advisory Centre on International Investment Law, Jean Monnet Papers 05/2023, https://www.uni-saarland.de/fileadmin/upload/lehrstuhl/bungenberg/Jean_Monnet_Papers/Advisory_Centre_on_International_Investment_Law__Johanna_Braun-Afolabi_Adekemi_.pdf. See also a short summary of the informal meetings held on 14-16 June 2021 on the establishment of an Advisory Centre, 1 July 2021, https://uncitral.un.org/sites/uncitral.un.org/files/media-documents/uncitral/en/summary_of_the_chair_and_rapporteur_-_informal_meeting_on_the_establishment_of_an_advisory_centre.pdf.

[35] The Submission from the Governments of Chile, Israel and Japan, A/CN.9/WG.III/WP.163, 15 March 2019, is particularly enlightening because it lists all the possible reform options that could be implemented rather quickly without the need for a MIC, https://documents-dds-ny.un.org/doc/UNDOC/LTD/V19/015/35/PDF/V1901535.pdf?OpenElement.

However, such an opt-in system will of course create new problems because most States will stay out of it with their old BITs, while a minority, let's say 30–40 States (the EU and Member States, Canada, Singapore, maybe some African States) will opt-in. However, the big economies such as the US, Japan, China, Russia will certainly not be part of the group of first movers. Compare this with the 150+ members of ICSID or the WTO, so the question arises: what will the authority be of this MIC with 30–40 signatories?

Moreover, what does that mean for consistency and predictability? Will they not become more rampant rather than less? Also, what would this mean for the enforcement of MIC awards? Could you enforce them for example in the US if the US is not a party to it?

All in all, this highlights that the MIC raises a host of new problems that have not yet been properly discussed and resolved.

11 Conclusion: The MIC Is Not Addressing the Elephant in the Room

Thus, my conclusion is that the MIC will be established in one form or another, but it will not address the real concerns, namely, to harmonise the substantive protection standards.

However, recently, the OECD members have embarked on exactly the issue of harmonizing substantive protection standards. The project is called the *Future of Investment Treaties* and within Track 2 of that project OECD investment experts have been discussing how to harmonise certain standards such as FET and indirect expropriation in their investment treaties.[36] The work is done in relative secrecy since as it is explicitly stated:

> It is conceived as a forum where governments' experts in their respective fields exchange among peers. Meetings under Track 2 are held in principle in private among governments unless non-governmental participation is explicitly sought. This format encourages and results in frank exchanges on a technical level in a cordial and collegial atmosphere. Governments contribute their expertise freely and informally.[37]

So far, only short summaries of the meetings held have been published. Accordingly, it could very well be that the elephant in the room is addressed in the OECD rather than in UNCITRAL.

As I mentioned above, this is what the EU has done in CETA and its other FTAs but also in the revised draft ECT, which has been abandoned by the EU and its

[36] See for more information the dedicated OECD website: https://www.oecd.org/investment/investment-policy/investment-treaties.htm.

[37] OECD, Work on the Future of Investment Treaties in the Track 2 Project - Frequently Asked Questions - Note by the Secretariat, 7 October 2022, p. 3, https://www.oecd.org/investment/investment-policy/oecd-future-investment-treaties-track2-faq.pdf.

Member States. However, the approach of revising existing treaties or negotiating new ones would take decades in order to achieve harmonization on a global level.

Indeed, the EU and its Member States are not waiting for that and are instead exiting the ISDS system by terminating intra-EU BITs,[38] by disapplying the ISDS provisions of the ECT[39] and even simply by withdrawing from the ECT as several EU Member States have announced and as Italy has done before.[40] That is of course a much more effective way for States to escape judicial scrutiny and international responsibility for their illegal acts and to avoid paying adverse awards, such as in particular Spain and other EU Member States.[41]

So, in conclusion, there is simply no compelling reason to create the MIC. Rather, in my view, the MIC is like the air conditioning in a concept car: it is nice to have it, but it is certainly not necessary to drive around with it.

References

Braun J, Adekemi A (2023) Advisory Centre on International Investment Law, Jean Monnet Papers 05/2023. Available at: https://www.uni-saarland.de/fileadmin/upload/lehrstuhl/bungenberg/Jean_Monnet_Papers/Advisory_Centre_on_International_Investment_Law__Johanna_Braun-Afolabi_Adekemi_.pdf

Lavranos N (2017) Mixed exclusivity: the CJEU's opinion on the EU-Singapore FTA. EILA Rev 2017:1–34

Lavranos N (2020) The changing ecosystem of Dutch BITs. Arbitr Int 2022:441–457

Lavranos N (2022) Green Power K/S and SCE Solar Don Benito APS v Kingdom of Spain: How EU Law Allegedly Trumps International Investment Law. EILA Rev 2022:166–174

Lavranos N et al (2023) The meltdown of the ECT: how the ECT was ruined by the EU and its Members States. SchiedsVZ (1):38–45

Leonard P (2022) Ratification of the ISDS provisions in CETA – current court and legislative challenges – an overview. EILA Rev:113–126

[38] Agreement for the termination of Bilateral Investment Treaties between the Member States of the European Union, OJ L 169, 29.5.2020, p. 1–41.

[39] As per CJEU *Komstroy* judgment and the envisaged disconnection clause in the revised draft ECT text.

[40] Lavranos et al, The meltdown of the ECT: How the ECT was ruined by the EU and its Members States, SchiedsVZ 2023, issue 1, pp. 38–45. As per April 2023, France, Germany, Poland, Spain, the Netherlands, Slovenia, Luxembourg and Denmark, have announced their intention to withdraw from the ECT. So far, however, the Energy Charter's Secretariat noted that only the first three of these states have officially submitted their withdrawal notices to the ECT's depositary. Most recently, the EU and its Member States have announced their intention to commonly withdraw from the ECT rather than sign up to the revised ECT text, see: IA Reporter, European Commission submits formal proposal for the EU to withdraw from the ECT, 7 July 2023, https://www.iareporter.com/articles/european-commission-submits-formal-proposals-for-the-eu-and-euratom-to-withdraw-from-the-ect-commission-opines-that-sunset-clause-never-applied-to-intra-eu-disputes-but-it-nevertheless-proposes-the/.

[41] See: International Law Compliance Report 2022, https://www.internationallawcompliance.com/.

Muchlinski PT (2000) The rise and fall of the multilateral agreement on investment: where now? Int Lawyer:1033–1053

OECD., Future of Investment Treaties, Track 2, available at: https://www.oecd.org/investment/investment-policy/investment-treaties.htm

UNCITRAL WG III (2019) Third-party funding – Possible solutions, A/CN.9/WG.III/WP.172, 2 August 2019. Available at: https://documents-dds-ny.un.org/doc/UNDOC/LTD/V19/083/90/PDF/V1908390.pdf?OpenElement

UNCITRAL WG III (2021) Standing multilateral mechanism: Selection and appointment of ISDS tribunal members and related matters, A/CN.9/WG.III/WP.213, 8 December 2021. https://documents-dds-ny.un.org/doc/UNDOC/LTD/V21/092/76/PDF/V2109276.pdf?OpenElement

UNCITRAL WG III (2022) Draft Code of Conduct, A/CN.9/WG.III/WP.216, 5 July 2022. Available at: https://documents-dds-ny.un.org/doc/UNDOC/LTD/221/033/8E/PDF/2210338E.pdf?OpenElement

UNCTAD Issue Note (2022) Facts on ISDS Arbitrations 2021: with a special focus on tax related ISDS cases. Available at: https://unctad.org/system/files/official-document/diaepcbinf2022d4_en.pdf

Nikos Lavranos is former Guest Professor, Free University Brussels – Brussels Diplomatic Academy; Secretary General of EFILA; founder of NL-Investmentconsulting; Partner at Herreveld van den Hurk & Partners. The views expressed are of the author alone and do not necessarily reflect the views of the organisations to which the author is affiliated with.

Modernisation of the Energy Charter Treaty: A View from the Inside

Yuriy Pochtovyk and Lukas Stifter

Contents

Abstract The energy sector is subject to complex political risks, including regulatory ones, making foreign investors vulnerable in long-term energy projects. In response, the Energy Charter Treaty (ECT) was negotiated in 1994, becoming the first sector-specific multilateral treaty with investment provisions. However, the

The views expressed in this chapter are solely those of the authors.

Y. Pochtovyk
Brussels, Belgium
e-mail: yuriy.pochtovyk@encharter.org

L. Stifter (✉)
Vienna, Austria
e-mail: lukas.stifter@bmaw.gv.at

M. Bungenberg, A. Reinisch (eds.), *New Frontiers for EU Investment Policy*, Special Issue, https://doi.org/10.1007/978-3-031-41977-5_5

international energy and international investment regime have evolved significantly since then. Concerns have arisen over the legitimacy of investment arbitration and states' regulatory flexibility, especially in light of growing awareness about threats of climate change and the environmental impact of the energy sector. To address some of these issues, the Energy Charter Conference embarked on an effort to reform the 1994 ECT, resulting in the Agreement in Principle (AIP) in June 2022. The AIP proposes amendments seeking a stronger climate focus and alignment with the goals of the Paris Agreement. It revises definitions, introduces detailed substantive protection standards, reinforces the right to regulate in the public interest, and pioneers the opt-in "Flexibility Mechanism" to gradually phase out investment protection for fossil fuels. Nevertheless, the AIP has faced criticism, prompting some Contracting Parties to announce their intention to withdraw or withdrawal from the ECT. This chapter explains the negotiation process and highlights the key achievements of the AIP. It further examines the most critical provisions with references to relevant arbitral jurisprudence and explores the potential outcomes of the proposed amendments.

1 Introduction

1.1 Context

The complex and ever-changing political environment and regulatory framework of the energy sector expose foreign investors in energy projects to a multitude of types of political risks. Given its economic and political importance and, more recently, the growing awareness of climate change and the environmental impact of energy-related activities, the energy sector has often been subject to some forms of intervention by the governments.

Against this backdrop, the Energy Charter Treaty (ECT) was negotiated in 1994 in the aftermath of the dissolution of the Soviet Union, being the first-of-its-kind sector-specific multilateral treaty with investment provisions.[1] The ECT provides for a detailed set of binding international legal rules and non-binding, "soft" or "best endeavours" provisions in three main areas: investment, trade, and transit. The Treaty also covers certain aspects of environmental protection and energy efficiency.[2]

[1] Energy Charter Treaty (adopted 17 December 1994, entered into force 16 April 1998). See also ECOWAS (Economic Community of West African States) Energy Protocol (adopted 31 January 2003, entered into force after the ninth instrument of ratification was deposited in accordance with Article 39) negotiated on the basis of the ECT.

[2] See Article 19 ECT (Environmental Aspects), further supplemented by the Energy Charter Protocol on Energy Efficiency and Related Environmental Aspects (PEEREA; adopted 17 December 1994, entered into force 16 April 1998).

Increasing attention, however, has been paid to investment protection (Part III ECT—Investment Promotion and Protection) and investment dispute resolution (Article 26 ECT—Settlement of Disputes between an Investor and a Contracting Party) provisions of the ECT, which have generated at least 157 arbitral proceedings in investment disputes known at the time of writing.[3] Indeed, with more than 50 Contracting Parties,[4] the ECT is known as the largest and most frequently used investment protection agreement.[5]

Nonetheless, in almost three decades following the negotiations of the 1994 ECT, both international energy and international investment regime have undergone a significant overhaul. Since then, increasing concerns over states' regulatory flexibility, including in climate change mitigation and adaptation, as well as the usefulness and legitimacy of investment arbitration, have led states to revisit their investment treaty policies.

It is this context in which the Energy Charter Conference (Conference), the main governing and decision-making body under the ECT, decided to join the global efforts to reform the international investment regime.[6] The negotiations were finished on 24 June 2022 with a proposal for draft amendments, technical changes and modifications to the text of the Treaty and its Annexes—the Agreement in Principle (AIP).[7] Among other things, the AIP has a stronger climate focus and seeks to align the Treaty with the goals of the Paris Agreement. [8] It does so by clarifying several definitions and introduces more detailed substantive protection standards. It further reinforces the Contracting Parties' right to regulate in the public interest. Moreover, the envisaged "Flexibility Mechanism" allows for the gradual phase-out of investment protection for fossil fuels—a novelty in the international investment regime.

[3] For more detailed statistics, see International Energy Charter (10 January 2023) Statistics. https://www.energychartertreaty.org/cases/statistics/.

[4] At the time of writing, the ECT's membership comprised 52 Contracting Parties, including the EU and the European Atomic Energy Community (EURATOM), as well as two signatories: see International Energy Charter (2023) Annual Report 2022. https://www.energycharter.org/fileadmin/DocumentsMedia/AR/IEC_Annual_Report_2022_WEB.pdf, pp. 4–5.

[5] The United Nations Conference on Trade and Development (UNCTAD) regards the ECT as the most frequently invoked international investment agreement in arbitral proceedings in investment disputes: see UNCTAD (2022a), p. 74.

[6] See Decision of the Energy Charter Conference (CCDEC 2018 15) Bucharest Energy Charter Declaration, 7 November 2018. https://www.energycharter.org/fileadmin/DocumentsMedia/CCDECS/2018/CCDEC201815_-_GEN_Bucharest_Energy_Charter_Declaration.pdf.

[7] See Decision of the Energy Charter Conference (CCDEC 2022 10) Public Communication explaining the main changes contained in the agreement in principle, 24 June 2022. https://www.energycharter.org/fileadmin/DocumentsMedia/CCDECS/2022/CCDEC202210.pdf.

[8] Paris Agreement to the United Nations Framework Convention on Climate Change (Paris Agreement; adopted 12 December 2015, entered into force 4 November 2016) UN Doc FCCC/CP/2015/L.9/Rev/1.

Despite these efforts, the AIP has already prompted a degree of criticism, including from the European Parliament, whereas some Contracting Parties have publicly announced their intention to withdraw or withdrawal from the Treaty.[9]

It is submitted that the modernisation of the ECT, being the most heavily used treaty, is of systemic importance for the general reform debate on the investment treaty regime. In addition, the modernisation efforts may offer broader implications for the following issues:

- **Feasibility of multilateral reform of substantive investment law**: Multilateral reform efforts outside the ECT have been limited to procedural rules, partly due to the commonly held belief that such an approach would constitute the "lowest common denominator".[10] The envisaged modernisation of the ECT aims at multilateral consensus on investment protection standards among a politically and economically heterogeneous group of Contracting Parties. The AIP may imply a greater degree of general convergence on substantive law than commonly held.
- **Investment protection and climate policy**: The ECT's alignment with the Paris Agreement, different climate ambitions and energy security priorities of the Contracting Parties were at the core of the negotiations.[11] The proposed phase-out of protection for fossil fuel-related investments by some Contracting Parties may serve as an inspiration for other pertinent investment policy discussions.[12]

---

[9] See International Energy Charter. Letter of the Secretary-General to the Parliament of the European Union. 13 February 2023. https://www.energycharter.org/fileadmin/DocumentsMedia/News/0047-SG-13022023-EP_President.pdf; Written notifications of withdrawal from the Energy Charter Treaty. 22 March 2023. https://www.energycharter.org/media/news/article/written-notifications-of-withdrawal-from-the-energy-charter-treaty/?tx_news_pi1%5Bcontroller%5D=News&tx_news_pi1%5Baction%5D=detail&cHash=da7935d6899f348360408dfaad518bc9, confirming the withdrawal of France, Germany and Poland; Written notification of withdrawal from the Energy Charter Treaty. 30 August 2023. https://www.energycharter.org/media/news/article/written-notification-of-withdrawal-from-the-energy-charter-treaty/?tx_news_pi1%5Bcontroller%5D=News&tx_news_pi1%5Baction%5D=detail&cHash=b0ed49a6364a7830b9a3185225716cec, confirming the withdrawal of Luzembourg.

[10] The mandate of the United Nations Commission on International Trade Law (UNCITRAL) Working Group III (Investor-State Dispute Settlement Reform) is limited to the potential reform of investor-state dispute settlement, leaving aside the issues of substantive investment law: see United Nations General Assembly (Fiftieth session, 3– 21 July 2017) Report of the United Nations Commission on International Trade Law. Seventy-second session, Supplement No 17, UN Doc. A/72/17, para 264.

[11] See, e.g. Article 2(1)(c) of the Paris Agreement ("This Agreement, in enhancing the implementation of the Convention, including its objective, aims to strengthen the global response to the threat of climate change, in the context of sustainable development and efforts to eradicate poverty, including by: [...] (c) Making finance flows consistent with a pathway towards low greenhouse gas emissions and climate-resilient development [emphasis added]").

[12] See, e.g. the Organisation for Economic Co-operation and Development (OECD) work programme on the Future of Investment Treaties https://www.oecd.org/investment/investment-policy/investment-treaties.htm. See also UNCTAD (2022b).

1.2 *Outline*

While leaving aside individual positions of the Contracting Parties and specific text proposals, the authors aim to shed light on the negotiation process and to explain the main achievements of the AIP.

Section 2 of the present chapter gives an account of the mandate, institutional setting and procedural aspects of the negotiations on the modernisation of the ECT. Sections 3 to 5 explain the main components of the modernised text proposed in the AIP. It is important to note that while the mandate for negotiations encompassed a list of topics beyond investment provisions, this chapter is limited to the components relevant to investment protection and investment dispute settlement. Finally, Sect. 6 provides an outlook on the possible future of the AIP.

Arbitral jurisprudence discussed throughout the chapter may explain the potential implications of the envisaged amendments. References made to the articles of the ECT concern the 1994 Treaty currently in force (e.g. "Article 1(6) ECT"). References to provisions contained in the AIP are marked separately (e.g. "Article 26(10) AIP").

2 Negotiations in the ECT Modernisation Group

2.1 *Institutional Setting, Mandate and Scope of Negotiations*

Pursuant to Article 34(5) ECT, the Conference establishes subsidiary bodies to assist it with the implementation of the Treaty commitments and administer the Energy Charter process.[13] On 6 November 2019, the Conference established the Modernisation Group and mandated it to conduct the negotiations on the modernisation of the ECT.[14] The Modernisation Group was composed of the delegates representing the Contracting Parties, the Chair and Vice-Chairs, and the Energy Charter Secretariat providing legal advice and technical assistance in the negotiations. In addition, an informal steering group comprised of interested delegations supported the work of the Chair and the Vice-Chairs.[15] The mandate of the Modernisation Group set out the objective and the scope of negotiations:

---

[13] For the full list of subsidiary bodies of the Conference, see International Energy Charter (4 January 2021) Subsidiary Bodies of the Energy Charter Conference. https://www.energycharter.org/who-we-are/subsidiary-bodies/overview/.

[14] See Decision of the Energy Charter Conference (CCDEC 2019 10) Modernisation of the Energy Charter Treaty: Mandate, Procedural Issues and Timeline for Negotiations, 6 November 2019. https://www.energycharter.org/fileadmin/DocumentsMedia/CCDECS/2019/CCDEC201910.pdf.

[15] Ibid, point d.

> [. . .] to reach the highest possible degree of convergence among the participants on the negotiation drafts starting from the identified list of topics (CCDEC2018 18) and suggested policy options (CCDEC2019 08) [emphasis added].[16]

These two documents, to the "List of Topics" and the "Policy Options" formed the substantive basis of the negotiations. The List of Topics limited discussions to 25 topics pertaining to the following categories: definitions, investment protection, dispute settlement, transit, sustainable development and corporate social responsibility, transit, pre-investment phase, Regional Economic Integration Organisation (REIO), and obsolete provisions.[17]

The List of Topics put a strong focus on investment protection. With respect to investment dispute settlement under Article 26 ECT, only incremental discussions were foreseen.[18] In particular, systemic reform of investment arbitration through the introduction of a standing investment court as propagated by the European Union (EU) in its treaty practice was not envisaged. It is worth noting, however, that consultations preceding the adoption of the List of Topics led to the inclusion of topics covering all areas of the ECT.[19] As a result, considerable attention in negotiations was paid to several other matters, in particular, energy transit and sustainability.

The second document, the Policy Options, offers an insight into the approaches and the initial levels of ambition of individual Contracting Parties.[20] The positions of Contracting Parties expressed therein range from rather detailed negotiating goals and text proposals to brief policy considerations.

This information is of certain value considering the limited transparency and reporting regime of the negotiations (see infra at Sect. 2.2). However, more in-depth information can be found in the publicly available text proposals introduced into the negotiations by the EU and its Member States.[21]

---

[16] Ibid, point e.

[17] See Decision of the Energy Charter Conference (CCDEC 2018 18) Modernisation of the Energy Charter Treaty, 27 November 2018. https://www.energycharter.org/fileadmin/DocumentsMedia/CCDECS/2018/CCDEC201818_-_STR_Modernisation_of_the_Energy_Charter_Treaty.pdf.

[18] The List of Topics included the following components related to investment dispute settlement: frivolous claims, transparency, security for costs, valuation of damages, and third-party funding: see Decision of the Energy Charter Conference (CCDEC 2019 10), supra n. 15.

[19] Decision of the Energy Charter Conference (CCDEC 2017 23) Modernisation of the Energy Charter Treaty, 28 November 2017. https://www.energycharter.org/fileadmin/DocumentsMedia/CCDECS/2017/CCDEC201723.pdf, para 3 ("[...] any discussion on updating, clarifying or modernising the ECT should take into consideration all the provisions of the ECT and not only the investment protection standards").

[20] See Decision of the Energy Charter Conference (CCDEC 2019 08) Policy Options for Modernisation of the ECT, 6 October 2019. https://www.energycharter.org/fileadmin/DocumentsMedia/CCDECS/2019/CCDEC201908.pdf.

[21] See infra n. 27. From the perspective of EU law, the ECT is a "mixed" agreement whose Contracting Parties are both the EU and its Member States. The 1994 ECT was negotiated and signed by the European Communities, comprised of the European Economic Community (later replaced by the EU), European Coal and Steel Community (ceased to exist in 2002) and

2.2 *Conduct of Negotiations, Agreement in Principle, and Conclusion of Negotiations*

The negotiations on the modernisation of the ECT were conducted through formal negotiation rounds. Due to the outbreak of the Coronavirus disease (COVID-19) in the spring of 2020, the first negotiation round on the modernisation of the ECT, expected to take place in April 2020, had to be postponed by three months.[22] In light of the global sanitary situation, travel restrictions, and other logistical complications caused by the pandemic, the Modernisation Group had to shift to digital communication and collaboration solutions. Following the start of the negotiations in July 2020, the Modernisation Group conducted 15 rounds of negotiations, 12 of which were held by videoconference, two in hybrid mode and one in the form of a physical meeting.

The discussions in negotiation rounds were based on text proposals, comments and other submissions by the Contracting Parties compiled in negotiation drafts for each respective round. Later, based on these submissions, compromise text proposals were developed.

Participation in the negotiations, including access to the submissions by the Contracting Parties, negotiation drafts and the meetings, was restricted to the delegates of the Contracting Parties.[23] However, in line with its mandate, following each of the negotiation rounds, the Modernisation Group issued a public communication with a summary of the discussions and the progress achieved.[24] In addition, the Modernisation Group reported annually on the progress achieved to the Conference.[25] Restricted public access to evolving treaty text in the process of negotiations,

---

EURATOM, on behalf of their Member States. The EURATOM has remained an independent entity but is represented in the Energy Charter process by the EU. Following Italy's withdrawal from the ECT in 2015, 26 EU Member States were Contracting Parties to the ECT at the time of writing. The EU as a REIO in the meaning of Article 1(3) ECT represents all EU Member States-Contracting Parties to the ECT in the Energy Charter process and exercises voting rights in accordance with Article 36 ECT—both subject to their internal coordination. See also infra Sect. 5.

[22] Decision of the Energy Charter Conference (CCDEC 2020 16) Report of the Modernisation Group on Progress Made in Fulfilling the Negotiations Mandate, 16 December 2020, para 5. https://www.energycharter.org/fileadmin/DocumentsMedia/CCDECS/2020/CCDEC202016.pdf. For initial provisional schedule of negotiation rounds in 2020, see Decision of the Energy Charter Conference (CCDEC 2019 10), supra n. 15.

[23] See point m of Decision of the Energy Charter Conference (CCDEC 2019 10), supra n. 15 ("Negotiation drafts, as well as comments and messages sent by delegates will be considered as restricted. After approval by consensus, a short summary on negotiations round will be made public without identifying the Delegations which made interventions").

[24] For a compilation of public communications, see International Energy Charter, 'Modernisation of the Treaty'. https://www.energychartertreaty.org/modernisation-of-the-treaty/.

[25] See Decision of the Energy Charter Conference (CCDEC 2020 16) supra n. 23 and Decision of the Energy Charter Conference (CCDEC 2021 21) Progress Report of the Modernisation Group 2021,14 December 2021. https://www.energycharter.org/fileadmin/DocumentsMedia/CCDECS/2021/CCDEC202121.pdf.

diplomatic communications and meetings of the negotiators resembles the practice of the Contracting Parties and the practice of trade and investment negotiations more broadly. At the same time, the Contracting Parties prepared their negotiation positions and publicised them in accordance with their internal procedures. For example, at the outset of the negotiations, the EU and its Member States published their initial text proposals on all the topics, followed by a more specific text regarding the carve-out for fossil fuel-related investments.[26]

In addition to formal negotiation rounds, the Modernisation Group held several preparatory meetings, informal drafting meetings to develop compromise text proposals and informal workshops to discuss issues of substance raised in the negotiations.

Within formal negotiation rounds, decisions were taken based on consensus, understood as the absence of objections.

On 24 June 2022, the Contracting Parties reached the AIP at the Ad Hoc Meeting of the Conference. The conclusion of the AIP was accompanied by a public communication explaining the main changes contained therein.[27]

Subsequently, a working document of the General Secretariat of the Council of the EU containing the AIP was leaked in the media.[28] In this respect, it is worth noting that the leaked document does not contain the complete agreement, as it lacks important parts relating to provisional application and entry into force. Moreover, the conclusion of the AIP did not amount to an amendment in the sense of Article 42 ECT. The AIP is a political acknowledgement by the Contracting Parties that the main goal set out in the mandate of the Modernisation Group—"to reach the highest possible degree of convergence"—was achieved.[29] After an editorial and legal review of the draft text, the final draft amendments, technical changes and modifications to the text of the Treaty and its Annexes were expected to be adopted at the annual meeting of the Conference on 22 November 2022 (see Sect. 6).[30]

---

[26] See European Union, 'European Union text proposal for the modernisation of the Energy Charter Treaty'. https://trade.ec.europa.eu/doclib/docs/2020/may/tradoc_158754.pdf and https://energy.ec.europa.eu/system/files/2021-02/eu_submission_-_revised_definition_of_economic_activity_in_the_energy_sector_0.pdf.

[27] See Decision of the Energy Charter Conference (CCDEC 2022 10), supra n. 8.

[28] The document was initially made available to subscribers of Politico Pro (https://www.politicopro.com/) on 12 September 2022. At the time of writing, the document was available at https://www.bilaterals.org/IMG/pdf/reformed_ect_text.pdf.

[29] See Decision of the Energy Charter Conference (CCDEC 2019 10), supra n. 15, point e.

[30] See Article 42(2) ECT ("The text of any proposed amendment to this Treaty shall be communicated to the Contracting Parties by the Secretariat at least three months before the date on which it is proposed for adoption by the Charter Conference").

3 New Investment Protection Regime Under the ECT

3.1 Scope of Application

The discussions on the scope of application of the ECT, in particular of Part III (Investment Protection), entailed a revision of the provisions on the definitions of "Economic Activity in the Energy Sector" (Article 1(5)), "Investment" (Article 1(6)) and "Investor" (Article 1 (7)).

3.1.1 Definition of "Economic Activity in the Energy Sector"

Article 1(5) determines the sectoral character of the ECT. This distinguishes the ECT from other investment agreements that do not require an investment to relate to a specific economic sector. A covered investment under Part III of the ECT is subject to a test with multiple layers:

- First, apart from the asset-based definition of a covered investment similar to other investment agreements, Article 1(6) ECT requires an investment to have a link to an Economic Activity in the Energy Sector as defined in Article 1(5) ECT.[31] Pursuant to arbitral practice, a covered investment must be only "factually associated"[32] with one of the activities described in Article 1(5).[33]
- Second, an Economic Activity in the Energy Sector must relate to "Energy Materials and Products" as defined in Article 1(4) ECT.[34]

[31] See Article 1(6) ECT ("[. . .] 'Investment' refers to any investment associated with an Economic Activity in the Energy Sector and to investments or classes of investments designated by a Contracting Party in its Area as 'Charter efficiency projects' and so notified to the Secretariat [emphasis added]").

[32] See, e.g. *Limited Liability Company Amto v. Ukraine*, SCC Case No. 080/2005, Final Award, 26 March 2008, para 42 ("[. . .] the interpretation of the words 'associated with' involves a question of degree, and refers primarily to the factual rather than legal association between the alleged investment and an Economic Activity in the Energy Sector [...] The associated activity of any alleged investment must be energy related, without itself needing to satisfy the definition in Article 1(5) of an Economic Activity in the Energy Sector"); see also Thomas W. Waelde, 'International Investment under the 1994 Energy Charter Treaty – Legal, Negotiating, and Policy Implications for International Investors within Western and Commonwealth of Independent States/Eastern European Countries' Journal of World Trade (Volume 29 No 5) 26–27 for discussion on the requirement of "associated with Economic Activity in the Energy Sector".

[33] It is worth noting that Article 1(5) ECT does not cover maritime transportation of Energy Materials and Products.

[34] See Article 1(5) ("'Economic Activity in the Energy Sector' means an economic activity concerning the exploration, extraction, refining, production, storage, land transport, transmission, distribution, trade, marketing, or sale of Energy Materials and Products except those included in Annex NI, or concerning the distribution of heat to multiple premises"). See also Understanding 2 to the Final Act of the European Energy Charter Conference with respect to Article 1(5), which includes the list of activities that are illustrative of an "Economic Activity in the Energy Sector".

- Third, the Energy Materials or Products in question must not be included in the list of exceptions of Annex NI but listed in Annexes EM I and EM II.[35]

While not "as 'user friendly' as might be wished",[36] the above structure does not present particular complications with its application. In essence, as long as a putative investment merits "association" with one or more broadly defined activities set out in Article 1(5) ECT, the list of Energy Materials and Products in Annexes EM I, EM II and NI will ultimately define whether the investment falls within the sectoral coverage of the Treaty.[37] So far, categories including fossil-fuel, nuclear and electrical energy regardless of the source of generation have been covered. Therefore, the ECT has often been regarded as a fuel- or technology-neutral agreement.

It is for this reason that the definition of "Economic Activity in the Energy Sector" and Annexes EM I, EM II and NI were at the centre of intense negotiations. In this regard, different climate ambitions and energy security priorities of the Contracting Parties came to the surface when the potential inclusion or exclusion of Energy Materials and Products was considered. Some of the Contracting Parties preferred to exclude new investments in fossil fuel-related projects from the scope of the modernised ECT and to gradually phase out the protection for already made investments in such projects.[38]

The compromise resulting from these discussions departs from the idea of reciprocity in the strict sense of agreeing upon one solution for all. It builds on the principle of Common but Differentiated Responsibilities underpinning the United Nations Framework Convention on Climate Change (UNFCCC) and the Paris Agreement, and aligns different national circumstances of the Contracting Parties by allowing differentiated treatment.[39] In this way, the AIP seeks to enable the

---

[35] See Article 1(4) ECT ("'Energy Materials and Products', based on the Harmonised System of the World Customs Organization and the Combined Nomenclature of the European Communities, means the items included in Annexes EM I or EM II") as amended by Article 2 of the Amendment to the Trade-Related Provisions 1998.

[36] See Bamberger (1996), p. 2, referring to the Chair of the Legal Advisory Committee of the Energy Charter Conference in negotiations of the 1994 ECT, who describes the Treaty as "not as 'user-friendly' as might be wished".

[37] See, e.g. *Electrabel v. Hungary*, ICSID Case No. ARB/07/19, Decision on Jurisdiction, Applicable Law and Liability, 30 November 2012, para 5.50 ("[. . .] in accordance with the definition contained in Article 1(5) ECT and the provisions of Annex EM paragraph 27.16 ECT and Annex NI ECT, the activities of 'production' and 'sale' of 'electrical energy' as 'energy materials' also constitute an 'economic activity in the energy sector' [. . .]").

[38] See, e.g. supra n. 7.

[39] See Article 3(1) UNFCCC ("The Parties should protect the climate system for the benefit of present and future generations of humankind, on the basis of equity and in accordance with their common but differentiated responsibilities and respective capabilities. Accordingly, the developed country Parties should take the lead in combating climate change and the adverse effects thereof") and Article 4(1) UNFCCC ("All Parties, taking into account their common but differentiated responsibilities and their specific national and regional development priorities, objectives and circumstances, shall [. . .]"). See also Article 2(2) Paris Agreement ("This Agreement will be implemented to reflect equity and the principle of common but differentiated responsibilities and

Contracting Parties to align their obligations under the ECT with the Paris Agreement at their "own pace" dictated by their respective capabilities and development needs. This compromise is based on three pillars.

Pillar 1: Updated Definition of "Economic Activity in the Energy Sector" and the List of "Energy Materials and Products"

Taking into account technological developments, the Contracting Parties decided to extend the definition of "Economic Activity in the Energy Sector" under Article 1(5) by adding the capture, utilisation and storage of carbon dioxide (CCUS). Furthermore, additional energy products relevant to clean energy transition were added to the list of Energy Materials and Products: hydrogen, anhydrous ammonia, biomass, biogas, and synthetic fuels. It is believed that the inclusion of the CCUS, none of whose components were earlier covered in the definition itself or the list of Energy Materials and Products, and the listing of additional energy products may facilitate investment needed for low-carbon development.

Pillar 2: Flexibility Mechanism

The novel Flexibility Mechanism proposed in the AIP would allow the Contracting Parties to carve out protection for investments associated with specific Energy Materials and Products listed in Annexes EM I and EM II. Similar to the nationally determined contributions under the Paris Agreement, and drawing inspiration from the drafting techniques used in free trade agreements,[40] the Contracting Parties would be able to exclude investment protection for fossil fuel-related investments. This mechanism makes use of the already existing Annex NI, which exempts certain

---

respective capabilities, in the light of different national circumstances"), Article 4(3) Paris Agreement ("Each Party's successive nationally determined contribution will represent a progression beyond the Party's then current nationally determined contribution and reflect its highest possible ambition, reflecting its common but differentiated responsibilities and respective capabilities, in the light of different national circumstances"), and Article 4(19) Paris Agreement ("All Parties should strive to formulate and communicate long-term low greenhouse gas emission development strategies, mindful of Article 2 taking into account their common but differentiated responsibilities and respective capabilities, in the light of different national circumstances").

[40] In multilateral negotiations, the lack of consensus on certain issues has resulted in specific drafting techniques, leaving a choice for states to decide to commit to particular obligations. The use of lists in free trade agreements is one of the examples. Such lists may take the form of a "positive list" (a state party undertakes full or partial commitments with respect to sectors specifically listed) or a "negative list" (an agreement covers all sectors unless a state party specifies a reservation related to a certain (sub-)sector).

Energy Materials and Products from the definition of "Economic Activity in the Energy Sector"[41] and existing forms of "flexibility" in the current ECT.[42] The proposed Annex NI would include sections with exclusions listed by specific Contracting Parties who choose to utilise the Flexibility Mechanism.[43]

Notably, the exclusions under the modernised Annex NI would only affect the investments in the territory of the excluding Contracting Party. The exceptions would not, in principle, affect investments of investors of the excluding Contracting Party in the territory of other Contracting Parties, unless the latter opt for reciprocal application of the exclusions. To this end, dedicated Annexes were introduced.

It is also worth noting that this drafting technique relies on the modification of Annex NI under Article 36(1)(d) ECT, which is to be distinguished from amendments to the Treaty pursuant to Article 42. Hence, the exclusions under Annex NI proposed in the AIP, as well as future exclusions, would not be subject to ratification, acceptance or approval under respective national procedures and entry into force pursuant to the provision of Article 42. Instead, the Conference would enjoy flexibility in deciding on any date of entry into force of the modification—subject to a unanimous decision of the Contracting Parties.[44]

In the AIP, the EU and its Member States and the United Kingdom opted for listing certain Energy Materials and Products in Annex NI to gradually phase out protection for fossil fuel-related investments. For these Contracting Parties, investment protection under Part III of the ECT would not cover fossil fuel-related investments made after 15 August 2023 with certain exceptions or extended deadlines for low-carbon "bridging" technologies that may be instrumental in the energy transition. Protection for existing projects would be phased out over ten years following the entry into force of the modification to Annex NI. Japan and Switzerland opted to apply these exclusions reciprocally to investors from the EU or United Kingdom in their territories.

Pillar 3: Review Mechanism

The proposed text aims at facilitating future adjustments to the coverage of the ECT's investment regime without triggering the cumbersome procedure for amending the Treaty under Article 42. To this end, the "Review Mechanism"

[41] See Article 1(5) ECT ("'Economic Activity in the Energy Sector' means an economic activity concerning the exploration, extraction, refining, production, storage, land transport, transmission, distribution, trade, marketing, or sale of Energy Materials and Products except those included in Annex NI, or concerning the distribution of heat to multiple premises [emphasis added]").

[42] Current Annexes ID and IA enable individual Contracting Parties to decide to introduce limitations on their consent to international arbitration or conciliation under Article 26 ECT.

[43] See Annex NI AIP, supra n. 9.

[44] See Article 36(1) ECT ("Unanimity of the Contracting Parties Present and Voting at the meeting of the Charter Conference where such matters fall to be decided shall be required for decisions by the Charter Conference [. . .]").

would commit the Contracting Parties to review the list of Energy Materials and Products and the list of exclusions under Annex NI five years after the entry into force of the modernised ECT and at five-year intervals thereafter, or at an earlier date determined by the Conference.

3.1.2 Definition of "Investment"

The modernised Article 1(6) ECT would maintain an asset-based definition of an "Investment" while subjecting a covered investment to an indicative list of certain characteristics. These characteristics stem from arbitral jurisprudence and recent EU treaty practice, and require a contribution of capital or other resources, the expectation of profit or return, a certain duration or the assumption of risk. In addition, the new definition expressly provides that a covered investment must be made in accordance with the host Contracting Parties' law.[45]

As to the assets falling under the definition of an "Investment", the proposed text excludes judicial and administrative decisions and arbitral awards from the definition as well as limits the coverage of loans. With respect to claims to money arising solely from commercial transactions for the sale of goods and services, Article 1(6) AIP clarifies that such claims are "less likely to have the characteristics of an investment". In the past, the coverage of such assets generated particular controversy in jurisprudence.[46]

Most recently, after almost ten years of setting-aside actions, the issue of debt acquisition in connection with a supply contract as an "Investment" under the ECT was determined by the Court of Justice of the European Union (CJEU). One of the

[45] See Article 1(6) AIP, supra n. 29 ("'Investment' means every kind of asset, owned or controlled directly or indirectly by an Investor of a Contracting Party in the Area of another Contracting Party ('host Contracting Party') that is made or acquired in accordance with the applicable laws in the latter and that have the characteristics of an investment, such as the commitment of capital or other resources, the expectation of gain or profit, a certain duration or the assumption of risk"). See also Article 8.1 Canada-European Union Comprehensive Economic and Trade Agreement (CETA; adopted 30 November 2016, not yet in force) ("investment means every kind of asset that an investor owns or controls, directly or indirectly, that has the characteristics of an investment, which includes a certain duration and other characteristics such as the commitment of capital or other resources, the expectation of gain or profit, or the assumption of risk"); Article 1.2(1) EU–Singapore Investment Protection Agreement (EU–Singapore IPA; adopted 19 October 2018, not yet in force); and Article 1.2(h) EU–Viet Nam Investment Protection Agreement (EU–Viet Nam IPA; adopted 30 June 2019, not yet in force).

[46] See, e.g. *State Enterprise Energorynok v. Moldova*, SCC Case No. 2012/175, Final Award, 29 June 2015, paras 62–70, where claimant argued that a succeeded debt claim was a "claim to money" in accordance with Article 1(6)(c) ECT and, by virtue of a Ukrainian court's decision in favour of the claimant, also a "right conferred by law" under Article 1(6)(f) ECT; and *Petrobart Limited v.Kyrgyz Republic*, SCC Case No. 126/2003, Arbitral Award, 29 March 2005, p. 68, where the claimant argued that its investment was comprised of a supply contract, claim to money for non-payment under the contract, and the judgment of a Kyrgyz court in the claimant's favour in connection with such non-payment.

claims in *Komstroy (former Energoalians) v. Moldova* arose from a trilateral contract involving the claimant as a supplier of electricity, an intermediate entity as a buyer and a Moldova state-owned enterprise as a payer. The payer's debt owed to the buyer for the electricity supplied was assigned to the claimant.[47] The tribunal agreed with the claimant that the assigned debt constituted a claim to money in the meaning of Article 1(6)(c) ECT.[48] By contrast, the tribunal declined jurisdiction with respect to the claimant's claim to money that the claimant had acquired from the buyer without participating in the underlying business activity.[49] Subsequently, the Paris Court of Appeal annulled the *Energoalians v. Moldova* award since the claimant's alleged investment under Article 1(6)(c) failed to meet the requirement of contribution and the condition of being "associated with an Investment".[50] This decision was overturned by the French Court of Cassation.[51] Following the request from the Paris Court of Appeal, the CJEU determined that, indeed, a claim to money under a contract as an "Investment" covered under Article 1(6)(c) must be "associated" with another qualified "Investment".[52] Second, the Court held that the disputed claim for money could not be "associated" with another "Investment" as it arose out of a supply contract—"a commercial transaction which cannot, in itself, constitute an 'investment' within the meaning of Article 1(6) ECT, irrespective of whether an economic contribution is necessary in order for a given transaction to constitute an investment".[53] Following the CJEU's interpretation, the Paris Court of Appeal set aside the award.[54] It is foreseen, that the changes proposed in the AIP would streamline the understanding and interpretation of the nature and types of assets covered by the Treaty's investment provisions.

Building on the EU's treaty practice, public debt remains covered in the AIP, albeit implicitly.[55] However, certain claims with respect to the restructuring of debt issued by a Contracting Party are excluded from the dispute resolution provisions.[56] The authors are not aware of any investment disputes under the ECT arising out of a

---

[47] See *Komstroy (formerly Energoalians) v. Moldova,* UNCITRAL, Arbitral Award, 23 October 2013, paras 69–74 for the factual background of the case; see also paras 193–262 for the tribunal's analysis of the contract at issue; see also Article 1(6)(c) ECT ("claims to money and claims to performance pursuant to contract having an economic value and associated with an Investment [emphasis added]").

[48] See ibid, para 251.

[49] See ibid, paras 268–272.

[50] Paris Court of Appeal, No 13/22531, Judgment, 12 April 2016.

[51] Court of Cassation of France, No 16-16568, Judgment, 28 March 2018.

[52] See CJEU, Case C-741/19. Judgment of the Court (Grand Chamber), 2 September 2021, paras 73–76.

[53] Ibid, para 77.

[54] Paris Court of Appeal, No 18/14721, Judgment, 10 January 2023.

[55] See Annex 8-B CETA, Annex 4 EU–Singapore IPA, and Annex 5 EU–Viet Nam IPA.

[56] See Article 26(12) ("A claim with respect to the restructuring of debt issued by a Contracting Party may only be submitted under Article 26(4) in accordance with Annex PD") and Annex PD (Public Debt) AIP, supra n. 28.

public debt instrument or operation. However, non-payment of public debt has generated certain complications with the interpretation and application of other investment agreements.[57] With the growing importance of sustainable finance and the potential role of debt instruments at a sovereign level for financing energy transition, clarification of the coverage of public debt under the ECT would offer greater legal certainty for both investors and the Contracting Parties.

3.1.3 Definition of "Investor"

The new provision of Article 1(7) AIP expressly excludes natural persons who are nationals or permanent residents of the host Contracting Party at the time of making an investment from the definition of a covered "Investor".[58] The 1994 ECT is silent on the issue of individuals with multiple nationalities, including the nationality of a host Contracting Party, as well as permanent residents of a host Contracting Party.[59] The current definition of "Investor" merely provides that a natural person may qualify as an "Investor" based on either "nationality" of, "citizenship" of or "permanently residing in" one of the Contracting Parties, whereas Article 26(1) includes a further jurisdictional requirement that such an individual has made an "Investment" in the "Area" of a Contracting Party other than the Contracting Party of citizenship, nationality or permanent residence. In the case of *Cem Cenzig Uzan v. Turkey*, a Turkish national sought to establish the tribunal's jurisdiction based on his alleged British and later—French permanent residence.[60] The tribunal determined that at the time of making the investment and until the time of the alleged breaches, Mr Uzan had been a national of Turkey and not claimed foreign resi-

[57] See, e.g. *Abaclat and others v. Argentina*, ICSID Case No. ARB/07/5, where the claimants argued that their interests in Argentine sovereign bonds purchased in the secondary market qualified as an investment under the 1990 Argentina–Italy bilateral investment treaty (BIT). See also *Poštová banka, a.s. and ISTROKAPITAL SE v. Greece*, ICSID Case No. ARB/13/8, where the claimants argued that their interests in Greek sovereign bonds purchased in the secondary market qualified as an investment under 1992 Cyprus–Greece BIT and 1991 Slovakia–Greece BIT.

[58] See Article 1(7)(i) AIP, supra n. 29 ("[. . .] a natural person having the nationality of or who is a permanent resident of a Contracting Party in accordance with its applicable law, provided that such person does not have the nationality or is not a permanent resident of the host Contracting Party at the time the investment was made or acquired").

[59] However, in case of dispute resolution under the Convention on the Settlement of Investment Disputes between States and Nationals of other States (ICSID Convention) pursuant to Article 26(4)(a)(i) ECT, Article 25(2)(b) ICSID Convention prohibits individuals to bring claims against the state of their nationality ("[...] 'National of another Contracting State' means: [...] but does not include any person who on either date also had the nationality of the Contracting State party to the dispute").

[60] See *Cem Cengiz Uzan v. Turkey,* SCC Case No. V 2014/023, Award on Respondent's Bifurcated Preliminary Objections, 20 April 2016, paras 79–86.

dence.[61] Therefore, he was merely a domestic investor not entitled to protection under the ECT.[62] Nonetheless, the arbitrators observed that Mr Uzan could have qualified as an investor based on his permanent residence in another Contracting Party if he had made an investment in Turkey while permanently residing in that Contracting Party.[63] The claimant sought to challenge the above award before the Svea Court of Appeal.[64] While upholding the award, the Court observed that it was "doubtful" that an investor from one Contracting Party could be at the same time considered as an investor from another Contracting Party based on their permanent residence.[65]

In addition, the new provision requires juridical persons to prove "substantial business activities" in their home Contracting Parties. The 1994 ECT makes a reference to "substantial business activities" in the denial-of-advantages clause of Article 17, allowing the Contracting Parties to deny the protection under Part III of the ECT to the entities with no "substantial business activities" in their home Contracting Party that are owned or controlled by nationals of a non-Contracting Party. This clause has been previously treated as an issue of admissibility or merits rather than jurisdiction.[66] As a consequence, at least initially, the burden of proving the circumstances relied upon when invoking the denial-of-advantages clause may lie on the respondent Contracting Party (see infra at Sect. 3.2.6). Under the new text, however, it is for a claimant to prove the jurisdictional requirement of "substantial business activities". This would require showing elements from the indicative list envisaged in the new definition, such as physical presence, employment of personnel, generation of turnover or payment of taxes in the territory of a host Contracting Party.[67]

[61] See ibid, paras 147–153.

[62] See ibid.

[63] See ibid, para 148.

[64] See Svea Court of Appeal, Case No T 6582-16, Judgment, 26 February 2018.

[65] See supra n. 64, p. 26 ("[. . .] it is highly doubtful that such an investor – in relation to the state of their citizenship – can at the same time be considered as an investor from another contracting state because he or she resides there [unofficial translation]").

[66] See, e.g. *Isolux Netherlands B.V. v. Spain*, SCC Case V2013/153, Final Award, 17 July 2016, para 711 ("[...] the Arbitral Tribunal does not doubt that the denial of benefits of Article 17 of the ECT raises a question of admissibility [unofficial translation]"); and *Khan Resources Inc., Khan Resources B.V., and Cauc Holding Company Ltd. v. Mongolia* (*Khan v. Mongolia*), UNCITRAL, Decision on Jurisdiction, 25 July 2012, para 411 ("The question of the application of Article 17 is therefore one for the merits not jurisdiction").

[67] See Article 1(7)(ii) AIP ("The existence of substantial business activities should be established by an overall examination, on a case-by-case basis, of the relevant circumstances, which may include w whether the enterprise (a) has a physical presence in the Area of that Contracting Party; (b) employs staff in the Area of that Contracting Party; (c) generates turnover in the Area of that Contracting Party; or (d) pays taxes in the Area of that Contracting Party"). It is worth noting that international investment agreements, including newer generation, do not normally provide any guidance on what constitutes "substantial business activities". Arbitral jurisprudence in investment disputes under the ECT does not provide any uniform list of elements indicative of "substantial

3.2 *Investment Protection*

3.2.1 Full Protection and Security

The "most constant protection and security" under Article 10(1) ECT has been predominantly understood by arbitral tribunals as an obligation of a Contracting Party to provide some form of physical protection against non-state parties and agents of the state.[68] Nevertheless, some tribunals noted that such standard may go beyond physical protection and include a certain level of legal protection.[69] For the avoidance of doubt, the new provision clarifies that "full protection and security" concerns only the "physical security" of investors and investments.[70]

---

business activities" either. However, in often cited *Limited Liability Company Amto v. Ukraine*, SCC Case No. 080/2005, Final Award, 26 March 2008, para 56, the tribunal observed that "'substantial' in this context means 'of substance, and not merely of form'. It does not mean 'large', and the materiality not the magnitude of the business activity is the decisive question". The tribunal concluded that the claimant maintained "substantial business activities" in its country of incorporation, Latvia, by conducting various investment-related activities concerning its shareholdings in foreign companies, paying taxes, using a bank account, having its office, and employing permanent staff in Latvia (paras 68–69). In contrast, the claimants in *Littop Enterprises Limited, Bridgemont Ventures Limited and Bordo Management Limited v. Ukraine*, SCC Case No. V 2015/092, Final Award, 4 February 2021, did not show evidence of any investment-related activities conducted in their country of incorporation, Cyprus, apart from holding shares in a Ukrainian company (paras 615–638). At the time of writing, the authors were not aware of any other arbitral proceeding in an investment dispute under the ECT where the claimant was found to have no "substantial business activities" in the country of their nationality.

[68] See, e.g. *AES Summit Generation Limited and AES-Tisza Erömü Kft v. Hungary*, ICSID Case No. ARB/07/22, Award, 23 September 2010, para 13.3.2 ("[...] a state's obligation to take reasonable steps to protect its investors (or to enable its investors to protect themselves) against harassment by third parties and/or state actors [...]") and *Liman Caspian Oil B.V. and NCL Dutch Investment B.V. v. Kazakhstan*, ICSID Case No. ARB/07/14, Excerpts of Award, 22 June 2010, para 289 ("[...] to protect the integrity of an investment against interference by the use of force and particularly physical damage").

[69] See, e.g. *Mohammad Ammar Al-Bahloul v. Tajikistan,* SCC Case No. V (064/2008), Partial Award on Jurisdiction and Liability, 2 September 2009, para 246 ("[...] while the concept of protection and security in investment treaties has developed principally in the context of physical security, some tribunals have applied it more broadly to encompass legal security as well. Therefore, it could arguably cover a situation in which there has been a demonstrated miscarriage of justice").

[70] See Article 10(3) AIP, supra n.29, ("The obligation to accord 'Full Protection and Security' refers to the physical security of Investors and Investments"). See also UNCTAD (2022c), p. 23, suggesting that "a definition of the standard could be included to clarify that the provision is limited to 'physical' or 'police' security. In the absence of such a clarification, arbitral tribunals are free to adopt a limited or expansive approach, leading to uncertainty for States and investors".

3.2.2 Transfers Related to Investments

The AIP clarifies Article 14 ECT (Transfers Related to Investments) and further introduces exceptions for temporary restrictions on transfers in case of serious balance-of-payments difficulties of a Contracting Party.[71] This is accompanied by a specific provision on safeguard measures in the event of serious difficulties in the functioning of the economic and monetary union of the EU or the monetary and exchange rate policies of other Contracting Parties. The revised Article 14 would offer the Contracting Parties greater flexibility in introducing certain restrictions on the transfer of capital in the implementation of their domestic law and taking macroeconomic measures to mitigate financial crises without violating the freedom-of-transfers clause.[72] Such a revision would also align the ECT with the most recent treaty practice of the EU and EU law.[73]

3.2.3 Fair and Equitable Treatment

The standard of fair and equitable treatment (FET) has been invoked in most arbitral proceedings in investment disputes under the ECT. At the time of writing, a breach of FET was alleged by claimants in 80 of 87 (or 92%) investment arbitration cases under the ECT in which such information was publicly available.[74] Furthermore, a breach of FET was found in 33 of 44 (or 75%) cases in which liability of a respondent Contracting Party was established and a precise protection standard breached was publicly known.[75] Accordingly, the ECT has generated ample body of jurisprudence on the interpretation of FET, including the conception of investors' "legitimate expectations", and received increasing attention from the Contracting Parties in the process of modernisation of the Treaty.

Article 10(1) ECT, second sentence includes an open-ended, unqualified FET clause typical for older generation investment agreements—a "commitment to accord at all times to Investments of Investors fair and equitable treatment". The

[71] See Article 14 AIP, supra n. 29.

[72] See UNCTAD (2018a), p. 100, suggesting that "an unqualified transfer-of-funds provision significantly reduces a host country's ability to deal with sudden and massive outflows or inflows of capital, balance-of-payments (BoP) difficulties and other macroeconomic problems" and that "[c] ountries may also need to reserve their right to restrict transfers if this is required for the enforcement of the [p]arty's laws (e.g. to prevent fraud on creditors etc.)".

[73] See, e.g, Articles 8.4 and 15.8 EU–Republic of Korea Free Trade Agreement (adopted 15 October 2009, entered into force 13 December 2015) and Articles 9.3 and 9.4 of EU–Japan Economic Partnership Agreement (adopted 17 July 2018, entered into force 1 February 2019); see also CJEU, Case C-205/06, Judgment of the Court (Grand Chamber), 3 March 2009 and CJEU, Case C-249/06, Judgment of the Court (Grand Chamber), 3 March 2009 finding that EU Member States were under obligation to take appropriate steps to eliminate incompatibilities of freedom-of-transfers clauses in their international agreements with EU law.

[74] See Statistics, supra n. 3.

[75] Ibid.

original text does not link the FET standard to international law or the minimum standard of treatment under customary international law. Among the types of conduct that may constitute a breach of the ECT's FET clause, the tribunals found arbitrariness, breach of due process, denial of justice, discrimination on wrongful grounds, and abusive conduct such as harassment.[76]

In many arbitral awards and decisions in ECT cases, the tribunals also considered the issue of investors' legitimate expectations as part of a claim for a breach of FET or under a different heading. However, while some tribunals regarded the protection of legitimate expectations as an "element" of FET, others saw legitimate expectations only as a "relevant factor" when considering FET claims or other claims under Article 10(1) of the ECT.[77] Notably, tribunals diverged on the question of whether investors' legitimate expectations covered by the ECT could derive from both the legal or regulatory framework of a host Contracting Party or only specific representations, assurances or promises given to an investor.[78]

It is also worth mentioning that the ECT has a particular purpose reflected in Article 2—"long-term cooperation in the energy field in accordance with the objectives and principles of the European Energy Charter", a non-binding political

[76] See, e.g. *AES Solar and others (PV Investors) v. Spain*, PCA Case No. 2012-14, Final Award, 28 February 2020, para 565 ("[. . .] the Tribunal likewise considers that FET encompasses [. . .] the protection against arbitrary, unreasonable, and disproportionate conduct"); *Mohammad Ammar Al-Bahloul v. Tajikistan,* SCC Case No. V (064/2008), Partial Award on Jurisdiction and Liability, 2 September 2009, para 221 ("It is recognized in literature and jurisprudence that the duty to provide due process is part of the obligation to provide fair and equitable treatment"); *Limited Liability Company Amto v. Ukraine,* SCC Case No. 080/2005, Final Award, 26 March 2008, para 75 ("Denial of justice is a concept of state responsibility afflicted by imprecision. It is a manifestation of a breach of the obligation of a State to provide fair and equitable treatment and the minimum standard of treatment required by international law"); *Infracapital F1 S.à r.l. and Infracapital Solar B.V. v. Spain*, ICSID Case No. ARB/16/18, Decision on Jurisdiction, Liability and Directions on Quantum, 13 September 2021, para 658 ("[. . .] the principle of non-discrimination referenced in the third sentence is part of the requirement of equality of treatment in the sense that it allows the possibility of different treatment but only on reasonable and justifiable ground [. . .] the impairment clause of the third sentence forms part of the FET obligation"); *Anatolie Stati, Gabriel Stati, Ascom Group SA and Terra Raf Trans Traiding Ltd. v. Kazakhstan* (*Stati v. Kazakhstan*), SCC Case No. V 116/2010, Award, 19 December 2013, para 1095 ("[. . .] Respondent's measures [. . .] constituted a string of measures of coordinated harassment by various institutions of Respondent. These measures must be considered as a breach of the obligation to treat investors fairly and equitably").

[77] See, e.g. *Electrabel S.A. v. Hungary*, supra n. 38, para 7.74 ("[. . .] the obligation to provide fair and equitable treatment comprises several elements, including an obligation [. . .] to refrain [. . .] from frustrating the investor's reasonable expectations with respect to the legal framework adversely affecting its investment") and *9REN Holding S.a.r.l v. Spain*, ICSID Case No. ARB/15/15, Award, 31 May 2019, para 308 ("[I]n addition to deciding that its legitimate expectations have been frustrated by the host State, a claimant must also prove a breach of the FET standard. The former does not necessarily lead to the latter. 'Legitimate expectations' based upon a specific representation are only 'a relevant factor' in assessing whether or not the Respondent violated the FET standard in Article 10(1) of the ECT").

[78] See, e.g. *Masdar Solar & Wind Cooperatief U.A. v. Spain,* ICSID Case No. ARB/14/1, Award, 16 May 2018, Award, paras 489–510 for a discussion on the two "schools of thought" on the sources of investors' legitimate expectations.

declaration of 1991. In its turn, the European Energy Charter recognises the importance of "stable, transparent legal framework" and "legal security" for foreign investments.[79] In a similar vein, the first sentence of Article 10(1) preceding the FET clause stipulates a pre-investment obligation to "encourage and create stable, equitable, favourable and transparent conditions to make Investments".[80]

These two factors, the purpose of the Treaty and the first sentence of Article 10(1), led some arbitral tribunals to the conclusion that the stability of the legal framework for energy investments is of particular importance when interpreting the standard of FET under the ECT.[81]

As reflected in the Policy Options initially submitted by the Contacting Parties, several of the Contracting Parties had certain concerns about the broad notion of FET in 1994 ECT and preferred to have a qualified standard instead.[82] Among the options proposed in the Policy Options were (i) limiting the scope of the FET to the minimum standard of treatment under customary international law, (ii) including a closed list of conduct that may constitute a breach of FET, and (iii) including a non-exhaustive list of obligations under the standard of FET.[83]

As a result of the negotiations, Article 10 AIP follows the following architecture:

[79] European Energy Charter (adopted 17 December 1991) Title II "Implementation", 4. Promotion and protection of investments.

[80] See Wälde (1996), pp. 277–284 and Wälde and Hamida (2008), pp. 174–190 for a discussion on the nature of obligation under Article 10(1) ECT, first sentence. However, some arbitral tribunals concluded that the obligation of Article 10(1), first sentence is connected to or forms part of the FET clause of the second sentence, or that the standard of FET under the ECT includes the conditions listed in Article 10(1), first sentence: see, e.g. *Electrabel v. Hungary*, supra n. 38, para 7.73 ("The first part of Article 10(1) ECT refers to the encouragement and creation of 'stable, equitable, favourable and transparent conditions for investors', which is said to include a commitment to accord at all times fair and equitable treatment to investments. Fair and equitable treatment is connected in the ECT to the encouragement to provide stable, equitable, favorable and transparent conditions for investors").

[81] See, e.g. *Infrastructure Services Luxembourg S.à.r.l. and Energia Termosolar B.V. (formerly Antin Infrastructure Services Luxembourg S.à.r.l. and Antin Energia Termosolar B.V.) v. Spain*, ICSID Case No. ARB/13/31, Award, 15 June 2018, para 526 ("[. . .] the stability of the conditions for Investors of other Contracting Parties to make Investments in another Contracting Party's Area is a leitmotiv in the text of the ECT and is clearly reinforced in the Charter") and para 532 ("[. . .] the obligation under Article 10(1) of the ECT to provide FET to protected investments comprises an obligation to afford fundamental stability in the essential characteristics of the legal regime relied upon by the investors in making long-term investments").

[82] See Decision of the Energy Charter Conference (CCDEC 2019 08), supra n. 21. See also UNCTAD (2022d), p. 16, suggesting "[c]larifying the content of investment protection standards with regard to climate action", "[c]arving-out climate action measures from investment standards and/or ISDS", and "[c]onsidering limiting the scope of FET or excluding it altogether, while detailing specific types of conduct against which sustainable investors and investments are protected".

[83] See Decision of the Energy Charter Conference (CCDEC 2019 08), supra n. 21.

- Paragraph 1 sets out the obligation to accord FET.[84]
- Paragraph 2 introduces, similar to EU treaty practice,[85] a closed list of measures that constitute a violation of FET: (i) arbitrariness, such as blatant unreasonableness; (ii) targeted discrimination on wrongful grounds, such as gender, race or religious beliefs; (iii) fundamental breach of due process, including a fundamental breach of transparency in judicial and administrative proceedings; (iv) denial of justice in criminal, civil or administrative adjudicatory proceedings; (v) abusive treatment such as harassment, duress or coercion; and (vi) frustration of an Investor's legitimate expectations.[86]

  The protection of investors' legitimate expectations is conditioned in the AIP upon (i) their central role in the decision to invest,[87] (ii) reasonableness,[88] and (iii) specific and clear representations of a host Contracting Party.[89] The revised FET clause explicitly excludes the protection of general expectations that a legal or regulatory framework will not change.[90]

3.2.4 Umbrella Clause

One of the most contentious aspects of investors' claims based on the "umbrella clause" of Article 10(1) ECT, last sentence has been the nature of the Contracting Parties' "obligations" covered by this clause. While some arbitral tribunals decided that the wording "any obligations" encompassed obligations under legal or regulatory acts, albeit specifically addressed to investors, others found that the phrase

---

[84] See Article 10(1) AIP, supra n. 29 ("Each Contracting Party shall accord to Investments of Investors of other Contracting Parties, and to such Investors with respect to their Investments, Fair and Equitable Treatment and Full Protection and Security in its Area").

[85] See, e.g. Article 8.10(2) CETA, Article 2.4(2) EU–Singapore IPA, and Article 2.5(2) EU–Viet Nam IPA.

[86] See Article 10(2) AIP, supra n. 29.

[87] See Article 10(2)(vi) AIP, supra n. 29 ("[. . .] where these were central to its Investment [emphasis added]").

[88] ibid ("[. . .] upon which the Investor reasonably relied in deciding to make or maintain the Investment [emphasis added]").

[89] ibid ("[. . .] arose from a clear and specific representation or commitment [emphasis added]"). See also Article 10(3)(vi), fn. 3 AIP, supra n. 29 ("For the purpose of this Article, the determination of whether there is a clear and specific representation or commitment requires a case-by-case, fact-based inquiry that considers, among other factors, laws and regulations and the Contracting Party's relevant publicly known policies and their objectives"). The reference to "publicly known polices" is deemed to balance investors' expectations against relevant political developments, including the Contracting Parties' energy and climate policies.

[90] See Article 10(2)(vi), fn. 2 AIP, supra n. 29 ("For greater certainty, an Investor's legitimate expectations do not include general expectations, such as an expectation (in the absence of clear and specific representations or commitments to that effect) that a Contracting Party's legal or regulatory framework will not change").

"entered into with" could only cover contractual arrangements and promises specifically directed at a particular investor.[91]

The revised umbrella clause of Article 10(12) AIP specifies that the obligations covered are those that are "written", "specific", and "entered into." In addition, the revised clause expressly provides that such obligations may only be breached "through the exercise of governmental authority". Such clarifications bring the ECT's umbrella clause in line with the initial objective of this type of provision, which is to protect contractual and contractual-like arrangements "entered into" with particular investors or investments from violations by states relying on their sovereign powers rather than acting as a counterparty in a commercial transaction.[92]

3.2.5 Indirect Expropriation

The protection against expropriation without compensation under Article 13 is one of the most common protection standards invoked in investment disputes under the ECT. At the time of writing, expropriation claims were advanced in 56 of 87 (or 64%) investment arbitration cases under the ECT in which such information was publicly available.[93] The success rate of such claims, however, appears to be somewhat low—a breach of Article 13 was reportedly found in 7 cases only (or 16% of cases in which liability of a respondent Contracting Party was established).[94]

Since the ECT entered into force, claimants have disputed a multitude of measures under the heading of expropriation. These disputes ranged from claims for expropriatory taxation brought by former shareholders and lenders of Yukos Oil Company to claims for indirect expropriation resulting from the phase-down of incentive schemes for renewable power generation.[95] Lately, the arbitral award in

[91] See, e.g. *Greentech Energy Systems A/S, NovEnergia II Energy & Environment (SCA) SICAR, and NovEnergia II Italian Portfolio S.A. v. Italy*, SCC Case No. V 2015/095, Final Award, 23 December 2018, para 464 ("[. . .] the Tribunal majority is inclined to interpret 'obligations' referred to in the ECT's umbrella clause as sufficiently broad to encompass not only contractual duties but also certain legislative and regulatory instruments that are specific enough to qualify as commitments to identifiable investments or investors") and *Stadtwerke München GmbH, RWE Innogy GmbH and others v. Spain*, ICSID Case No. ARB/15/1, Award, 2 December 2019, para 380 ("[. . .] the ECT negotiators intended the umbrella clause to cover only contractual obligations or contractual-like arrangements, that is to say obligations assumed specifically in respect of a particular individual or legal person").

[92] See Wälde (2006), pp. 214–219, on the "original intentions" of the drafters; see also UNCTAD (2018b), p. 45 ("[. . .] States can clarify that the clause covers only 'written obligations' and that the obligations must be 'entered into' with respect to specific investments. They can also indicate that the umbrella clause applies only to conduct that constitutes an exercise of sovereign powers by a government, i.e. not an ordinary breach of contract by the State").

[93] See Statistics, supra n. 3.

[94] Ibid.

[95] *Hulley Enterprises Limited (Cyprus) v. Russian Federation*, PCA Case No. AA 226; *Yukos Universal Limited (Isle of Man) v. Russian Federation*, PCA Case No. AA 227; *Veteran Petroleum Limited (Cyprus) v. Russian Federation*, PCA Case No. AA 228; *Yukos Capital S.à.r.l v. Russian Federation*, PCA Case No. 2013-31; *Luxtona Limited v. Russian Federation*, PCA Case

Rockhopper v. Italy, concerning a concession for offshore exploration of hydrocarbons within the protected coastal area, has received much attention.[96]

While tribunals confirmed that Article 13 in the 1994 ECT covered the cases of *de facto*, "indirect" and "creeping" expropriation, they also established that a finding of expropriation or a measure "having equivalent" to expropriation requires showing "substantial deprivation" of the use or enjoyment of an investment, or value equivalent to the deprivation of an investment.[97]

The revised Article 13 in the AIP provides an express differentiation between the cases of "direct" and "indirect" expropriation. For an indirect expropriation to occur, the AIP explicitly requires a "substantial deprivation" of "the value of [Investor's] Investment or of the fundamental attributes of property in its Investment, including the right to use, enjoy and dispose of its Investment".[98] The text specifies that an arbitral tribunal would have to take into account the character, object and context of a disputed measure, and that the sole economic impact of the measure in itself would not warrant a finding of indirect expropriation. Importantly, following EU treaty practice, the AIP stipulates that non-discriminatory measures adopted to protect legitimate public policy objectives do not constitute indirect expropriation as a general rule.[99] In this connection, the modernised ECT specifically refers to "climate change mitigation and adaptation" as one of such objectives.[100]

No. 2014-09. For the Energy Charter Secretariat's database of arbitral proceedings in investment disputes under the ECT, see International Energy Charter, List of Cases. https://www.energychartertreaty.org/cases/list-of-cases/. Accessed 11 March 2023.

[96] See *Rockhopper Italia S.p.A., Rockhopper Mediterranean Ltd., and Rockhopper Exploration Plc v. Italy*, ICSID Case No. ARB/17/14, Final Award, 23 August 2022.

[97] See, e.g. *Petrobart Limited v. Kyrgyz Republic,* supra n. 47, p. 77 ("[...] this provision gives protection not only in respect of expropriation but also in regard to measures having effect equivalent to expropriation. Such measures are sometimes referred to as 'indirect', 'creeping' or 'de facto' expropriation and are frequently assimilated to formal expropriation as regards their legal consequences [references omitted]") and *Electrabel S.A. v. Hungary,* supra n. 38, para 6.62 ("[...] the requirement under international law for the investor to establish the substantial, radical, severe, devastating or fundamental deprivation of its rights or the virtual annihilation, effective neutralisation or factual destruction of its investment, its value or enjoyment").

[98] See Article 13(3) AIP, supra n. 29.

[99] See, e.g. Annex 8-A (Expropriation) CETA, para 3. Similar clarifications are contained in Annex 4 (Understanding on Expropriation) EU–Viet Nam IPA and Annex 1 (Expropriation) EU–Singapore IPA. See also UNCTAD (2018b), p. 39, suggesting public policy exceptions to allow states to regulate in public interest with greater legal certainty and reduced exposure to investment claims and particularly noting the 1994 ECT ("[...] the relationship between an exceptions clause and each IIA obligation needs to be considered carefully. The Energy Charter Treaty's Article 24 on 'Exceptions' for example, does not apply to the article on expropriation").

[100] See Article 13(4) AIP, supra n. 28. ("Except in rare circumstances when the impact of a measure or series of measures is so severe in light of its purpose that it is manifestly excessive, non-discriminatory measures by a Contracting Party that are designed and applied to protect legitimate policy objectives, such as public health, safety and the environment (including with respect to climate change mitigation and adaptation), do not constitute indirect expropriations [emphasis added]"). In this connection, see, e.g. UNCTAD (2022d), p. 16, suggesting "[c]larifying

3.2.6 Denial of Benefits

Previously, arbitral tribunals in investment disputes under the ECT confirmed that (i) the Contracting Parties' right to deny investment protection under Part III of the ECT pursuant to the provision of Article 17 does not apply automatically but must be actively exercised[101] and that (ii) the denial of benefits under Article 17 must not be invoked retroactively and, in any case, no later than when a dispute with a subject investor arises.[102] Such jurisprudence has often been contested by the disputing Contracting Parties and subject to criticism among the commentators.[103] It has been observed that states often have no knowledge about the corporate structure and the nature of business activities of foreign investors prior to the materialisation of a legal dispute, making it hardly attainable to deny benefits to specific investors prospectively.[104] Most recently, the tribunal in *Littop v. Ukraine* concluded that the right to deny benefits under Article 17 may be exercised retrospectively, within a reasonable

---

the content of investment protection standards with regard to climate action" and "[c]arving-out climate action measures from investment standards and/or ISDS".

[101] See, e.g. *Plama Consortium Limited v. Bulgaria* (*Plama v. Bulgaria*), ICSID Case No. ARB/03/24, Decision on Jurisdiction, 8 February 2005, para 157 ("By itself, Article 17(1) ECT is at best only half a notice; without further reasonable notice of its exercise by the host state, its terms tell the investor little; and for all practical purposes, something more is needed") and *Khan v. Mongolia*, supra n. 68, para 420 ("If Article 17(1) were to provide for an automatic denial of benefits, it would effectively create an exception to this broad definition. Such exception would more logically be found within the definition at Article 1(7) itself"). See also *Plama v. Bulgaria*, para 150, on how the right to deny benefits may be excercised ("[. . .] a general declaration in a Contracting State's official gazette could suffice; or a statutory provision in a Contracting State's investment or other laws; or even an exchange of letters with a particular investor or class of investors"). For Ukraine's notification on the denial of benefits under Article 17(2) of the ECT, see International Energy Charter, 'Ukraine denies advantages under Article 17(2) of the ECT' (19 August 2022). https://www.energycharter.org/media/news/article/ukraine-denies-advantages-under-article-172-of-the-ect/?tx_news_pi1%5Bcontroller%5D=News&tx_news_pi1%5Baction%5D=detail&cHash=f522138c347edda150bdaca599ba25f4.

[102] See, e.g. *Stati v. Kazakhstan*, supra n. 78, para 745 ("Art. 17 ECT would only apply if a state invoked that provision to deny benefits to an investor before a dispute arose"). Other tribunals suggested that the right to deny advantages under Article 17 may need to be exercised before the making of investments by the subject investor—see, e.g. *Luxtona Limited v. Russian Federation*, PCA Case No. 2014-09, Interim Award on Respondent's Objections to the Jurisdiction of the Tribunal, 22 March 2017, para 282 ("[. . .] the Tribunal decides that the invocation of Article 17(1) does not reach back in time to deprive existing Investments of the protections of Part III of the ECT").

[103] See, e.g. Jagusch and Sinclair (2008), pp. 35–42 and Baltag (2012), pp. 154–159 for a discussion on the requirement of prior notification.

[104] See, e.g. Jagusch and Sinclair (2008). See also UNCTAD (2015), p. 94 ("To ensure the effectiveness of the denial-of-benefits clause in light of the contradictory arbitral practice, it may be useful to clarify that the clause can be invoked also after the commencement of arbitral proceedings").

time after an arbitral proceeding has commenced and information giving rise to the denial of benefits surfaced.[105]

Considering the above jurisprudence and practical complications associated with the denial-of-benefits clause in the ECT, the modernised text revises the provision to ensure its effectiveness and greater legal certainty. To this end, the AIP introduces a timeframe for invoking the denial of-benefits clause. It provides the possibility to deny benefits after the commencement of arbitration but no later than the date a tribunal or court determines for the submission of arguments on preliminary questions.[106] Also, the exercise of this right would not be subject to prior formal notification. In addition, the new provision extends its scope to Article 26 (Settlement of Disputes between an Investor and a Contracting Party), arguably making the denial of benefits a matter of jurisdiction rather than merits or admissibility (see supra at Sect. 3.1.3).

With "substantial business activities" being considered under the definition of "Investor", the modernised text envisages that the Contracting Parties may deny benefits of Part III and Article 26 ECT with respect to the entities owned or controlled by nationals of a state as to which the denying Contracting Party (i) does not maintain diplomatic relation or (ii) adopts or maintains measures for the maintenance of international peace and security, including the protection of human rights, in line with the the Charter of the United Nations and other international commitments.

3.2.7 Most-Favoured-Nation Treatment

The most-favoured-nation (MFN) treatment provision in the modernised ECT excludes dispute settlement provisions contained in other international agreements from its scope of application.[107] This clarification is important considering previous arbitration practice, where the controversy arose regarding the extent to which MFN clauses allow claimants to invoke more favourable dispute settlement provisions from other agreements.[108]

---

[105] *Littop Enterprises Limited, Bridgemont Ventures Limited and Bordo Management Limited v. Ukraine*, SCC Case No. V 2015/092, Final Award, 4 February 2021, para 601. See also *NextEra Energy Global Holdings B.V. and NextEra Energy Spain Holdings B.V. v. Spain*, ICSID Case No. ARB/14/11, Decision on Jurisdiction, Liability and Quantum Principles, 12 March 2019, paras 264–269, where the tribunal determined that the respondent for the first time invoked the denial of benefits in its memorial on jurisdiction in the arbitral proceeding, having been aware for several years about the investors' corporate structure.

[106] See Article 17(1) AIP, supra n. 29.

[107] See Article 10(8)(i) AIP, supra n. 29.

[108] See *Emilio Agustín Maffezini v. Spain*, ICSID Case No. ARB/97/7, Decision of the Tribunal on Objections to Jurisdiction, 25 January 2000, finding that the MFN clause of 1991 Argentina Spain BIT allowed importing more favourable dispute resolution provisions of another agreement. See also *Técnicas Medioambientales Tecmed, S.A. v. Mexico*, ICSID Case No. ARB (AF)/00/2, Award, 29 May 2003; *Siemens A.G. v. Argentina*, ICSID Case No. ARB/02/8, Decision on Jurisdiction,

In addition, following EU treaty practice,[109] substantive provisions in other international agreements would not in themselves constitute "treatment" to be granted under the MFN clause, confining its application to actual measures undertaken by a Contracting Party with respect to investments.[110]

3.2.8 Right to Regulate

The AIP envisages a number of amendments to the text of the Treaty reaffirming and strengthening the Contracting Parties' "right to regulate" in line with recent international treaty practice.[111] Most notably, for greater legal certainty, a new standalone article is included in Part III to safeguard the Contracting Parties' right to regulate under customary international law.[112] To this end, the "Contracting Parties reaffirm the right to regulate within their territories to achieve legitimate policy

3 August 2004; *Camuzzi International S.A. v. Argentina*, ICSID Case No. ARB/03/2, Decision on Objections to Jurisdiction, 11 May 2005; *Gas Natural SDG, S.A. v. Argentina*, ICSID Case No. ARB/03/10, Decision of the Tribunal on Preliminary Questions on Jurisdiction, 17 June 2005; and *Suez, Sociedad General de Aguas de Barcelona, S.A. and Vivendi Universal, S.A. v. Argentina*, ICSID Case No. ARB/03/19, Decision on Jurisdiction, 3 August 2006. While the authors are not aware of any arbitral decision interpreting the MFN provision of Article 10(7) ECT vis-à-vis dispute resolution provisions of other treaties, the issue of operation of another MFN clause was considered in *Plama v. Bulgaria*, supra n. 103. In this case, the claimant sought to overcome Bulgaria's invocation of the denial-of-benefits clause under Article 17 ECT by invoking 1987 Cyprus–Bulgaria BIT, albeit lacking ICSID arbitration among the dispute resolution avenues offered. By way of operation of the MFN clause in Cyprus–Bulgaria BIT, Plama pursued to establish Bulgaria's consent to ICSID arbitration found in 1997 Bulgaria–Finland BIT. Nevertheless, the tribunal concluded that an MFN clause in a basic agreement could not be read as covering dispute resolution provisions of other treaties in the absence of evidence to the opposite.

[109] See, e.g. Article 8.7(4) CETA and Article 2.4(5) EU–Viet Nam IPA. See also UNCTAD (2020), p. 19, observing that "[t]he MFN clause can potentially have the effect of rolling back substantive treaty reform. A number of arbitral decisions have read the MFN obligation as allowing investors to invoke more investor-friendly provisions from third treaties [...] States may wish to exclude this possibility by clarifying what constitutes "treatment" for the purposes of the MFN clause".

[110] See Article 10(8)(ii) AIP, supra n. 29.

[111] See, e.g. Article 8.9 CETA or Article 9.16 Comprehensive and Progressive Agreement for Trans-Pacific Partnership (CPTPP; adopted 8 March 2018, entered into force 30 December 2018).

[112] Previously, tribunals in arbitral proceedings in investment disputes under the ECT confirmed the Contracting Parties' right to regulate: see, e.g. *Antaris Solar GmbH and Dr. Michael Göde v. Czech Republic*, PCA Case No. 2014-01, Award, 2 May 2018, para 360 ("The requirements of legitimate expectations and legal stability as manifestations of the FET standard do not affect the State's rights to exercise its sovereign authority to legislate and to adapt its legal system to changing circumstances"). However, the tribunals observed that the degree of the Contracting Parties' regulatory flexibility may be limited by their obligations under the ECT: see, e.g. *Foresight Luxembourg Solar 1 S.à.r.l. and others v. Spain*, SCC Case No. 2015/150, Final Award, para 364 ("[. . .] the right to regulate must be subject to limitations if investor protections are not to be rendered meaningless").

objectives, such as the protection of the environment, including climate change mitigation and adaptation, protection of public health, safety or public morals".[113]

Moreover, a new structure for exceptions is envisaged, drawing inspiration from WTO law:[114] Article 24 AIP is now solely devoted to "General Exceptions". Notably, environmental measures, including climate change mitigation and adaptation measures, are added to the existing general exceptions.[115] They now would apply to a broader range of provisions in Part III, including the FET clause of Article 10 ECT. New Article 24bis envisages "Security Exceptions" and, in particular, reaffirms the right to take measures for the maintenance of international peace and security.[116]

4 Dispute Settlement

In accordance with the mandate of the Modernisation Group, rules concerning dispute settlement were considered in negotiations only to a limited extent. Discussions were inspired by the Contracting Parties' treaty practice as well as the ICSID Rules and Regulations Amendment of 2022 with the following results.[117]

4.1 Transparency

The proposal for the modernised ECT incorporates the Rules on Transparency in Treaty-based Investor-State Arbitration of the United Nations Commission on

[113] See New Article "Right to Regulate" AIP, supra n.29. See also UNCTAD (2022d), p. 16, suggesting "[c]larifying the content of investment protection standards with regard to climate action", "[c]arving-out climate action measures from investment standards and/or ISDS," and "[r] eferencing commitment to combat climate change and undertake climate action" in treaties' preambles.

[114] See Articles XX and XXI General Agreement on Tariffs and Trade (GATT; signed 30 October 1947, entered into force 1 January 1948).

[115] See Article 24(1)(b), fn.10 AIP, supra n. 29 ("paragraph (i)(b) includes environmental measures (including climate change mitigation and adaptation measures) necessary to protect human, animal or plant life or health"). See UNCTAD (2022d), p. 16, suggesting "[i]ncluding general climate action exceptions".

[116] See Article 24bis(1) AIP, supra n. 29 ("Nothing in this Treaty shall be construed to prevent any Contracting Party from taking any measure in pursuance of maintenance of international peace and security, or to require a Contracting Party to furnish any information, the disclosure of which it considers contrary to its essential security interests").

[117] For an overview of the ICSID 2022 Rules and Regulations and relevant resources, see ICSID, 'ICSID 2022 Rules and Regulations: Resources'. https://icsid.worldbank.org/rules-regulations/2022-rules-and-regulations/resources.

International Trade Law (UNCITRAL).[118] This addresses the criticism concerning the lack of transparency in investment arbitration under Article 26(3) ECT.

Also, for disputes between Contracting Parties under Article 27 ECT, the new provision of Article 27(4) AIP ensures that procedural documents and hearings are, in principle, publicly accessible.

4.2 *Frivolous Claims*

To ensure the efficiency of arbitration proceedings and to reduce the costs of litigation, the AIP includes a new article on frivolous claims to allow for the early dismissal of certain claims through the following mechanisms:

- **Claims manifestly without legal merit**: Building on ICSID Arbitration Rule 41, the AIP provides for the dismissal of claims lacking legal merit, either as a matter of jurisdiction or substance, *a limine litis*.[119] The introduction of this provision would allow for the early dismissal of claims in non-ICSID proceedings as well.
- **Claims unfounded as a matter of law**: Following recent treaty practice of some Contracting Parties,[120] the AIP includes a provision on expedited dismissal of unfounded claims as a preliminary issue on merits.[121]
- **Forum-shopping:** It is clarified that the tribunal should decline jurisdiction over claims brought as a result of the acquisition or restructuring of an investment for the sole purpose of establishing jurisdiction under Article 26 ECT.[122]

4.3 *Security for Costs*

The AIP introduces the right of a respondent Contracting Party to request the tribunal to order the claimant to post security for costs in certain cases. The new article particularly addresses the risk of non-compliance with adverse cost decisions.[123]

---

[118] See Article 26(6) AIP, supra n. 29. See also UNCITRAL, UNCITRAL Rules on Transparency in Treaty-based Investor-State Arbitration (2014). https://uncitral.un.org/sites/uncitral.un.org/files/media-documents/uncitral/en/rules-on-transparency-e.pdf.

[119] See New Article "Frivolous Claims" (1) AIP, supra n. 29.

[120] See, e.g. Article 27(2) Argentina–Japan BIT (adopted 1 December 2018, not yet in force), Article 9.23(4) CPTPP, and Article 8.33 CETA.

[121] See New Article "Frivolous Claims" (2) AIP, supra n. 29.

[122] See ibid, (1).

[123] See New Article "Security for Costs" AIP, supra n. 29.

4.4 *Third-Party Funding*

The new provision directs both disputing parties to disclose information on a third party funding their litigation costs.[124] This provision is particularly aimed at preventing any conflict of interest. It also allows the tribunal to request further information concerning the funding agreement if the need arises.

4.5 *Valuation of Damages*

Under this heading, the Contracting Parties refrained from regulating the methods for the valuation of damages but made several clarifications on the awards of compensation. First, the AIP allows the respondent Contracting Party found in breach of the expropriation provision of Article 13 to choose between restitution of the investor's property or paying monetary damages.[125] Second, monetary damages are limited to the loss actually suffered by the investor and may not include punitive damages.[126] Third, the new cost allocation rules provide that the costs of proceedings and other reasonable party costs are, in principle, borne by the losing disputing party.[127]

5 Regional Economic Integration Organisation

Article 1(2) ECT stipulates that a "Contracting Party" to the ECT may be either a state or a REIO. It further follows from Article 36(7) that both a REIO and its member states may become Contracting Parties to the ECT in their own right.[128] The current ECT is silent on the issue of application of the Treaty among Contracting Parties that are members of a REIO in their mutual relations, including with respect to Article 26, allowing for investment arbitration.

In contrast, Article 24(3) AIP expressly provides that Articles 7 (Transit), 26 (Settlement of Disputes between an Investor and a Contracting Party), 27 (Settlement of Disputes between Contracting Parties) and 29 (Interim Provisions on Trade-Related Matters) do not apply among Contracting Parties that are members of the same REIO

[124] See New Article "Third Party Funding" AIP, supra n. 29.

[125] See Article 26(9)(b) AIP, supra n. 29.

[126] See Article 26(10) AIP, supra n. 29.

[127] See Article 26(11) AIP, supra n. 29.

[128] See Article 36(7) ECT ("A Regional Economic Integration Organisation shall, when voting, have a number of votes equal to the number of its member states which are Contracting Parties to this Treaty; provided that such an Organisation shall not exercise its right to vote if its member states exercise theirs, and vice versa").

in their mutual relations.[129] The practical relevance of the new provision in Article 24 is limited to the EU as the only Contracting Party-REIO at the time of writing and its Member States-Contracting Parties to the ECT. Nevertheless, the implication of such an amendment in many respects would be significant. For instance, over 60% of arbitral proceedings in investment disputes under the ECT initiated before 10 January 2023 were between an EU investor and an EU Member State ("intra-EU").[130]

It is worth noting that the contemplated clarifications are not mere policy choices. From the perspective of EU law, they are sought out of constitutional necessity to bring the ECT in line with the jurisprudence of the CJEU, which has qualified investment arbitration under international investment agreements, including the ECT, in the intra-EU context as incompatible with the EU Treaties.[131]

6 Outlook

The contemplated adoption of the modernised ECT did not take place at the meeting of 22 November 2022. Prior to the meeting, the EU Member States did not reach consensus within the Council of the EU to mandate the European Commission to adopt the amendments.[132] Therefore, the European Commission requested to remove this item from the agenda of the meeting.[133] The adoption of the amendments was rescheduled for an ad hoc meeting in April 2023.[134] Given the difficult political landscape within the EU, the modernisation of the ECT has not advanced so far. After all, the 1994 ECT and its "sunset clause" of Article 47(3) may be around far longer as one may have expected at the time of the adoption of the AIP.[135]

[129] See Article 24(3) AIP, supra n. 29 ("For greater certainty, Articles 7, 26, 27, 29 shall not apply among Contracting Parties that are members of the same Regional Economic Integration Organisation in their mutual relations").

[130] See Statistics, supra n. 3.

[131] See CJEU, Judgement, 6 March 2018, C-284/16 (Slovak Republic/Achmea B.V.); CJEU, Judgement, 2 September 2021, C-741/19 (Republic of Moldova/Komstroy LLC).

[132] Euractive, 'Brussels calls for pause in ECT reform talks after losing key EU vote' (21 November 2022). https://www.euractiv.com/section/energy/news/brussels-calls-for-pause-in-ect-reform-talks-after-losing-key-eu-vote/.

[133] See supra n. 134.

[134] Energy Charter Conference Decision (CCDEC 2022 32) of 22 November 2022 at https://www.energycharter.org/fileadmin/DocumentsMedia/CCDECS/2022/CCDEC202232.pdf.

[135] See Article 47(3) ECT ("The provisions of this Treaty shall continue to apply to Investments made in the Area of a Contracting Party by Investors of other Contracting Parties or in the Area of other Contracting Parties by Investors of that Contracting Party as of the date when that Contracting Party's withdrawal from the Treaty takes effect for a period of 20 years from such date").

References

Baltag C (2012) The energy charter treaty: the notion of investor. Kluwer Law International

Bamberger CS (1996) Chapter 1: overview. In: Wälde TW (ed) The energy charter treaty: an east-west gateway for investment & trade. Kluwer Law International

Jagusch S, Sinclair A (2008) Denial of advantages under Article 17(1). In: Coop G, Ribero C (eds) Investment protection and the energy charter treaty. JurisNet

UNCTAD (2015) Investment Policy Framework for Sustainable Development. https://unctad.org/system/files/official-document/diaepcb2015d5_en.pdf

UNCTAD (2018a) Investment Policy Framework for Sustainable Development. https://investmentpolicy.unctad.org/uploaded-files/document/UNCTAD_Reform_Package_2018.pdf

UNCTAD (2018b) UNCTAD's Reform Package for the International Investment Regime (2018). https://investmentpolicy.unctad.org/uploaded-files/document/UNCTAD_Reform_Package_2018.pdf

UNCTAD (2020) International Investment Agreement Accelerator. https://unctad.org/system/files/official-document/diaepcbinf2020d8_en.pdf

UNCTAD (2022a) World Investment Report 2022. https://unctad.org/system/files/official-document/wir2022_en.pdf

UNCTAD (2022b) International Investment in Climate Change Mitigation and Adaptation. https://unctad.org/system/files/official-document/diaeinf2022d2_en.pdf

UNCTAD (2022c) International Investment Agreements Reform Accelerator. https://unctad.org/system/files/official-document/diaepcbinf2020d8_en.pdf

UNCTAD (2022d) International Investment Agreements Issue Note. The International Investment Treaty Regime and Climate Action (Issue 3, September 2022). https://unctad.org/system/files/official-document/diaepcbinf2022d6_en.pdf

Wälde TW (1996) International investment under the 1994 energy charter treaty. In: Waelde TW (ed) The energy charter treaty: an east-west gateway for investment & trade. Kluwer Law International

Wälde TW (2006) Contract claims under the energy charter treaty's umbrella clause: original intentions versus emerging Jurisprudence. In: Ribeiro C (ed) Investment arbitration and the energy charter treaty. JurisNet

Wälde TW, Hamida WB (2008) The energy charter treaty and corporate acquisition. In: Coop G, Riberio C (eds) Investment protection and the energy charter treaty. JurisNet

Yuriy Pochtovyk is a Junior Legal Official at the Energy Charter Secretariat. He was a member of the Secretariat's core team providing legal advice and facilitating negotiations on the modernisation of the Energy Charter Treaty.

Lukas Stifter is a Senior Investment Policy Officer at the Austrian Federal Ministry of Labour and Economy. He served as Chair of the Modernisation Group of the Energy Charter Conference since July 2020.

The Substantive Protection of Intra-EU Investors Under International Investment Law and EU Law: Convergence and Divergence on the Protection of Property and Legitimate Expectations

Christina Binder and Philipp Janig

Contents

Abstract The dismantling of the system of intra-EU investment arbitration raises the question whether affected investors are provided with comparable protection under EU law. This contribution examines substantive aspects of that question, including the differences in personal and material scope of these fields of law, and focusses on the question of property rights and interests. It additionally discusses the *Photovoltaic Energy* cases, in which both the CJEU and investment tribunals dealt with the protection of legitimate expectations under the respective legal regime. The contribution highlights that the answer to the question of comparable protection depends to a great extent on the specific comparator chosen on the side of international investment law, both in terms of treaty provisions as well as arbitral case law.

C. Binder (✉) · P. Janig
Universität der Bundeswehr München, Neubiberg, Germany
e-mail: c.binder@unibw.de; philipp.janig@unibw.de

M. Bungenberg, A. Reinisch (eds.), *New Frontiers for EU Investment Policy*, Special Issue, https://doi.org/10.1007/978-3-031-41977-5_6

It then concludes by arguing that a potentially lower standard of protection under EU law is not necessarily undesirable for policy reasons.

1 Introduction

The dismantling of the system of intra-EU investment arbitration in the wake of the *Achmea* judgment,[1] and largely implemented through the 2020 termination agreement,[2] has kicked off a debate on alternative avenues for investor protection. The question arose whether that decline would leave the affected investors without appropriate protection—or whether EU law sufficiently takes account of their interests. While the Commission itself essentially considered that there were no significant issues for investors in a communication from July 2018 (and thus briefly after *Achmea*),[3] it held a public consultation on the need for a regulation concerning intra-EU investments in 2020. However, so far, no further action was taken on the issue.[4]

This contribution assesses to what extent the substantive protection under EU law conforms with the protection under treatment standards typically found in investment treaties. While undoubtedly important, we are not concerned with issues of procedure and enforcement. Thus, the question whether investor-state arbitration or domestic courts and the CJEU provide for better procedural safeguards and remedies is outside the scope of this paper. Rather, we examine whether intra-EU investors will enjoy a comparable *substantive* protection under the EU legal framework (in particular the fundamental rights and freedoms) as those under investment law. In that context, the contribution—after a brief discussion on the differences in personal and material scope of these two fields of law—mainly focuses on the question of property rights and interests. It then examines a rare instance in which the CJEU and investment tribunals both had to deal with the same matter under comparable legal standards, namely the protection of legitimate interests in the *Photovoltaic Energy* Cases.

The following discussions will show that the outcome of that comparison depends to a great extent on the specific comparator chosen on the side of international investment law, both in terms of treaty provisions as well as arbitral case law. This contribution takes account of various international investment agreements (including CETA and ECT), as well as arbitral awards based on different

[1] *Achmea B.V. v. The Slovak Republic (formerly Eureko B.V. v. The Slovak Republic)*, UNCITRAL, PCA Case No. 2008-13, Award on Jurisdiction, Arbitrability and Suspension, 26 October 2010.

[2] Agreement for the Termination of Bilateral Investment Treaties between the Member States of the European Union (signed 5 May 2020, entered into force 29 August 2020) OJ L169.

[3] European Commission (2018).

[4] European Commission (2020a).

agreements. It should further be highlighted that the finding that a given protection standard is not fully reflected in EU law does not necessarily imply a judgment on the *desirability* of that substantive protections for intra-EU investors. These issues will be briefly touched upon in the conclusion.

2 Difference of Application *Ratione Materiae* and *Ratione Personae*

2.1 *The Material Scope of Application*

2.1.1 Overview

The factor relevant for the application of international investment law is the existence of an 'investment' as defined by the applicable international investment agreement (IIA). In general, treaties provide for an asset-based definition of 'investments' and include a non-exhaustive list of protected 'assets'.[5] These definitions in particular include rights in tangible assets, shareholding, financial instruments and intellectual property rights.[6] Such investments are generally considered to also fall within the scope of EU law during their full-life cycle, thus the entire process of entering, operating and exiting the market. For instance, Julien Berger noted that 'an intra-European cross-border economic situation such as an intra-EU investment activity will always fall within the formal scope of application of EU law.'[7] They may in particular be protected by two fundamental freedoms in EU law, namely the freedom of establishment (Art 49 TFEU) and the free movement of capital (Art 63 TFEU). As will be seen, their scope of application overlaps in significant ways with the notion of 'investments'. In addition, sector-specific EU legislation covers a wide range of issues relevant for foreign investments, such as the energy sector or

[5] See, *e.g.*, Art 1(1) 2008 Germany Model BIT https://investmentpolicy.unctad.org/international-investment-agreements/treaty-files/2865/download ('the term "investments" comprises every kind of asset [...] [and] include in particular: [...]'); Art 1(1) 2020 Italy Model BIT https://edit.wti.org/document/show/2cb70b93-9d50-4541-a092-8127562e9257 ('The term "investment" shall mean any kind of asset [...] [and] shall include in particular, but not exclusively [...]'); Art 1(1) 2006 France Model BIT https://edit.wti.org/document/show/4dd30824-38f3-4e5e-9d05-79a9d1bfb422 ('The term "investment" means every kind of assets [...] and in particular though not exclusively [...]').

[6] Dolzer et al. (2022), pp. 96–99. See also in more detail below in Sect. 4.2.

[7] Berger (2021), p. 48; see also Andersen and Hindelang (2016), pp. 984, 992 ('In case of intra-EU investments, which concern cross-border economic activities related to both, the freedom of capital movement as well as the freedom of establishment, it is hard to imagine a situation in which the EU Treaties would in fact not apply.'); Moskvan (2022), p. 16 (contending that 'it can be argued that [...] EU law is much more liberal than protection under BITs'); see also European Commission (2018), pp. 5–9.

intellectual property.[8] Insofar as EU member states 'are implementing Union law', the fundamental rights enshrined in the CFEU will also apply.[9] The following discussions will first address the two most relevant fundamental freedoms and then address the situation with regard to fundamental rights.

2.1.2 The Fundamental Freedoms

Many forms of foreign direct investments fall within the scope of the freedom of establishment, while the free movement of capital covers portfolio investments and certain direct investments. However, the distinction between the two freedoms is not always clear-cut and they overlap in some regards.

The freedom of establishment applies to 'any activity that has commercial and economic nature' that 'is actually pursued from an established professional base in another MS on a stable and continuous basis'.[10] According to the CJEU, 'the definition of establishment [. . .] involves the actual pursuit of an economic activity through a fixed establishment in another Member State for an indefinite period'.[11] The purchase of shares in a company is protected by the freedom of establishment only insofar as those shares provide a 'definite influence over the company's decisions'.[12]

The CJEU consistently holds that 'all measures which prohibit, impede or render less attractive the exercise of that freedom [of establishment] must be regarded as restrictions within the meaning of that article'.[13] Most importantly, although it traditionally has been understood as an expression of the principle of non-discrimination, it is not necessary for measures to be discriminatory. In addition, it also covers circumstances in which the 'restriction identified is of limited scope or of minor importance'.[14]

[8] European Commission (2018), p. 3.

[9] Article 51(1) Charter of Fundamental Rights of the European Union (26 October 2012) OJ C 326/391.

[10] Tomkin (2019), Article 49 TFEU, p. 650, para. 14; see also Enzinger (2022), mn. 10.

[11] ECJ, Case C-438/05 *The International Transport Workers' Federation und The Finnish Seamen's Union* [2007] ECLI:EU:C:2007:772, para. 70; ECJ, Case C-171/02 *Commission v Portugal* [2004] ECLI:EU:C:2004:270, para. 25; Khan and Eisenhut (2018), Artikel 49 AEUV, p. 442, mn. 12–13.

[12] ECJ, Case C-251/98 *Baars* [2000] ECLI:EU:C:2000:205, para. 22; see also Moskvan (2022), p. 10; Khan and Eisenhut (2018), Artikel 49 AEUV, p. 442, mn. 7.

[13] ECJ, Case C-389/05 *Commission v France* [2008] ECLI:EU:C:2008:411, para. 52; Tomkin (2019), Article 49 TFEU, p. 650, paras. 29–30; Khan and Eisenhut (2018), Artikel 49 AEUV, p. 442, mn. 18; Enzinger (2022), Art 49 AEUV, mn. 18.

[14] Tomkin (2019), Article 49 TFEU, p. 650, para. 30.

In comparison, the free movement of capital is concerned with the prohibition of 'all restrictions on the movement of capital between Member States and between Member States and third countries' (Art 63(1) TFEU). According to case law, it applies to financial transactions undertaken for the primary purpose of investing.[15] In order to define the term, the CJEU often consults the (non-exhaustive) list in Annex I of Directive 88/361/EEC as having indicative value, although the Directive is no longer in effect.[16] This includes foreign direct investments, the purchase of shares, investments in real estate, loans and credits, guarantees and securities, the receipt of dividends or the physical import and export of financial assets.[17]

The prohibition of restrictions covers any measures 'likely to discourage non-residents from making investments in a Member State'[18] and may be relevant when making as well as holding the investment. It applies regardless of whether restrictions are discriminatory. In addition, their level of severity is irrelevant, as also transitory restrictions or those of limited importance are covered.[19]

2.1.3 The Applicability of the CFEU

Article 51(1) CFEU provides that EU member states are bound by EU fundamental rights 'only when they are implementing Union law'.[20] According to the CJEU, this is the case if the relevant measure of the state 'falls within the scope of European Union law'.[21] Thus, it will fundamentally depend on the subject matter concerned. The requirement has been subject to an expansive, albeit not always entirely coherent, jurisprudence by the CJEU.[22]

The applicability of the CFEU is undisputed in instances where the member states act as 'agents' of the EU. Thus, the enforcement of Regulations or the implementation of Directives must comply with fundamental rights. This also applies if member states exercise discretion awarded to them by EU legislation in choosing the specific manner of implementation. In contrast, the CFEU will not apply if the matter is explicitly excluded from the scope of EU law (e.g. on the basis of an

---

[15] Schneider (2020), Art 63 AEUV, mn. 12.

[16] Steiblytė and Tomkin (2019), Article 63 TFEU, p. 743, para. 9; Moskvan (2022), p. 11; Schneider (2020), Art. 63 AEUV, mn. 13.

[17] For a comprehensive list with references to case law, see Schneider (2020), Art. 63 AEUV, mn. 14; see also Moskvan (2022), p. 11.

[18] ECJ, Joined Cases C-52/16 and C-113/16 *SEGRO and Horváth* [2018] ECLI:EU:C:2018:157, para. 65 (with further references).

[19] Schneider (2020), Art. 63 AEUV, mn. 30–31; Steiblytė and Tomkin (2019), Article 63 TFEU, p. 743, paras. 24–26.

[20] Art 51(1) Charter of Fundamental Rights of the European Union (26 October 2012) OJ C 326/391.

[21] ECJ, Case C-617/10 *Åkerberg Fransson* [2013] ECLI:EU:C:2013:105, para. 19; ECJ, Case C-235/17 *Commission v Hungary (Usufruct Over Agricultural Land)* [2019] ECLI:EU:C:2019:432, para. 63.

[22] See also Lock (2019a), Art 51 CFEU, p. 2241, paras. 5–6.

express provision in a Directive) or if the subject matter nexus between the state measure in question and the (allegedly) 'implemented' part of EU law is insufficient.[23] In addition, member states are not bound by the CFEU if they act collaboratively on the basis of international law, and thus outside the EU legal order.[24]

The second line of jurisprudence (partly criticized in the literature) concerns situations where a measure constitutes a restriction of one of the fundamental freedoms. According to the CJEU, if 'national legislation is such as to obstruct one or more of the fundamental freedoms guaranteed by the FEU Treaty' it has to comply with fundamental rights.[25] More specifically, the reliance on an exception to a fundamental freedom provided for by EU law 'must be regarded as "implementing Union law" within the meaning of Article 51(1) of the Charter'.[26]

That may be particularly relevant in the context of those matters that essentially remain in the competence of member states, such as direct taxation or criminal law. It is the settled case-law of the CJEU that these competences must be exercised 'consistently with EU law and, in particular, with the fundamental freedoms'.[27]

2.1.4 Conclusions

The freedom of establishment (Art 49 TFEU) and the free movement of capital (Art 63 TFEU) will arguably cover the different types of investments typically protected by international investment law. As noted before, the applicability of the CFEU might follow from EU legislation covering a particular sector or subject matter, or from the state measure in question constituting a restriction of one of the freedoms. While it remains to be seen whether the CJEU is open to consider *all* types of measures that an intra-EU investor would be protected against under international investment law as such restrictions, the material applicability of EU law should generally not provide an obstacle.

The applicability of these protections to intra-EU investors after the establishment phase of investments is exemplified by *Commission v Hungary*. The case concerned

---

[23] See e.g., ECJ, Case C-206/13 *Siragusa* [2014] ECLI:EU:C:2014:126, para. 24 ('requires a certain degree of connection above and beyond the matters covered being closely related or one of those matters having an indirect impact on the other').

[24] ECJ, Case C-370/12, *Pringle* [2012] ECLI:EU:C:2012:756, paras. 178–181; Holoubek and Oswald (2019), Art 51 GRC, mn. 20–25; Lock (2019a), Art 51 CFEU, p. 2241, paras. 5–8; see also Ward (2021), Article 51, p. 1413.

[25] ECJ, Case C-235/17 *Commission v Hungary (Usufruct Over Agricultural Land)* [2019] ECLI:EU:C:2019:432, para. 64; ECJ, Case C-201/15 *AGET Iraklis* [2016] ECLI:EU:C:2016:972, para. 63; ECJ, Case C-235/17 *Commission v Hungary (Usufruct Over Agricultural Land)* [2019] ECLI:EU:C:2019:432, para. 65; ECJ, Case C-201/15 *AGET Iraklis* [2016] ECLI:EU:C:2016:972, para. 64.

[26] See also Holoubek and Oswald (2019), Art 51 GRC, mn. 26.

[27] Case C-48/15 *NN (L)* [2016] ECLI:EU:C:2016:356, para. 43; see also Case C-251/98 *Baars* [2000] ECLI:EU:C:2000:205, para. 17; Case C-319/02 *Manninen* [2004] ECLI:EU:C:2004:484, para. 19.

the extinguishment of rights of usufruct over agricultural land by persons who could not demonstrate a close family tie with the owner of the land. The CJEU held that when nationals of other member states 'have [. . .] acquired, directly or indirectly, a right of usufruct over agricultural land' for the purposes of farming, 'that right constitutes [. . .] the corollary of the exercise of those nationals' right of establishment'.[28] In addition, given that such transactions generates capital movements—which include 'investments in real estate on the territory of a Member State by non-residents'[29]—they also fall within the scope of the free movement of capital.[30]

2.2 *The Personal Scope of Application*

The substantive (as well as procedural) protections of international investment law notably only extend to *foreign* investors. Thus, foreign nationality (and, given that the field is largely governed by bilateral treaties, the nationality of a *particular* state) is a fundamental prerequisite for international investment law to apply.[31]

The pertinent fundamental rights under EU law (discussed in more detail below), as well as the free movement of capital apply to *everyone*, including third-state nationals as well as entities established in third states.[32] In contrast, the personal scope of application of the freedom of establishment is more limited. Pursuant to Art 54 TFEU it only applies to '[c]ompanies and firms formed in accordance with the law of a Member State' that have 'their registered office, central administration or principal place of business within the Union'. Thus, third-state companies as such can under no circumstances enjoy the protection of that fundamental freedom.[33]

However, certain intra-EU BITs also extended the notion of 'investors' to certain entities established under the law of third states. For instance, the Austria-Bulgaria BIT defined 'investors' as including 'any juridical person established and having its seat outside the jurisdiction of one of the Contracting Parties and being controlled by an investor of the other Contracting Party'.[34] While EU nationals (or companies) that have structured their investments through corporations outside of the EU were protected by these treaties, they cannot base themselves on the freedom of establishment.

---

[28] ECJ, Case C-235/17 *Commission v Hungary (Usufruct Over Agricultural Land)* [2019] ECLI: EU:C:2019:432, para. 52.

[29] Ibid, para. 54.

[30] Ibid, para. 53.

[31] See in more detail, Dolzer et al. (2022), pp. 58ff.

[32] See with regard to the free movement of capital, Steiblytė and Tomkin (2019), p. 743, para. 6 (highlighting that a different level of protection might apply with regard to third countries).

[33] Tomkin (2019), Article 54 TFEU, p. 686, paras. 3–5.

[34] Art 1(3)(c) Austria-Bulgaria BIT https://investmentpolicy.unctad.org/international-investment-agreements/treaty-files/3319/download; see similarly Art 1(b)(iii) Netherlands-Poland BIT https://investmentpolicy.unctad.org/international-investment-agreements/treaty-files/2074/download.

The relevance of this should not be overstated. For one, investment chapters negotiated by the EU itself, such as in CETA, do not include similar language.[35] In addition, the presumably only small sub-set of 'foreign investors' concerned by this may well continue to enjoy protection under a BIT concluded with the relevant third state. The discussions above have further shown that many investment activities protected by the freedom of establishment simultaneously fall within the scope of application of the free movement of capital.

3 Different Standards of Treatment and Their Reflection in Primary EU Law: A Short Mapping Exercise

The question whether (and to what extent) EU fundamental rights and freedoms may provide for comparable protection to investment agreements is subject to considerable debate. For instance, the tribunal in *Achmea v Slovakia* considered that 'EU law does not provide substantive rights for investors that extend as far as those provided for by the BIT'.[36] More specifically, it asserted that not all claims relating to Fair and Equitable Treatment (FET) 'necessarily lie within the scope of the protections afforded by EU law',[37] that Full Protection and Security (FPS) 'is not exhausted by the rights flowing from the freedom of establishment under EU law'[38] and that the protection against expropriation is also 'by no means covered by the EU freedom of establishment'.[39] With regard to expropriation, the tribunal further noted:

> While it certainly overlaps with the right to property secured by Article 17 of the EU Charter of Fundamental Rights [...], the BIT provision on expropriation is not obviously co-extensive with it. Both the considerable body of jurisprudence on indirect takings that has emerged in the context of BITs, and also the fact that the BIT protects 'assets' and 'investments' rather than the arguably narrower concepts of 'possessions' and 'property' protected by the EU Charter on Fundamental Rights, give rise to the possibility of wider protection under the BIT than is enjoyed under EU law.[40]

In contrast, in a Communication from 2018, the European Commission considered that intra-EU investments were protected by EU law throughout their entire life-

[35] See definition of 'investor' in Art 8.1 Comprehensive Economic and Trade Agreement (CETA) [2017] OJ L 11/23; see also Art 1.2(3) and (5) EU-Singapore Investment Protection Agreement https://eur-lex.europa.eu/resource.html?uri=cellar:55d54e18-42e0-11e8-b5fe-01aa75ed71a1.0002.02/DOC_2&format=PDF.

[36] *Achmea B.V. v. The Slovak Republic (formerly Eureko B.V. v. The Slovak Republic)*, UNCITRAL, PCA Case No. 2008-13, Award on Jurisdiction, Arbitrability and Suspension, 26 October 2010, para. 262.

[37] Ibid, para. 259.

[38] Ibid, para. 260.

[39] Ibid, para. 261.

[40] Ibid.

cycle and that the substantive standards do not fall short of those existing in investment law.[41]

The actual picture is more complex than both positions suggest. It is possible to discern a direct counterpart in EU law for certain of the traditional investment standards—such as the right to property (Art 17 CFEU) with regard to protections against expropriation; the principle of equality before the law (Art 20 CFEU) and the right to non-discrimination (Art 21 CFEU) with regard to non-discrimination standards in investment law; or the free movement of capital with regard to transfer provisions. While this does not imply that protections will be congruent in all circumstances,[42] the provisions of EU law roughly protect similar legal interests or against similar types of state intrusions.

When it comes to the *physical* protection under FPS,[43] states might have similar positive obligations under the CFEU to protect individuals, such as investors (under the right to integrity of the person in Art 3 CFEU and the right to liberty and security in Art 6 CFEU), as well as property rights (under the right to property in Art 17 CFEU).

However, the most complicated issue concerns FET, which encompasses protection against a variety of different interferences by the state.[44] Whether EU law includes a comparable substantive protection thus depends on the specific type of case. For instance, questions of 'procedural propriety and due process' are likewise addressed by the right to an effective remedy and to fair trial in Art 47 CFEU. It grants individuals the right to challenge the legality of measures by states before courts,[45] establishes minimum standards for the organization of those courts,[46] and provides for rights of disputing parties.[47] Similarly, issues of 'stability and consistency' in the domestic legal framework are object of the general principle of legal certainty in EU law. That principle requires that norms are 'clear and precise' and 'their application foreseeable by those subject to them'.[48]

The arguably clearest divergence exists with regard to contractual obligations, which international investment law protects through umbrella clauses or (according

41 European Commission (2018).

42 See also below in Sect. 4.

43 Dolzer et al. (2022), pp. 234–236.

44 For instance, Dolzer, Kriebaum and Schreuer list eight 'specific applications' of FET, namely 'stability and consistency', 'legitimate expectations', 'transparency', 'compliance with contractual obligations', 'procedural propriety and due process', 'application of domestic law', 'freedom from coercion and harassment' and 'good faith', see Dolzer et al. (2022), pp. 205–228.

45 ECJ, Case C-64/16 *Associação Sindical dos Juízes Portugueses* [2018] ECLI:EU:C:2018:117, para. 31.

46 See e.g., ECJ, Case C-585/18 *A.K. (Independence of the Disciplinary Chamber of the Supreme Court)* [2019] ECLI:EU:C:2019:982, paras. 115ff; ECJ, Case C-619/18 *Commission v Poland (Independence of the Supreme Court)* [2019] ECLI:EU:C:2019:531, para. 58.

47 See e.g., ECJ, Case C-199/11 *Otis et al* [2012] ECLI:EU:C:2012:684, paras. 71ff.

48 ECJ, Case T-227/21 *Illumina* [2022] ECLI:EU:T:2022:447, para. 173.

to some tribunals) as an aspect of FET.[49] In contrast, EU law has no comparable general standard that protects against interferences with contractual relationships. Nevertheless, in certain circumstances they might be protected by the freedom to conduct a business under Art 16 CFEU. That provision covers the 'freedom of contract', which 'includes, in particular, the freedom to choose with whom to do business'.[50]

While the discussions above remain somewhat cursory, it becomes clear that EU law, when viewed through the lens of investment protection standards, presents a complex and fragmented picture. Whether its legal protections will be comparable very much depends on the specific circumstances. The following part will address the issue of expropriation and examine in more detail how far the right to property in Article 17 CFEU may provide for comparable protection. In this context, reference will also be made to the case law of the ECtHR, which (in accordance with Article 52(3) CFEU) constitutes the minimum threshold of protection.[51] Thereafter, the contribution will delve into how the CJEU and investment arbitration have construed the protection of 'legitimate expectations' under EU law and investment law in one specific context.

4 Expropriation and the Right to Property

4.1 Overview

The oldest, and most fundamental, protection of international investment law is the protection against the expropriation of investments. For instance, Article 8.12 CETA provides that parties 'shall not nationalise or expropriate a covered investment either directly, or indirectly through measures having an effect equivalent to nationalisation or expropriation'. The provision thus applies to 'investments' and protects them against direct and indirect expropriation, which are lawful if they are undertaken '(a) for a public purpose; (b) under due process of law; (c) in a non-discriminatory manner; and (d) on payment of prompt, adequate and effective compensation'.[52]

Similarly, Article 17 CFEU enshrines the right to property and provides that '[e]veryone has the right to own, use, dispose of and bequeath his or her lawfully acquired possessions'. The deprivation of possessions may only occur 'in the public interest and in the cases and under the conditions provided for by law, subject to fair compensation being paid in good time for their loss'. In addition, '[t]he use of property may be regulated by law in so far as is necessary for the general interest'.

[49] Dolzer et al. (2022), pp. 214–216.

[50] ECJ, Case C-283/11 *Sky Österreich* [2013] ECLI:EU:C:2013:28, paras. 42–43.

[51] See also ECJ, Case C-235/17 *Commission v Hungary (Usufruct Over Agricultural Land)* [2019] ECLI:EU:C:2019:432, para. 72.

[52] Art 8.12 Comprehensive Economic and Trade Agreement (CETA) [2017] OJ L 11/23.

The following will first discuss the notion of 'possessions' and compare it with the definition of 'investments' as enshrined in CETA. The contribution then turns to three differences: the protection of minority shareholders for reflective losses,[53] the question of 'indirect expropriations'[54] and the issue of compensation.

4.2 *Material Scope: Investments and the Notion of 'Possessions'*

As already noted above, what constitutes an 'investment' depends on the definition enshrined in the applicable IIA. In general, treaties provide for an asset-based definition of 'investments' and include a non-exhaustive list of protected assets. For instance, Article 8.1 CETA defines an investment as 'every kind of asset [...] that has the characteristics of an investment, which includes a certain duration and other characteristics such as the commitment of capital or other resources, the expectation of gain or profit, or the assumption of risk.' As examples of such assets, the provision then lists:

(a) an enterprise;
(b) shares, stocks and other forms of equity participation in an enterprise;
(c) bonds, debentures and other debt instruments of an enterprise;
(d) a loan to an enterprise;
(e) any other kind of interest in an enterprise;
(f) an interest arising from:

  (i) a concession conferred pursuant to the law of a Party or under a contract, including to search for, cultivate, extract or exploit natural resources,
  (ii) a turnkey, construction, production or revenue-sharing contract; or.
  (iii) other similar contracts;

(g) intellectual property rights;
(h) other moveable property, tangible or intangible, or immovable property and related rights;

(i) claims to money or claims to performance under a contract.

For greater certainty, claims to money does not include:

(a) claims to money that arise solely from commercial contracts for the sale of goods or services by a natural person or enterprise in the territory of a Party to a natural person or enterprise in the territory of the other Party.
(b) the domestic financing of such contracts; or
(c) any order, judgment, or arbitral award related to sub-subparagraph (a) or (b).

Returns that are invested shall be treated as investments. [...]

---

[53] Kriebaum and Schreuer (2007), pp. 743, 753–759 (with regard to ECtHR case law).
[54] See e.g., Sattorova (2016), pp. 895, 904–907; Berger (2021), pp. 51–54.

In comparison, Article 17 CFEU applies to 'lawfully acquired possessions',[55] which the CJEU defined as 'rights with an asset value creating an established legal position under the legal system, enabling the holder to exercise those rights autonomously and for his [or her] benefit'.[56] Thus, rights only constitute 'possessions' if they simultaneously have an 'asset value' and create a specific 'established legal position'.

The asset value of rights or interests may follow in particular from them being granted for consideration.[57] However, 'mere commercial interests or opportunities'—which are by their very nature uncertain—cannot constitute possessions.[58] This includes market shares[59] or 'the mere possibility of being able to market' certain products in the EU.[60] Such interests might fall under the scope of the freedom to conduct business of Article 16 CFEU, but are not protected by the right to property.

The term 'possessions' encompasses immovable and movable property as traditionally understood,[61] as well as other rights *in rem* such as rights of *usufruct*,[62] liens[63] or other security rights.[64] In addition, it includes financial instruments, such

---

[55] On the basis of that legality requirement, the obligation to repay state aid due to the failure to satisfy the eligibility conditions does not amount to an infringement of Article 17 CFEU, see ECJ, Case C-273/15 *Ezernieki* [2016] ECLI:EU:C:2016:364, paras. 47, 49.

[56] ECJ, Case C-283/11 *Sky Österreich* [2013] ECLI:EU:C:2013:28, para. 34; ECJ, Case C-398/13 P *Inuit Tapiriit Kanatami and Others v Commission* [2015] ECLI:EU:C:2015:535, para. 60; ECJ, Case C-235/17 *Commission v Hungary (Usufruct Over Agricultural Land)* [2019] ECLI:EU:C:2019:432, para. 69; ECJ, Joined Cases C-798/18 and C-799/18 *Federazione nazionale delle imprese elettrotecniche ed elettroniche (Anie) and Others and Athesia Energy and Others* [2021] ECLI:EU:C:2021:280, para. 33.

[57] ECJ, Case C-283/11 *Sky Österreich* [2013] ECLI:EU:C:2013:28, para. 35; Wollenschläger (2021), Article 17(1), p. 465, para. 17(1).16; see also ECJ, Joined Cases C-798/18 and C-799/18 *Federazione nazionale delle imprese elettrotecniche ed elettroniche (Anie) and Others and Athesia Energy and Others* [2021] ECLI:EU:C:2021:280, paras. 34–54 (concerning incentives for the production of photovoltaic energy, which have an asset value, but do not constitute an established legal position).

[58] ECJ, Case C-398/13 P *Inuit Tapiriit Kanatami and Others v Commission* [2015] ECLI:EU:C:2015:535, para. 60.

[59] ECJ, Joined Cases C-120/06 P and C-121/06 P *FIAMM and Others v Council and Commission* [2008] ECLI:EU:C:2008:476, para. 185.

[60] ECJ, Case C-398/13 P *Inuit Tapiriit Kanatami and Others v Commission* [2015] ECLI:EU:C:2015:535, paras. 62–63.

[61] Lock (2019b), Article 17 CFR, p. 2149, para. 4; Kriebaum and Schreuer (2007), pp. 743, 748–749.

[62] ECJ, Case C-235/17 *Commission v Hungary (Usufruct Over Agricultural Land)* [2019] ECLI:EU:C:2019:432, para. 70 (emphasizing that it permitted the 'usufructuary to use and enjoy that property' and to 'exercise those rights [. . .] independently, even if the possibility of transferring such rights is limited or precluded under the applicable national law').

[63] Wollenschläger (2021), Article 17(1), p. 465, para. 17(1).16 (with further references).

[64] *Gasus Dosier- und Färdertechnik GmbH v the Netherlands* App no 15375/89 (ECtHR, 23 February 1995) para. 53.

as company shares and bonds tradable on the capital markets,[65] as well as sovereign bonds.[66] The protection of intellectual property is explicitly affirmed by Article 17(2) CFEU, which encompasses patents,[67] trademarks[68] as well as (rights related to) copyright.[69]

The ECtHR has further applied the right to property to certain other rights, in particular business licenses or permits,[70] as well as intangible interests, such as the value and goodwill of a business[71] or an existing professional clientele.[72] However, it remains to be seen whether the CJEU will also address these issues under the right to property, or rather resort to the freedom to conduct a business under Article 16 CFEU.[73]

The CJEU has moreover confirmed that 'future income' may be protected insofar as 'it has already been earned, it is definitely payable or there are specific circumstances that can cause the person concerned to entertain a legitimate expectation of obtaining an asset'.[74] In accordance with the case law of the ECtHR, this includes enforceable judgments or awards, as well as certain contractual rights (e.g. the contractual right to renew a long-term lease[75]).

In *Sky Österreich*, the CJEU accepted that exclusive broadcasting rights granted on a contractual basis in return for payment had an 'asset value', however did not constitute an 'established legal position' in the specific circumstances of the case. This followed from the fact that the specific measures complained against were foreseeable in light of existing legislation.[76]

While many rights and interests protected against expropriation in international investment law are equally protected by Article 17 CFEU, it should not be overlooked that the object of protection is fundamentally different. Article

---

[65] ECJ, Case C-83/20 *BPC Lux 2 and Others* [2022] ECLI:EU:C:2022:346, paras. 39–43.

[66] ECJ, Case T-107/17 *Steinhoff and Others v ECB* [2019] ECLI:EU:T:2019:353, paras. 94ff.

[67] ECJ, Case C-307/18 *Generics (UK) and Others* [2020] ECLI:EU:C:2020:52, para. 41.

[68] ECJ, Case C-220/17 *Planta Tabak* [2019] ECLI:EU:C:2019:76, paras. 91–92.

[69] See on the 'right [of music performers] to a single equitable remuneration', ECJ, Case C-265/19 *Recorded Artists Actors Performers* [2020] ECLI:EU:C:2020:677, paras. 57, 85.

[70] ECtHR (2022), paras. 43–46.

[71] Reinisch and Schreuer (2020), Ch 1 Expropriation, para. 91.

[72] ECtHR (2022), paras. 42.

[73] Wollenschläger (2021), Article 17(1), p. 465, para. 17(1).21.

[74] ECJ, Case C-398/13 P *Inuit Tapiriit Kanatami and Others v Commission* [2015] ECLI:EU:C:2015:535, para. 61; ECJ, Joined Cases C-798/18 and C-799/18 *Federazione nazionale delle imprese elettrotecniche ed elettroniche (Anie) and Others and Athesia Energy and Others* [2021] ECLI:EU:C:2021:280, para. 39; on the case law of the ECtHR on this see ECtHR (2022), paras. 17–25; Reinisch and Schreuer (2020), Ch 1 Expropriation, paras. 89–91.

[75] *Stretch v the United Kingdom* App no 44277/98 (ECtHR, 24 March 2003) paras. 32–35.

[76] ECJ, Case C-283/11 *Sky Österreich* [2013] ECLI:EU:C:2013:28, paras. 35–40; see also ECJ, Joined Cases C-798/18 and C-799/18 *Federazione nazionale delle imprese elettrotecniche ed elettroniche (Anie) and Others and Athesia Energy and Others* [2021] ECLI:EU:C:2021:280, paras. 45–47.

17 CFEU applies to certain individual legal positions (to the extent that is not altogether clear whether an economic enterprise as such is protected).[77] Thus, it may also protect legal positions that do not constitute investments, such as pensions or other social security benefits.[78]

In contrast, provisions in international investment law apply to 'investments' as entire economic operations. This might entail the protection of legal interests that presumably are not covered by Article 17 CFEU (although potentially under other provisions), such as market access.[79] Whether IIAs will protect against interferences with specific legal positions, not constituting an investment as such, very much depends on the circumstances.[80]

4.3 *The Rights of Shareholders*

Company shares constitute 'possessions' protected by Article 17 CFEU as well as (typically) 'investments' covered by investment treaties. As a result, both legal regimes protect shareholders against interferences with rights directly stemming from those shares, such as voting rights or the right to influence the company's policy.[81] However, investment arbitral tribunals have additionally recognized the right of investors to bring claims for 'reflective' or 'indirect' losses.[82]

Thus, shareholders may bring claims against host states due to measures affecting the company (leading to direct damage of the company), for depreciation of the value of their shares (*i.e.* indirect damage). This constitutes a separate cause of action, which is independent of the existence of a claim by the company itself. Moreover, it is not contingent on control exercised by the shareholder over the company, also allowing minority shareholders to bring claims.[83]

The ECtHR has adopted the opposite position, namely that shareholders are in principle not considered victims of measures affecting the company.[84] Thus, they have to show that the measures complained against directly affected their rights

[77] Wollenschläger (2021), Article 17(1), p. 465, para. 17(1).20; Ziniel (2019), Art 17 GRC, mn. 29.

[78] ECJ, Case C-258/14 *Florescu and Others* [2017] ECLI:EU:C:2017:448, para. 50; Case C-130/19 *Court of Auditors v Pinxten* [2021] ECLI:EU:C:2021:782, para. 888.

[79] Reinisch and Schreuer (2020), paras. 132–134.

[80] Dolzer et al. (2022), pp. 147–151.

[81] ECtHR (2022), paras. 32; see, e.g., *Reisner v Turkey* App no 46815/09 (ECtHR, 21 July 2015) para. 45 (applying the right to property because shares lost entirety of their value due to the respective state measures).

[82] Vanhonnaeker (2020), pp. 6–7.

[83] Vanhonnaeker (2020), pp. 137–138.

[84] ECtHR (2022), para. 33.

stemming from those shares or the ability to exercise them. In contrast, a mere (indirect) effect on their economic interests is insufficient.[85] The ECtHR has only accepted two exceptions to this principle: firstly, instances in which the shareholders and the company are so closely connected that a distinction between them would be considered artificial.[86] This essentially applies in the context of small or family-owned companies, *e.g.* where the application is brought by the sole shareholder.[87] However, it is generally not sufficient that the shareholders complaining are representative of a majority of shares.[88] The second exception includes certain other specific circumstances, in particular the impossibility of the company to complain about the measures itself.[89] Thus, if the organs of the company or its liquidators are not able to bring an application, the shareholders might.[90]

Under the assumption that the CJEU will likewise adopt this line of jurisprudence from the ECtHR, the rights of shareholders under EU law are significantly curtailed vis-á-vis the investment regime.[91] This is particularly relevant for minority shareholders, who are unable to determine how the company itself reacts to state measures, and thus cannot ensure that legal actions are brought.

However, there are also factors that put into question whether that should give rise to legislative action with regard to intra-EU investors. Firstly, regardless of the rights of shareholders, the company itself can always avail itself of the protections of EU law. This is not necessarily the case in international investment law, given its limited scope of applicability *ratione personae*. Secondly, the approach of investment law constitutes the outlier, departing from the general approach adopted within international and domestic (corporate) law. In *Barcelona Traction*, the ICJ confirmed the status of corporations as separate legal entities, and that lifting the corporate veil is only possible in exceptional circumstances.[92] Thirdly, the possibility of shareholder claims for reflective loss has been under critique more generally, in light of the associated risks of multiple (parallel) proceedings and potential double recovery, and currently is being discussed in UNCITRAL Working Group III.[93]

---

[85] *Albert and Others v Hungary* App no 5294/14 (ECtHR (GC), 7 July 2020) paras. 131–134.

[86] ECtHR (2022), para. 35.

[87] See, *e.g.*, *KIPS DOO and Drekalović v Montenegro* App no 18766/06 (ECtHR, 26 June 2018) paras. 86–87 (accepting this where the shareholder held 99% of the shares).

[88] Kriebaum and Schreuer (2007), pp. 743, 754–755.

[89] ECtHR (2022), para. 36.

[90] See, e.g., *Agrotexim and Others v Greece* App no 14807/89 (ECtHR, 24 October 1995) para. 66.

[91] Which has been criticized by in the context of EU law, see Reuter (2021), pp. 681, 700.

[92] *Barcelona Traction, Light and Power Company, Limited (Belgium v. Spain) (New Application: 1962)* [1970] ICJ Rep 3, paras. 56–58.

[93] See UNCITRAL (2019).

4.4 Substantive Protection: Indirect Expropriation

The protection against expropriation in international investment law also covers indirect expropriations. Thus, any (set of) measures by the host state that do not affect the legal title of the foreign investor as such, but nevertheless 'deprives the investor of the possibility to utilize the investment in a meaningful way'.[94] That being said, arbitral practice has not been uniform in how to examine (alleged) indirect expropriations resulting from regulatory measures of the host state.[95] In line with the 'sole effect' doctrine, some tribunals only examine the effects of those measures, without taking into account other contextual factors.[96] In contrast, under the 'police powers doctrine' adopted by other tribunals, measures are not considered expropriatory, if taken in the 'exercise of functions that are generally considered part of the government's powers to regulate the general welfare'.[97]

The latter approach has also found reflection in a number of more recent IIAs that emphasize the host state's right to regulate.[98] For instance, Article 8.9 CETA provides that 'the mere fact that a Party regulates, including through a modification to its laws, in a manner which negatively affects an investment or interferes with an investor's expectations, including its expectations of profits, does not amount to a breach of an obligation'.[99]

In comparison, the right to property under Article 17(1) CFEU has a broader scope of application, as it entails two separate guarantees: namely the protection against deprivation (*i.e.* expropriation) of property on the one hand, and the protection against regulations of the use of property on the other hand. With regard to both guarantees, the provision lists requirements that interferences have to meet in order to be lawful, in addition to the general requirements listed in Article 52(1) CFEU.[100]

In order for a measure to be qualified as a deprivation of property, the right-holder has to be deprived in a 'compulsory, complete and definitive manner' of their rights to a given asset.[101] In that context, the ECtHR considered that.

---

[94] Dolzer et al. (2022), p. 153.

[95] See also Sattorova (2016), pp. 895, 904–907.

[96] Dolzer et al. (2022), pp. 169–171.

[97] Dolzer et al. (2022), pp. 174–180; see, *e.g.*, *Técnicas Medioambientales Tecmed, S.A. v. The United Mexican States*, ICSID Case No. ARB (AF)/00/2, Award, 29 May 2003, para. 122 (taking account of the case law of the ECtHR).

[98] See Berger (2021), p. 52 (noting that 'the great majority of intra-EU BITs continues to guarantee an absolute and categorical protection against expropriation').

[99] See also Art 5(2) 2020 Italy Model BIT https://edit.wti.org/document/show/2cb70b93-9d50-4541-a092-8127562e9257.

[100] Ziniel (2019), Art 17 GRC, mn. 37–38; see also ECJ, Case C-83/20 *BPC Lux 2 and Others* [2022] ECLI:EU:C:2022:346, para. 38 (considering the general clause in Art 17 first sentence as an additional, separate guarantee).

[101] ECJ, Case C-235/17 *Commission v Hungary (Usufruct Over Agricultural Land)* [2019] ECLI:EU:C:2019:432, para. 81; see also ECJ, Case C-363/01 *Flughafen Hannover-Langenhagen* [2003] ECLI:EU:C:2003:548, paras. 55, 58 (indicating that that includes the possibility 'to exploit

> it is necessary not only to consider whether there has been a formal taking or expropriation of property but to look behind the appearances and investigate the realities of the situation[.][102]

Thus, the ECtHR[103] and (at least in principle) the CJEU[104] have acknowledged that—in addition to formal expropriations—state measures may amount to *de facto* deprivations of property. This occurs where 'the owner has lost all of the economic value of the property affected'[105] and could not legitimately expect that it would be affected by the state measure in question.[106] Nevertheless, the case law concerning *de facto* deprivations has been conceptually inconsistent, and it is not entirely clear where the distinction between 'deprivations' and 'regulations of the use' of property is drawn.[107] For instance, orders to (preventively) kill livestock for the purposes of disease control are consistently regarded as a regulation of the use of property, rather than a deprivation.[108]

In general, investment tribunals are more willing than the ECtHR to qualify state measures as amounting to an indirect expropriation—which may be seen in the *Yukos*-saga. Yukos was faced with tax reassessments of the Russian state and the imposition of large penalties and fines, the enforcement of which eventually led to the liquidation of the company.[109] While investment tribunals considered the totality of circumstances to amount to an indirect expropriation,[110] the ECtHR did not entertain the notion.[111]

However, in contrast to protections against expropriations in international investment law, the right to property covers interferences *below* the threshold of a 'deprivation', as 'regulations of the use of property'. This encompasses all state measures that require or prohibit a certain use of property, in a functional, temporal

---

[...] property in such a way as to make a profit'); *Immobiliare Saffi v Italy* App no 22774/93 (ECtHR, 28 July 1999) para. 46 (noting—in context of an apartment—that the applicant 'was at no stage deprived of the right to let or to sell the property').

[102] *Brumărescu v. Romania* App no 28342/95 (ECtHR (GC), 28 October 1999) para. 76; see also *Depalle v France* App no 34044/02 (ECtHR (GC), 29 March 2010) para. 78.

[103] *Sarıca and Dilaver v Turkey* App no 11765/05 (ECtHR, 27 May 2010), paras. 38–52 (on the physical seizure of real property).

[104] ECJ, Case C-83/20 *BPC Lux 2 and Others* [2022] ECLI:EU:C:2022:346, para. 44.

[105] Perkams (2010), pp. 107, 121.

[106] ECJ, Case T-107/17 *Steinhoff and Others v ECB* [2019] ECLI:EU:T:2019:353, paras. 107–111.

[107] See, arguing in favor of dismissing the category of *de facto* deprivations altogether, Wollenschläger (2021), Article 17(1), p. 465, paras. 17(1).35–36; Ziniel (2019), Art 17 GRC, mn. 41.

[108] ECJ, Joined Cases C-20/00 and C-64/00 *Booker Aquaculture and Hydro Seafood* [2003] ECLI:EU:C:2003:397, paras. 80, 92–93; *En l'affaire S.A. Bio d'Ardennes v Belgium* App no 44457/11 (ECtHR, 12 November 2019) para. 48.

[109] See also Kriebaum (2022), pp. 481, 495–499 (attributing the divergence in findings to differences in the evidentiary procedure).

[110] See, *i.a.*, *Yukos Universal Limited (Isle of Man) v The Russian Federation*, PCA Case No AA 227, Final Award, 18 July 2014, paras. 1580–1585.

[111] *OAO Neftyanaya Kompaniya Yukos v Russia* App no 14902/04 (ECtHR, 20 September 2011).

or spatial manner. In case law, this has *inter alia* included the court-ordered revocation of a building and operating permit, the freezing of assets or limitations on production.[112] With regard to these types of interferences, the payment of compensation is not an absolute requirement. The ECtHR has only acknowledged that under certain circumstances compensation may be necessary in order for interferences not to become disproportionate. This would be the case if it constitutes a disproportionate burden for the individual, taking account of the severity of the interference, legitimate expectations and whether the owner is in a different situation as other comparable individuals.[113] For instance, the *Ouzounoglou v Greece* case before the ECtHR concerned the effects of the construction of a freeway close to the applicant's house on its value. After noting the close vicinity to the house, the magnitude of the project and the negative effects of traffic on the applicant when using the home, the Court determined that the applicant had to be compensated for the reduction of the property's value.[114]

In conclusion, both under the CFEU as well international investment law, adjudicative bodies are in principle open to examine the expropriatory nature of state measures short of a formal taking of property or investments. However, while investment tribunals have developed a sophisticated (and partly diverging) case law on the issue, the ECtHR has resorted to the category on a rather exceptional basis. In most cases, the Court examined the exercise of regulatory or administrative powers of the state as 'regulations of the use of property'. This is arguably unlikely to be different under the CFEU, in light of the absolute requirement of compensation for a deprivation of property.[115] That being said, the right to property has a broader scope of application than the protections against expropriations in international investment law. Thus, even if the CJEU is less likely to consider state measures as *de facto* deprivations, the CFEU might nevertheless provide protection against regulations of the use of property—including a requirement of compensation.

4.5 Compensation

In order for an expropriation to be lawful, international investment law typically requires the payment of 'prompt, adequate and effective compensation', although treaty language partly significantly differs.[116] In that context, 'adequate' compensation is generally considered to correspond to the fair market value of the investment.[117]

---

[112] See with further references, Ziniel (2019), Art 17 GRC, mn. 42.

[113] Perkams (2010), pp. 107, 121; see also on the case law of the ECtHR (2022), paras. 190–192.

[114] *Ouzounoglou v Greece* App no 32730/03 (ECtHR, 24 November 2005) paras. 30–32.

[115] Ziniel (2019), Art 17 GRC, mn. 45.

[116] Reinisch and Schreuer (2020), Ch 1 Expropriation, para. 1116–1117.

[117] Reinisch and Schreuer (2020), Ch 1 Expropriation, para. 1178, see also paras. 1121–1122.

In comparison, Article 17 CFEU provides for the payment of '*fair* compensation [...] in good time' in order for deprivations to be lawful.[118] This is typically the 'true',[119] 'current' or 'full'[120] market value of an asset at the time of the deprivation.[121] When examining the totality of cases before the ECtHR, the amounts awarded are typically considerably smaller than those in investment awards. To a large extent, this arguably follows from the differences in the types of cases being brought before these fora, rather than reveals diverging approaches to the calculation of damages.[122]

Nevertheless, there are cases in which the ECtHR has explicitly held that public interests might justify a compensation below the market value.[123] Thus, 'measures of economic reform or measures designed to achieve greater social justice, may call for less than reimbursement of the full market value'.[124] The same applies to 'fundamental changes of a country's constitutional system [such] as the transition from a monarchy to a republic'.[125] In *Jahn and Others v Germany*, the ECtHR even considered that 'in light of the unique context of German reunification' a total lack of compensation was justified, also taking account of 'the grounds of social justice relied on by the German authorities'.[126] However, this exception typically only applies to general measures and not to individual measures of expropriations.[127]

The case law of the CJEU itself on the issue of compensation is so far extremely limited. Whether (or to what extent) it will follow the ECtHR's jurisprudence is open to question, as the payment of fair compensation is an explicit requirement for the legality of an expropriation under Article 17 CFEU, rather than one (albeit central) element of a proportionality assessment. Nevertheless, it is reasonable to assume that compensation due under Article 17 CFEU will be lower than under international investment law insofar as intra-EU investors are affected by general reform measures.

---

[118] Emphasis added.

[119] ECJ, Case T-570/17 *Algebris (UK) and Anchorage Capital Group v Commission* [2022] ECLI:EU:T:2022:314, para. 427; ECJ, Case T-680/13 *Chrysostomides, K. & Co. and Others v Council and Others* [2018] ECLI:EU:T:2018:486, para. 314 (also speaking of 'an amount reasonably related to the value of the assets at issue').

[120] Wollenschläger (2021), Article 17(1), p. 465, para. 17(1).41.

[121] See on the discussions during the drafting, Ziniel (2019), Art 17 GRC, mn. 2.

[122] Kriebaum (2009), pp. 219, 244.

[123] See, *e.g.*, *The Former King of Greece and Others v Greece* App no 25701/94 (ECtHR (GC), Just Satisfaction, 28 November 2002) paras. 78, 89; see generally on the ECtHR's approach, ECtHR (2022), paras. 178–192.

[124] *James and Others v the United Kingdom* App no 8793/79 (ECtHR, 21 February 1986) para. 54.

[125] *The Former King of Greece and Others v Greece* App no 25701/94 (ECtHR (GC), Merits, 23 November 2000) para. 87.

[126] In addition to a number of further considerations, see *Jahn and Others v Germany* App nos 46,720/99, 72,203/01 and 72,552/01 (ECtHR (GC), 30 June 2005) paras. 112–117.

[127] Wollenschläger (2021), Article 17(1), p. 465, para. 17(1).41; Ziniel (2019), Art 17 GRC, mn. 47.

5 The Photovoltaic Energy Cases against Italy Before the CJEU and Investor-State Tribunals

In the early 2000s, several European states introduced incentive schemes to spur investments in renewable energy, in particular photovoltaic (PV) power plants. These schemes were later revised to ease financial burdens for the respective state, leading to litigation by several intra-EU investors before domestic courts as well as investor-state arbitral tribunals. In particular, investors argued before arbitral tribunals that the subsequent changes violated their legitimate expectations and, thus, the FET standard in the Energy Charter Treaty.[128] With regard to Italy, the legality of the respective changes to the domestic legal framework was also addressed by the CJEU, in which it took account of the CFEU as well as the general principle of EU law protecting legitimate expectations.[129] This allowed arbitral tribunals as well as the CJEU to weigh in on the legality of Italy's measures, making it one of few instances in which these bodies judged essentially the same factual dispute against the background of comparable legal standards.

The Italian incentive scheme consisted of framework legislation that foresaw that (1) incentives should not burden the state budget, (2) their amounts should decrease over time (in light of sinking investment and operating costs of PV plants), and (3) should be of sufficient duration to guaranteed investors a 'fair return' on their investments and operating costs. In addition, ministerial decrees (the *Conto Energia* decrees) set down the specific incentive tariffs—to be paid on top of the market price—and foresaw that those should *remain constant* for a period of 20 years, from the date of initiation of operations. The costs of those incentives were passed on to the consumer. In order to receive the incentives, operators had to apply to a state-owned company (*Gestore dei Servizi Energetici S.p.A.* or GSE), which (if all requirements were met) would first issue a confirmation letter on the entitlement to the incentives and then conclude a standard contract, which indicated the rate and the 20-year duration of the incentives.[130] Starting in 2012, the Italian state revised its incentive scheme through several measures. This in particular included the so-called *Spalma-incentivi* decree (Law Decree No 91/2014) in 2014, which cut the incentive tariffs from 1 January 2015 onwards, offering investors three different options.[131]

The CJEU has addressed the matter in its judgment of 15 April 2021, in Joined Cases C-798/18 and C-799/18 *Anie and Others and Athesia Energy and Others*, following the request on a preliminary ruling by an Italian court.[132] The request in

[128] For a comprehensive overview over these arbitral cases, see Biggs (2021), p. 99.

[129] ECJ, Joined Cases C-798/18 and C-799/18 *Federazione nazionale delle imprese elettrotecniche ed elettroniche (Anie) and Others and Athesia Energy and Others* [2021] ECLI:EU:C:2021:280.

[130] Dall'Agnola (2021), pp. 789, 792–794; Schmidl (2021); Balakrishnan (2019).

[131] Dall'Agnola (2021), pp. 789, 794–795.

[132] ECJ, Joined Cases C-798/18 and C-799/18 *Federazione nazionale delle imprese elettrotecniche ed elettroniche (Anie) and Others and Athesia Energy and Others* [2021] ECLI:EU:C:2021:280; see also Dall'Agnola (2021), p. 789.

particular posed the question whether the measures could be unlawful in light of Articles 16 (freedom to conduct a business) and 17 CFEU (the right to property), the general principles of legal certainty and legitimate expectations in EU law as well as Article 10(1) ECT (which the CJEU considered inapplicable). The CJEU ultimately found that

> Articles 16 and 17 of the Charter of Fundamental Rights of the European Union, read in the light of the principles of legal certainty and of the protection of legitimate expectations, must be interpreted as not precluding national legislation which provides for the reduction or delay of the payment of incentives for energy produced by solar photovoltaic installations which were previously granted by administrative decisions and confirmed by special agreements concluded between the operators of those installations and a public company, where that legislation concerns incentives for which provision has previously been made but which are not yet due.[133]

In the context of the right to property under Article 17 CFEU, the Court confirmed its existing case-law that 'possessions' protected by the provision are 'rights with an asset value creating an established legal position under the legal system, enabling the holder to exercise those rights autonomously and for his or her own benefit'.[134] The proceedings concerned incentives for the production of photovoltaic energy 'which have not yet been paid but which were granted in the context of an existing support scheme'.[135] While the Court considered that those incentives had an asset value in the given circumstances,[136] the question whether such rights constituted 'an established legal position'[137] had to be determined in light of the *principles of legitimate expectations* and *legal certainty*.[138]

The principle of legitimate expectations protected the 'reasonable expectations' of an economic operator created by national authorities. However, the CJEU laid down two limits to that protection: First, if the adoption of a measure could have been foreseen by a 'prudent and circumspect economic operator' and, second, states retain a certain 'discretionary power'.[139] With regard to the specific circumstances, the Court considered that framework legislation showed that the incentives were not guaranteed to all operators, given that it provided for a decreasing amount of tariffs, a limited duration for the incentives and 'the setting of a maximum limit on the cumulative electrical power eligible for that incentive'.[140] These circumstances would have indicated to a 'prudent and circumspect economic operator' that the

---

[133] ECJ, Joined Cases C-798/18 and C-799/18 *Federazione nazionale delle imprese elettrotecniche ed elettroniche (Anie) and Others and Athesia Energy and Others* [2021] ECLI:EU:C:2021:280, para. 72; for the specific reasoning in the context of Article 16 CFEU, see ibid., paras. 55–66.

[134] Ibid, para. 33.

[135] Ibid, para. 34.

[136] Ibid, paras. 35–37.

[137] Ibid, para. 38.

[138] Ibid, para. 41.

[139] Ibid, para. 42.

[140] Ibid, paras. 45–46.

incentive scheme might be altered in light of changing circumstances.[141] Moreover, the Court considered that the contractual agreements with GSE did not give rise to expectations that would find protection: it held that those concluded *before* 31 December 2012 only laid down 'practical conditions for the payment of incentives', while the incentives themselves were granted on basis of an earlier administrative decision. In addition, the contractual agreements concluded *after* 31 December 2012 enshrined the right of GSE to change their terms unilaterally.[142] In light of these circumstances, the Court held that changes to the legislation were *foreseeable* for 'a prudent and circumspect economic operator', that the right of PV plant operators to receive incentives for the entire duration of their agreements with GSE was not an 'established legal position' and that it therefore was not a protected 'possession' under Article 17 CFEU.[143]

The measures by Italy were also subject to several arbitrations brought by intra-EU investors under the Energy Charter Treaty. While the CJEU extended its *Achmea*-reasoning—*i.e.* that investor-state arbitration in an intra-EU context violated EU law—also to the ECT in its 2021 judgment in *Komstroy*,[144] investment arbitral tribunals themselves rejected that it had any bearing on their competence to decide on case brought by intra-EU investors.

The ECT more generally has been used by a number of investors to challenge comparable changes in incentive regimes for renewables by other countries (in particular Spain and the Czech Republic), and arbitral tribunals have notably adopted different approaches to the question of legitimate expectations.[145] In cases against Italy, tribunals in part found that the *Spalma-incentivi* decree led to a violation of legitimate expectations protected by FET (*Greentech Energy v Italy*,[146] *CEF v Italy*[147] and *ESPF and Others v Italy*[148]), while others rejected the claim (*Belenergia v Italy*,[149] *Sun Reserve v Italy*[150] and *Silver Ridge v Italy*[151]).[152]

---

[141] Ibid, para. 47; referring to its findings in ECJ, Joined Cases C-180/18, C-286/18 and C-287/18 *Agrenergy and Fusignano Due* [2019] ECLI:EU:C:2019:605, para. 44.

[142] Ibid, paras. 49–51.

[143] Ibid, paras. 53–54; the CJEU subsequently confirmed its findings in Case C-306/19 *Milis Energy* [2022] ECLI:EU:C:2022:164.

[144] ECJ, Case C-741/19 *République de Moldavie* [2021] ECLI:EU:C:2021:655.

[145] See Schmidl (2021).

[146] *Greentech Energy Systems A/S, et al v. Italian Republic*, SCC Case No. V 2015/095, Final Award, 23 December 2018.

[147] *CEF Energia BV v. Italian Republic*, SCC Case No. 158/2015, Award, 16 January 2019.

[148] *ESPF Beteiligungs GmbH, ESPF Nr. 2 Austria Beteiligungs GmbH, and InfraClass Energie 5 GmbH & Co. KG v. Italian Republic*, ICSID Case No. ARB/16/5, Award, 14 September 2020.

[149] *Belenergia S.A. v. Italian Republic*, ICSID Case No. ARB/15/40, Award, 28 August 2019.

[150] *Sun Reserve Luxco Holdings SRL v. Italy*, SCC Case No. 132/2016, Award, 25 March 2020.

[151] *Silver Ridge Power BV v. Italian Republic*, ICSID Case No. ARB/15/37, Award, 26 February 2021.

[152] In addition, at least two arbitrations are still pending: *Encavis AG, Fano Solar 1 S.r.l., DE Stern 10 S.r.l. and others v Italian Republic*, ICSID Case No. ARB/20/39; *CIC Renewable Energies Italy*

These diverging outcomes—apart from the specific circumstances of each case—in particular follow from differences in how tribunals approach the emergence of legitimate expectations and the relevance of the state's right to regulate. This may be seen in the awards in *Greentech* (decided by a majority) and *Sun Reserve*.

The first question related to whether the conduct of Italy created legitimate expectation and, if so, what these specifically encompassed. The claimants in both cases based their arguments on the framework legislation, the *Conto Energia* decrees (implementing the framework legislation), certain representation by public officials, as well as the letters and contractual agreements that the GSE issued to and concluded with individual operators.[153] The majority in the *Greentech* tribunal (somewhat summarily) held that these constituted 'repeated and precise assurances to specific investors', which 'amounted to guarantees that the tariffs would remain fixed for two decades'.[154]

In contrast, the *Sun Reserve* was concerned with investments in different PV power plants, most of which had not received a confirmation letter by (or concluded a contract with) GSE at the time of investment. The tribunal rejected the argument that the abstract legislation by itself, together with public representations, could create *legitimate* expectations, as the payment of incentive tariffs was not automatic, but dependent on the application to the GSE.[155] It was only the state's conduct with regard to the Fiumicino power plant (which had already obtained a confirmation letter by GSE at the time of investment in June 2011) that had created legitimate expectations on part of the investor.[156] However, contrary to *Greentech*, and in line with two other awards,[157] the *Sun Reserve* tribunal considered that the GSE confirmation letter did not constitute a specific commitment to maintain the specific feed-in tariffs.[158] This followed from the fact that instruments issued by GSE did not constitute 'true' private law contracts, but rather 'accessory contracts' dependent on an administrative concession.[159] Thus, they 'cannot create any commitments or expectations above and beyond the administrative or public acts that they are

GmbH, Enernovum Asset 1 GmbH & Co. KG, Enernovum GmbH & Co. KG and others v Italian Republic, ICSID Case No. ARB/16/39.

[153] See *Greentech Energy Systems A/S, et al v. Italian Republic*, SCC Case No. V 2015/095, Final Award, 23 December 2018, para. 408; *Sun Reserve Luxco Holdings SRL v. Italy*, SCC Case No. 132/2016, Award, 25 March 2020, para. 770.

[154] *Greentech Energy Systems A/S, et al v. Italian Republic*, SCC Case No. V 2015/095, Final Award, 23 December 2018, para. 450, see also paras. 447–449, 453.

[155] *Sun Reserve Luxco Holdings SRL v. Italy*, SCC Case No. 132/2016, Award, 25 March 2020, paras. 838–839.

[156] Ibid, para. 840.

[157] *CEF Energia BV v. Italian Republic*, SCC Case No. 158/2015, Award, 16 January 2019, paras. 254–255; *Belenergia S.A. v. Italian Republic*, ICSID Case No. ARB/15/40, Award, 28 August 2019, paras. 579–580.

[158] *Sun Reserve Luxco Holdings SRL v. Italy*, SCC Case No. 132/2016, Award, 25 March 2020, paras. 827–828.

[159] Ibid, paras. 820–822.

sourced in'.[160] Thus, the investor only had legitimate expectations to receive 'fair remuneration' in accordance with the framework legislation.

The second question concerned the relevance of host states' right to regulate in light of legitimate expectations. The majority in *Greentech* considered that 'Italy had effectively waived its right to reduce the value of the tariffs' due to the 'repeated and precise assurances' it had given.[161] While states would 'retain the sovereign prerogative to amend their laws', the violation of 'express assurances that no amendment would occur' necessitated the fair compensation of the investor.[162] The tribunal further considered that, even if one would engage in a balancing exercise, there were no 'reasonable and valid policy justification for the changes'.[163] In contrast, the *Sun Reserve* tribunal explicitly held that determining a violation of FET *always* required balancing the investor's expectations with the right to regulate,[164] even if the latter made specific commitments to the investor.[165] The tribunal then found that the *Spalma-incentivi* decree did not interfere with or frustrate the investor's legitimate expectations of 'fair remuneration', in light of its specific (economic) impact, the rise in costs for end consumers, the reduction in operating costs for PV plants and the benefits granted by other European states.[166]

When comparing the CJEU's reasoning with the arbitral case law, a number of points can be made. In terms of substance, the CJEU's approach is certainly closer to the more state-friendly tribunals—as represented here by *Sun Reserve*. This in particular follows from the fact that legitimate expectations never enjoy absolute protection and the corresponding relevance of public interests. However, *Sun Reserve* also shows the further (temporal) limitations of protecting legitimate expectations. In light of the emphasis on the GSE confirmation letter, the particular timing of investments became crucial. That consideration does not play a role under legitimate expectations as a general principle of EU law.

6 Conclusion

When assessing the protection of intra-EU investors under EU law, three caveats should be made: *First*, much of the analysis depends on the specific comparator on the side of international investment law. While the discussions above focused on the

---

[160] Ibid, para. 823.

[161] *Greentech Energy Systems A/S, et al v. Italian Republic*, SCC Case No. V 2015/095, Final Award, 23 December 2018, para. 450.

[162] Ibid, para. 452.

[163] Ibid, para. 454.

[164] *Sun Reserve Luxco Holdings SRL v. Italy*, SCC Case No. 132/2016, Award, 25 March 2020, paras. 685–686.

[165] Ibid, para. 703.

[166] Ibid, paras. 849–855.

'traditional' standards of treatment, treaty practice partly widely diverges, and arbitral tribunals might reach diametrically opposed results even when concerned similarly worded treaty provisions. With regard to the present context, Catherine Titi has considered that BITs of EU member states 'contain some of the last vestiges of international economic law's *laissez-faire* liberalism'.[167] In contrast, investment chapters in FTAs negotiated by the EU itself are noticeably more state-friendly and in particular emphasize the right to regulate of host states.[168] Thus, in certain constellations, the substantive protections of intra-EU investors under EU law might fall short of those under now-defunct intra-EU BITs, but nevertheless resemble more recently concluded IIAs.

Second, the jurisprudence of the CJEU based on the CFEU on matters directly relevant for intra-EU investors is still somewhat limited. In particular fundamental rights are malleable to specific situations and much will depend on whether the CJEU is willing to develop its own case law in an investor-friendly direction or not. *Third*, to the extent that such jurisprudence exists, and in light of the nature of the preliminary ruling procedure, the factual determinations are often left to domestic courts. That particularly complicates a detailed comparison in fact-intensive disputes (which investment cases often are).

That being said, a few general observations can be made. Firstly, when viewed through the lens of investment protection standards, EU law presents a complex and fragmented picture. IIAs typically enshrine a few—more or less abstractly formulated—substantive standards. These standards, and in particular FET and FPS, generally do not have direct counterparts in EU primary law. Moreover, the fundamental freedoms and the CFEU are complemented by a significant body of specific rules within EU secondary law that might likewise become relevant. Thus, when the CJEU deals with investors, it does so against the background of a complex legal system with inter-dependent rules, which necessarily has implications for its legal reasoning.

Secondly, in the context of EU law it is unquestionable that interferences with fundamental rights and freedoms may (in principle) be justified in light of overriding public interests.[169] For instance, the CJEU consistently maintains that the right to property 'must be considered in relation to its function in society'.[170] While investment tribunals may also take account of such public interests in their determinations—and more recent IIAs often put greater emphasis thereon—the specific extent to which that will happen very much depends on the particular arbitrators. Thirdly, when it comes to the available redress, investment law is typically limited to compensation for the specific claimant bringing a case. In contrast, insofar as the violation of EU fundamental rights and freedoms stems

[167] Titi (2015), pp. 639, 647; which also applies to intra-EU BITs, see Berger (2021), p. 61.

[168] Ibid.

[169] Berger (2021), p. 61.

[170] ECJ, Case C-579/19 *Food Standards Agency* [2021] ECLI:EU:C:2021:665, para. 96.

from secondary EU law or domestic legislative acts, it may not only lead to compensation, but more broadly entail the inapplicability of those acts.

To the extent that EU law is considered to provide fewer protections than international investment law, questions arise whether that outcome is *undesirable* for policy reasons and, if so, whether the EU should take legislative action to enact rules specifically applicable to intra-EU investors. While only tentative answers will be provided to the first question at this moment, it is argued that the second question should be answered in the negative.

With regard to the first question, there are typically two (policy) narratives advanced to serve as underlying rationales of investment protection: the promotion of economic development and (more recently) of the rule of law in the host state. The pursuit of these two objectives is undoubtedly also relevant when it comes to the regulation of economic activities within the Union, and the EU Commission has highlighted them when it comes to intra-EU investment protection.[171] However, *to what extent* investment protection actually promotes these objectives and, in turn, whether the dismantling of intra-EU investment protection will lead to undesirable policy outcomes is much more difficult to assess. On a general level, the data on the (positive) economic impact of IIAs is inconclusive at best—with a recent meta-analysis finding 'robust evidence that [the] effect of international investment agreements [on foreign direct investment] is so small as to be considered zero'.[172] These difficulties in measuring a positive impact of IIAs on economic development are core to why narratives in support of investment protection have more recently shifted to rule of law-concerns.

At any rate, the limitation *ratione personae* of investment protection in IIAs arguably does not stem from policy preferences, but rather from *structural* factors in treaty negotiations: *i.e.* the result of states seeking to ensure protection for their investors on a bilateral level, with limited (if any) political incentives to go beyond that. These structural considerations simply do not apply for the Union, which is in a fundamentally different position to 'holistically' regulate intra-EU (economic) relationships in order to pursue these two rationales. Moreover, to the extent that the current legal framework within the Union is considered to fall short of a desired standard, there is no apparent *policy* reason to limit legislative responses to *intra*-EU investors. This is particularly the case in the context of the rule of law: the increasing rule of law-concerns in certain member states of the EU[173] might well make legislative action desirable. However, these concerns apply with similar force to any other (economic) actor within the EU as well, making it unclear why they should be met with legislation only applying to a certain group—i.e. *intra*-EU investors.

---

[171] The 'Inception Impact Assessment' by the European Commission focusses on matters of economic development, although it also projects benefits for the rule of law, see European Commission (2020b), pp. 4–5.

[172] However, the paper also acknowledges the limitations of underlying data, see Brada et al. (2021), p. 34.

[173] See e.g., ECJ, Case C-156/21 Hungary v Parliament and Council [2022] ECLI:EU:C:2022:97.

As a result, this paper argues that the promotion of economic development as well as rule of law objectives should be pursued through more 'holistic' approaches to legislative action, encompassing (economic) actors within the Union more generally. This might also pre-empt concerns being raised by those civil society actors with a notably skeptical position towards investment protection.

References

Andersen TT, Hindelang S (2016) The day after: alternatives to intra-EU BITs. J World Invest Trade 17:984

Balakrishnan S (2019) Italy found liable for change in renewable energy policy in intra-EU arbitration. Investment Treaty News, 23 April 2019. www.iisd.org/itn/en/2019/04/23/italy-found-liable-for-change-in-renewable-energy-policy-in-intra-eu-arbitration-shyam-balakrishnan/

Berger J (2021) International investment protection within Europe: The EU's assertion of control. Routledge

Biggs J (2021) The scope of investors' legitimate expectations under the FET in the European renewable energy cases. ICSID Rev 36(1):99

Brada JC, Drabek Z, Iwasaki I (2021) Does investor protection increase foreign direct investment? A meta-analysis. J Econ Surv 35(1):34–70

Dall'Agnola G (2021) Italy's reduction of existing renewable energy incentives: the ruling of the CJEU on the compatibility of the *Spalma-incentivi* decree with EU law. Diritto Del Commerico Internazionale XXXV(3):789, 792–789, 794

Dolzer R, Kriebaum U, Schreuer C (2022) Principles of international investment law. CUP

Enzinger M (2022) Art 49 AEUV. In: Jaeger T, Stöger K (eds) EUV/AEUV unter Berücksichtigung der österreichischen Judikatur und Literatur. Manz

European Commission (2018) Communication from the Commission to the European Parliament and the Council: protection of intra-EU investment, COM(2018) 547 final

European Commission (2020a) Cross-border investment within the EU – clarifying and supplementing EU rules. https://ec.europa.eu/info/law/better-regulation/have-your-say/initiatives/12403-Cross-border-investment-within-the-EU-clarifying-and-supplementing-EU-rules_en

European Commission (2020b) Inception impact assessment (26 May 2020), Ares(2022)2716046

European Court of Human Rights (2022) Guide on Article 1 of Protocol No. 1 to the European Convention on Human Rights: Protection of Property, 31 August 2022

Holoubek M, Oswald M (2019) Art 51 GRC. Anwendungsbereich. In: Holoubek M, Lienbacher G (eds) GRC Kommentar: Charta der Grundrechte der Europäischen Union: Kommentar. Manz

Khan DE, Eisenhut D (2018) Artikel 49 AEUV. In: Vedder C, Heintschel von Heinegg W (eds) Europäisches Unionsrecht. Nomos, p 442

Kriebaum U (2009) Is the European Court of Human Rights an alternative to investor-state arbitration? In: Dupuy PM, Petersmann EU, Francioni F (eds) Human rights in international investment law and arbitration. OUP

Kriebaum U (2022) The European Court of Human Rights' case law on international investment issues. In: Ruiz Fabri H, Stoppioni E (eds) International investment law: an analysis of the major decisions. Hart

Kriebaum U, Schreuer C (2007) The concept of property in human rights law and international investment law. In: Breitenmoser S et al (eds) Human rights, democracy and the rule of law: Liber Amicorum Luzius Wildhaber. Nomos

Lock T (2019a) Art 51 CFEU. In: Kellerbauer M, Klamert M, Tomkin J (eds) The EU treaties and the charter of fundamental rights: a commentary. OUP

Lock T (2019b) Article 17 CFR. In: Kellerbauer M, Klamert M, Tomkin J (eds) The EU treaties and the charter of fundamental rights: a commentary. OUP

Moskvan D (2022) Protection of foreign investments in an intra-EU context: not one BIT? Edward Elgar

Perkams M (2010) The concept of indirect expropriation in comparative public law – searching for light in the dark. In: Schill SW (ed) International investment law and comparative public law. OUP, p 107

Reinisch A, Schreuer C (2020) International protection of investments: the substantive standards. CUP

Reuter A (2021) Systematically flogging the wrong: EU corporate fines violate the fundamental rights of shareholders – the European Commission as revenant of the Persian Great King Xerxes. Eur Bus Law Rev 32(4):681

Sattorova M (2016) Investor rights under EU law and international investment law. J World Invest Trade 17:895

Schmidl M (2021) The renewable energy saga from Charanne v. Spain to the PV Investors v. Spain: trying to see the wood for the trees. Kluwer Arbitration Blog, 1 February 2021. http://arbitrationblog.kluwerarbitration.com/2021/02/01/the-renewable-energy-saga-from-charanne-v-spain-to-the-pv-investors-v-spain-trying-to-see-the-wood-for-the-trees/

Schneider C (2020) Art 63 AEUV. In: Jaeger T, Stöger K (eds) EUV/AEUV unter Berücksichtigung der österreichischen Judikatur und Literatur. Manz

Steiblytė A, Tomkin J (2019) Article 63 TFEU. In: Kellerbauer M, Klamert M, Tomkin J (eds) The EU treaties and the charter of fundamental rights: a commentary. OUP

Titi C (2015) International investment law and the European Union: towards a new generation of international investment agreements. EJIL 26(3):639

Tomkin J (2019) Article 49 TFEU. In: Kellerbauer M, Klamert M, Tomkin J (eds) The EU treaties and the charter of fundamental rights: a commentary. OUP

UNCITRAL (2019) Possible reform of investor-state dispute settlement (ISDS): shareholder claims and reflective loss. Note by the Secretariat (9 August 2019), UN Doc A/CN.9/WG.III/WP.170

Vanhonnaeker L (2020) Shareholders' claims for reflective loss in international investment law. CUP

Ward A (2021) Article 51. In: Peers S et al (eds) The EU charter of fundamental rights: a commentary. Hart

Wollenschläger F (2021) Article 17(1). In: Peers S et al (eds) The EU charter of fundamental rights: a commentary. Hart

Ziniel T (2019) Art 17 GRC. Eigentumsrecht. In: Holoubek M, Lienbacher G (eds) GRC Kommentar: Charta der Grundrechte der Europäischen Union: Kommentar. Manz

Enforcement (Deficits) of Substantive Investment Standards under EU Law

Christoph Herrmann and Tim Ellemann

Contents

Abstract The protection of foreign investment under EU law is systemically different from that under international investment law, both in substance and in enforcement. With the CJEU having closed the door to investor-state arbitration in intra-EU disputes, fundamental freedoms, the EU Charter of Fundamental Rights and their enforcement by Member State courts are gaining importance. In theory, EU law is capable of providing adequate investment protection. However, substantive and procedural prerequisites under EU and national law render protection difficult to obtain. The stringent requirements for state liability as established in *Francovich* create greater barriers for claiming monetary compensation before national courts compared to international tribunals. Even if an investor successfully pursues their case before a national court—whose independence from political interference is perceived unevenly across Europe—there is no system for the recognition of domestic judgments in other Member States comparable to the enforcement of international awards. As a result, investors will only be satisfactorily protected if all national

C. Herrmann
University of Passau, Passau, Germany
e-mail: christoph.herrmann@uni-passau.de

T. Ellemann (✉)
European University Institute, Florence, Italy
e-mail: tim.ellemann@eui.eu

M. Bungenberg, A. Reinisch (eds.), *New Frontiers for EU Investment Policy*, Special Issue, https://doi.org/10.1007/978-3-031-41977-5_7

courts apply the *Francovich* conditions adequately and consistently, if they interpret the legal margins left for domestic laws on procedure and compensation strictly and if other Member States were to accept the enforcement of the judgments. Current practice still shows deficits to this ideal.

1 Introduction

Intra-EU Investor-State Dispute Settlement (ISDS) cases account for one fifth of all known treaty-based arbitration cases worldwide.[1] They are initiated by investors from one EU Member State against another EU Member State (Intra-EU). Investors claim the violation of a substantive standard of protection arising from an international law treaty between their home country and the other EU Member State, for instance bilateral or multilateral investment treaties (BITs/MITs), in particular the Energy Charter Treaty (ECT). As of 2018, there exist around 200 intra-EU BITs.[2]

However, the system by which intra-EU ISDS cases are being arbitrated is likely coming to an end once and for all.[3] With its 2018 judgment in the *Achmea* case,[4] the Court of Justice of the European Union (CJEU) kicked off their demise. The Court decided that the ISDS clause contained in an intra-EU BIT was incompatible with EU law since the clause allowed the arbitral tribunal to apply EU law directly without being able to refer the case to the CJEU.[5] In the wake of the judgment, 23 EU Member States agreed to terminate (all)[6] bilateral investment treaties between them.[7] But the CJEU was not finished yet. *Achmea* was followed up by its 2021 judgment in *PL Holdings*[8] where it found an *ad hoc* arbitration agreement—instead of a BIT arbitration clause—between Poland and an investor to be incompatible with EU law as well.[9] Multilateral treaty arbitration did not fare much better. In

[1] UNCTAD (2018).

[2] Ankersmit (2018); Wiedmann (2018), p. 225.

[3] Fermeglia and Mistura (2020).

[4] Case C-284/16 *Achmea* (6 March 2018) ECLI:EU:C:2018:158.

[5] Case C-284/16 *Achmea* (6 March 2018) ECLI:EU:C:2018:158, paras 58–59; see in detail Glinski (2018), p. 47.

[6] See only Scheu (2020).

[7] Agreement for the termination of Bilateral Investment Treaties between the Member States of the European Union, OJ L 169, 29.5.2020, p. 1–41. They European Commission already started initiating infringement proceedings against several EU Member States in 2015 regarding their opposition to terminate intra-EU BITs, European Commission (2015).

[8] Case C-109/20 *PL Holdings* (26 October 2021) ECLI:EU:C:2021:875.

[9] Case C-109/20 *PL Holdings* (26 October 2021) ECLI:EU:C:2021:875, para 54; see also Zasheva and Lentner (2021).

Komstroy,[10] the CJEU extended its *Achmea* ruling to the ECT[11] and found that its arbitration clause "must be interpreted as not being applicable to disputes between a Member State and an investor of another Member State".[12] It is noteworthy, however, that arbitral tribunals have almost unanimously rejected the "intra-EU objection"[13] in cases heard under international investment law.[14] So far, the only notable exceptions affirming the intra-EU objection are the arbitral decision in *Green Power v. Spain*[15] and the US District Court ruling in *AES Solar Energy et al. v. Spain.*[16] Nevertheless, Spain has already refused to fulfil its payment obligation arising out of an ISDS award.[17]

With the intra-EU ISDS system having been practically dismantled from an EU perspective and no alternative system having been set up in the EU or the Member States,[18] the legal protection of investments within the EU rests solely upon the national law of the Member States and that of the EU. According to the European Commission, this result is not by fault but by design. It rejects the idea of a new tailor-made mechanism for intra-EU ISDS and instead proposes an EU-wide mechanism to find "amicable solutions"[19] or prevent investment disputes from arising in the first place. Stakeholders, on the other hand, largely consider this form of protection to be insufficient.[20] They argue that binding dispute settlement

---

[10] Case C-741/19 *République de Moldavie v Komstroy* (2 September 2021) ECLI:EU:C:2021:655.

[11] While the EU still negotiated the "modernisation" of the ECT in June of 2022, by November of the same year the European Parliament issued a joint motion for a resolution on "coordinated [. . .] withdrawal" from the ECT (JOINT MOTION FOR A RESOLUTION on the outcome of the modernisation of the Energy Charter Treaty, 23.11.2022—(2022/2934(RSP)), following a number of Member States' governments announcing their intention to withdraw from the ECT—largely due to climate concerns; see Lavranos et al. (2023), p. 38; Liebscher (2022).

[12] Case C-741/19 *République de Moldavie v Komstroy* (2 September 2021) ECLI:EU:C:2021:655, para 66; see also van der Beck (2022), p. 260.

[13] E.g. Reinisch and Tropper (2021).

[14] *Vattenfall AB and others v. Federal Republic of Germany*, ICSID Case No ARB/12/12, Decision on the Achmea Issue (31 August 2018) stands out as being the most lengthy discussion of the *Achmea* judgment by arbitral tribunals, but in no case the only one; see also Lavranos et al. (2023), p. 40; Sullivan and Ingle (2021), p. 333.

[15] *Green Power K/S and Obton A/S v. Spain*, SCC Case No V 2016/135, Award (16 June 2022) paras 172, 422; discussed by Levy (2022).

[16] United States District Court of Columbia, AES SOLAR ENERGY COÖPERATIEF U.A. and AMPERE EQUITY FUND B.V. v. Kingdom of Spain, Civil Action No 1:21-cv-3249-RJL https://jusmundi.com/en/document/pdf/other/en-aes-solar-and-others-pv-investors-v-the-kingdom-of-spain-the-kingdom-of-spains-opposition-to-petitioners-motion-for-substitution-monday-6th-march-2023.

[17] Newman (2023).

[18] European Commission (2017).

[19] ibid.

[20] E.g. Association of German Chambers of Industry and Commerce (DIHK e.V.) (2017).

mechanisms prevail over mediation or negotiation proceedings and stress that intra-EU BITs remain important for businesses in Europe.[21]

This contribution sets out to show the systemic differences between EU law and international investment law (Sect. 2). By analysing the principles of state liability within the national and EU legal framework, it outlines the pitfalls of claiming damages for "investment claims" without traditional investment law arbitration (Sect. 3). It then highlights the difficulties of enforcing such claims under national law (Sect. 4). It concludes that the EU legal framework alone—including the Member States' laws—does not satisfactorily protect investors' interests in practice and needs to be complemented by an alternative system of protection (Sect. 5).

2 Systemic Differences Between EU Law and Investment Law

In modern foreign investment law, the lines between international and domestic law have always been blurry.[22] Domestic laws govern the rules on the nationality of an investor, labour standards, property and taxation, to name but a few.[23] On the other hand, international law has shaped domestic investment frameworks, beginning with customary rules on the law of aliens up until the "treatification"[24] of international investment law since the 1960s.

In the context of the European Union, distinguishing international from domestic law is even more difficult. To some extent, EU law is both: the treaties establishing the European Union and their functioning are public international law treaties which, *inter alia*, include investment protection provisions.[25] At the same time, the Member States conferred parts of their national sovereignty to the Union and, with direct effect of its law in the Member States' national legal systems, EU law is also inextricably part of domestic law. To further complicate things, the CJEU has famously concluded in *Van Gen den Loos* that the Community (today: Union) constitutes a "new legal order of international law".[26]

However, for the purposes of this contribution, the system of international investment law as traditionally understood (Sec. 2.1) shall be contrasted with the

[21] ibid.

[22] Dolzer et al. (2022), p. 15.

[23] ibid.; Börnsen (2016), p. 275.

[24] Salacuse (2010), p. 3.

[25] Georgaki (2023), p. 10–12; see also Gött (2023), p. 37.

[26] Case C-26/62 *Van Gend en Loos v Administratie der Belastingen* (5 February 1963) ECLI:EU:C:1963:1, p 12.

separate system of EU law governing investment protection (Sec. 2.2), notwithstanding the fact that the EU itself is bound by international investment treaties.[27]

2.1 International Investment Law

Starting with agreements on friendship, commerce and navigation in the late eighteenth century,[28] international treaties on investment protection have become the fundamental source of international investment law today.[29] The first modern BIT was signed between Germany and Pakistan in 1959.[30] In many ways, it already resembled later BITs, having included a definition of investments, treaty-based substantive protection standards and a dispute resolution clause. However, it still lacked one of the key characteristics of today's investment agreements: ISDS by way of arbitration.[31]

Investor-state arbitration has key features which fundamentally distinguish it from domestic court proceedings. First, it is inherently international in nature.[32] After having been agreed upon in an international treaty between two or more states, individual investors are given the right to sue that sovereign state under international law for its exercise of public authority.[33] Second, while investment arbitration tribunals can, in principle, grant requests for declaratory relief or even restitution in kind,[34] the primary form of remedy is the award of financial compensation.[35] Third, awards issued as a result of investment arbitration are typically easy to enforce globally. In particular, the pecuniary obligations of awards issued under the ICSID

---

[27] Investment treaties of the EU include, among others, the Agreement between the European Union and Japan for an Economic Partnership, OJ L 330, 27.12.2018, p. 3–899 or the Trade and Cooperation Agreement between the European Union and the European Atomic Energy Community, of the one part, and the United Kingdom of Great Britain and Northern Ireland, of the other part, OJ L 149, 30.4.2021, p. 10–2539.

[28] Dolzer et al. (2022), p. 8.

[29] Salacuse (2010) p. 4; Wälde (2007), p. 44.

[30] Treaty between the Federal Republic of Germany and Pakistan for the Promotion and Protection of Investments, Federal Law Gazette 6 July 1961-II, 793, available at https://investmentpolicy.unctad.org/international-investment-agreements/treaty-files/1387/download.

[31] The first BIT to include an ISDS clause was the 1969 BIT between Chad and Italy, available at https://investmentpolicy.unctad.org/international-investment-agreements/treaty-files/659/download; Dolzer et al. (2022), p. 9.

[32] van Harten (2010), p. 630.

[33] E.g. Salacuse (2010), p. 387; van Harten and Loughlin (2006), p. 121, 127–128.

[34] E.g. *Ioan Micula, Viorel Micula, S.C. European Food S.A, S.C. Starmill S.R.L. and S.C. Multipack S.R.L. v. Romania [I]*, ICSID Case No ARB/05/20, Decision on Jurisdiction and Admissibility (24 September 2008) paras 166–168; Schreuer (n.d.), para 112.

[35] van Harten and Loughlin (2006), p. 131; Dolzer et al. (2022), p. 425–428; Schreuer (n.d.), para 112.

Convention[36] can be enforced in any of its 158 contracting states like final judgments of their respective courts, Art. 54(1) ICSID Convention.[37] For most other awards, the 1958 New York Convention[38] offers the relevant framework for the recognition and enforcement, subject to certain requirements (Art. III–IV) and a limited list of grounds for refusal (Art. V).[39] While state immunity under public international law can still bar the execution of awards (e.g. explicitly Art. 55 ICSID Convention),[40] investment arbitration awards are exceptionally well enforceable.[41]

In substance, treaty-based investment protection is largely based on broad open-ended protection standards.[42] These include prohibitions of discriminatory treatment, such as most favoured nation treatment (MFN) and national treatment (NT), guarantees of full protection and security (FPS), fair and equitable treatment (FET), free transfer of funds and compensation for expropriation. Such compensation must typically be paid out in full, promptly, adequately and effectively. Especially the first generation BITs do not—at least expressly[43]—allow much room for public interest considerations when making policy decisions.[44] By requiring an investment to be "made in accordance with the applicable law of the host Contracting Party at the time the investment is made",[45] most treaty-based protection standards only apply to the post-establishment phase of an investment.[46] Pre-establishment protection is rarely covered by the agreements,[47] with the notable exceptions, however, of some

[36] Convention for the Settlement of Settlement of Investment Disputes between States and Nationals of other States (adopted 18 March 1965, entered into force 14 October 1966) 575 UNTS 159.

[37] Schreuer (2010), para 49; Kröll (2015), p. 1496 et seq.

[38] Convention on the Recognition and Enforcement of Foreign Arbitral Awards (adopted 10 June 1958, entered into force 7 June 1959) 330 UNTS 3, with 172 state parties to the New York Convention as of 20 March 2023.

[39] In more detail Stanič (2020), p. 147–152.

[40] Bjorklund (2009), pp. 302, 306.

[41] van Harten and Loughlin (2006), pp. 134–135.

[42] Sattorova (2016), p. 917.

[43] Kulick (2013), p. 435.

[44] Kriebaum (2007), p. 734; Sattorova (2016), p. 899.

[45] Exemplary Article on the scope of application from the 2019 Dutch Model BIT typical for many other BITs, available https://investmentpolicy.unctad.org/international-investment-agreements/treaty-files/5832/download.

[46] Schreuer (n.d.), para 68.

[47] See Voon and Merriman (2022), p. 75, who also analyse the arbitration case of *Global Telecom Holding S.A.E. v. Canada*, ICSID Case No ARB/16/16, Award (27 March 2020) which appears to be an outlier from this general rule when it reviewed a decision by Canada under its national security screening under the FET clause of the applicable BIT.

non-discrimination clauses[48] or Art. 8.4–8.5 CETA.[49] For an international investment law claim to be successful, any such breach of a substantive standard stemming from international law which is attributable to the state (again under international law)[50] is sufficient. While some features of treaty-based investor-state arbitration draw criticism from various angles, it is largely effective.

2.2 *EU Investment Law*

Whereas the primary goal of BITs is generally the reciprocal protection of investments, the EU legal framework is much broader, factoring in both economic and non-economic interests.[51] Emerging out of the European Economic Community (EEC) from 1958, one pillar of today's EU law is still the promotion of economic activity in the internal (then: common) market, comprising of a customs union and an area "without internal frontiers" for goods, persons, services and capital (Art. 26(2) TFEU).[52]

Within the legal framework of the EU internal market, the fundamental freedoms (Titles II–IV of the TFEU) and the Charter of Fundamental Rights of the EU (CFR) are the primary sources of standards protecting investments.[53] Today, the CJEU interprets both Art. 49 TFEU on the freedom of establishment and Art. 63 TFEU on freedom of the movement of capital and funds not only as non-discrimination standards but also as comprehensive prohibitions of restrictions.[54] Within their respective scope of application,[55] they are offering a broad range of protection. However, this range may not always align with the scope of protection in BITs.[56] As *Basener* points out for instance, the guaranteed transfer of funds found in many BITs may pose a challenge to the possible implementing restrictions on the free movement

---

[48] For instance, Art. 4.2 of the 2012 US Model BIT: "Each Party shall accord to covered investments treatment no less favorable [. . .] with respect to the *establishment, acquisition, expansion*, management, conduct, operation, and sale or other disposition of investments.", emphasis added, available https://ustr.gov/sites/default/files/BIT%20text%20for%20ACIEP%20Meeting.pdf.

[49] Comprehensive Economic and Trade Agreement (CETA) between Canada, of the one part, and the European Union and its Member States, of the other part, OJ L 11, 14.1.2017, p 23–1079; however, Art. 8.4 and 8.5 CETA fall outside CETA's ISDS mechanism, see Art. 8.18 CETA and de Mestral and Vanhonnaeker (2022), Art. 8.4, p. 173.

[50] In lack of more special provisions, the requirements for attributability are laid out in Art. 4–11 of the Articles on the Responsibility of States for Internationally Wrongful Acts (General Assembly, Resolution 56/83, 28 January 2002) which reflect, in large parts, customary international law.

[51] Andersen and Hindelang (2016), p. 998.

[52] Art. 26 et seq. TFEU; Basener (2017), pp. 58–63.

[53] ibid. 110; Gonin and O'Reilly (2020), pp. 64 et seq.

[54] See e.g. Caro de Sousa (2015), pp. 87 et seq.

[55] See Basener (2017), pp. 111 et seq.

[56] Berger (2023), p. 63.

of capital under Art. 64–66 and 75 TFEU.[57] This might lead the protection under EU law being lower than under BITs.[58] Where BITs seldomly include explicit public policy exceptions, the CJEU developed a broad range of public policy factors which might justify the infringement of fundamental freedoms since its judgment in *Cassis de Dijon*.[59,60]

In contrast to the typical international investment law standards, the fundamental freedoms are interpreted by the CJEU explicitly to aim at reducing market-access restrictions.[61] Hence, they are in essence also protection standards for the pre-establishment phase of investments. Additionally, general principles of EU law and fundamental rights include conditions on due process (Art. 47 CFR) and good administration (Art. 41 CFR), protect against unjustified infringements upon the freedom to choose an occupation and the right to engage in work (Art. 15 CFR) as well as the freedom to conduct business (Art. 16 CFR).[62] Art. 17(1) CFR protects the right to property, prescribing that "fair compensation [must be] paid in good time" if someone is deprived of his or her possessions in the public interest. However, while this provision resembles expropriation clauses in BITs to a certain extent, the CJEU has traditionally interpreted property protection in the EU more narrowly, to be "viewed in relation to their social function [. . .] provided that any restrictions in fact correspond to objectives of general interest pursued by the European Community and do not constitute in relation to the aim pursued a disproportionate and intolerable interference".[63]

Hence, while EU substantive standards will most likely not leave an "enormous gap"[64] in investment protection, it certainly leaves more room for public interest considerations than under many (particularly first generation) BITs.[65] This appears to be acknowledged by the European Commission:

---

[57] Basener (2017), p. 169.

[58] Andersen and Hindelang (2016), p. 996.

[59] Case 120/78 *Rewe v Bundesmonopolverwaltung für Branntwein* (20 February 1979) ECLI:EU:C:1979:42, paras 8, 14.

[60] Berger (2023), p. 63.

[61] E.g. Case C-112/05 *Commission v Germany* (23 October 2007) ECLI:EU:C:2007:623, para 19: "national measures must be regarded as 'restrictions' within the meaning of Article 56(1) EC [today Art. 63(1) TFEU] if they are liable to *prevent or limit the acquisition* of shares in the undertakings concerned or to *deter investors of other Member States from investing* in their capital", emphasis added; see also in depth Dietz and Streinz (2015), p. 50.

[62] European Commission (2018), p. 16.

[63] Case C-200/96 *Metronome Musik v Music Point Hokamp* (28 April 1998) ECLI:EU:C:1998:172, para 21.

[64] As claimed by the foreign investor in the arbitration which would later lead to the CJEU's *Achmea* judgment, see *Eureko B.V. v. The Slovak Republic*, PCA Case No 2008–13, Award on Jurisdiction, Arbitrability and Suspension (26 October 2010), para 84.

[65] Kleinheisterkamp (2012), p. 99; Sattorova (2016), pp. 905–907; Andersen and Hindelang (2016), p. 998.

> "In the aftermath of the Achmea judgment, the unlawfulness of intra-EU investor-State arbitration may result in the perception that EU law does not provide for adequate substantive and procedural safeguards for intra-EU investors. *However, the EU legal system protects cross-border investors in the single market, while ensuring that other legitimate interests are duly taken into account.*"[66]

In terms of procedure, investors seeking the protection for their investment under EU law must seek remedy within the system of EU courts formed by the complex interplay between national courts of the Member States and the CJEU.[67] In all but a few cases, where an act by the Union directly affects the investment,[68] investors have to go to the Member States' courts. Here, two principally different forms of remedies are obtainable: challenging the Member State's action infringing EU law directly with the goal of eliminating the infringement itself (*primary* remedies) or seeking monetary compensation for the damage suffered in accordance with the rules on state liability (*secondary* remedies).[69] In contrast to investment arbitration, where the first and only claim is typically on monetary compensation, the CJEU has indicated that to claim state liability under EU law the claimant needs to exhaust the *primary* remedies without success under national law beforehand.[70] This is in line with many state liability regimes of the Member States.[71] The CJEU finds that "it is a general principle common to the legal systems of the Member States that the injured party must show reasonable diligence in limiting the extent of the loss or damage, or risk having to bear the damage himself".[72] Others argue that the CJEU has further emphasised the primacy of primary redress implicitly in its case of *Kühne & Heitz*[73] where it ruled on the conditions for national authorities to review final administrative decisions—one being that the administrative decision has become final only as a result of a judgment of a national court against whose decision there is no judicial remedy left.[74] In any case, Member States which do require the exhaustion of primary redress under their national state liability rules may—subject to the principle

---

[66] European Commission (2018), p. 3, emphasis added.

[67] Berger (2023), p. 73 et seq.; Andersen and Hindelang (2016), p. 991.

[68] Art. 340(2)–(3) TFEU in conjunction with Art. 268 TFEU vests jurisdiction regarding claims for non-contractual liability of the Union to the CJEU, see also Kellerbauer (2019), Article 340 TFEU, p. 2033.

[69] On the distinction, see van Aaken (2010).

[70] Joined cases C-46/93 and C-48/93 *Brasserie du pêcheur v Bundesrepublik Deutschland and The Queen / Secretary of State for Transport, ex parte Factortame and Others* (5 March 1996) ECLI: EU:C:1996:79, para 85; Karpenstein and Sangi (2021), p. 3232; Streinz (2002), p. 351.

[71] van Aaken (2010), p. 726.

[72] Joined cases C-46/93 and C-48/93 *Brasserie du pêcheur v Bundesrepublik Deutschland and The Queen / Secretary of State for Transport, ex parte Factortame and Others* (5 March 1996) ECLI: EU:C:1996:79, para 85.

[73] Case C-453/00 *Kühne & Heitz NV v Produktschap voor Pluimvee en Eieren* (13 January 2004) ECLI:EU:C:2004:17, para 26.

[74] Rennert (2007), p. 408.

of equivalence—set forth the same condition in state liability cases for breaches of EU law.[75]

3 EU Law on Damages for "Investment Claims": *Francovich* revisited

Whilst it can be said that the substantive standards of protection under EU law and international investment law do not diverge dramatically, and EU law may even offer more protection with the regard to the pre-establishment phase as well as primary redress, it is highly questionable whether the same is true for claims for damages once a breach of a substantive guarantee has taken place. In order to establish whether the requirements and hurdles of claiming compensation for breaches *of* EU law *under* EU law match with those in international investment law, it is necessary to examine the EU law's two-pillar approach: While the "right for reparation [. . .] flows directly from EU law, where those conditions are satisfied"[76] (Sec. 3.1), the basis on which the state must make reparation for the consequences of the loss or damage caused is up to the national rules of state liability as interpreted by the national courts, subject only to the EU law principles of equivalence and effectiveness (Sec. 3.2).[77]

3.1 Conditions of the Right for Reparation Under EU Law

In its landmark judgment in the *Francovich*[78] case, the CJEU ascertained "that it is a principle of Community law that the Member States are obliged to make good loss and damage caused to individuals by breaches of Community law for which they can be held responsible."[79] With its judgment in the joined cases of *Brasserie du Pêcheur* and *Factortame*,[80] the Court cemented the four conditions for reparation under EU law continually applied afterwards: the breach of EU law must be attributable to the Member State (1), the rule must intend to confer rights upon the

[75] Cf. Breuer (2011), p. 473.

[76] Case C-429/09 *Fuß* (25 November 2010) ECLI:EU:C:2010:717, para 62.

[77] Case C-160/14 *Ferreira da Silva e Brito and Others* (9 September 2015) ECLI:EU:C:2015:565, para 50; C-429/09 *Fuß* (25 November 2010) ECLI:EU:C:2010:717, para 62; Paparinskis (2016), p. 930.

[78] Case C-6/90 *Francovich and Bonifaci v Italy* (19 November 1991) ECLI:EU:C:1991:428.

[79] Case C-6/90 *Francovich and Bonifaci v Italy* (19 November 1991) ECLI:EU:C:1991:428, para 37.

[80] Joined cases C-46/93 and C-48/93 *Brasserie du pêcheur v Bundesrepublik Deutschland and The Queen / Secretary of State for Transport, ex parte Factortame and Others* (5 March 1996) ECLI:EU:C:1996:79.

individual (2), the breach must be sufficiently serious (3) and there must be a direct causal link between the breach and the damage sustained by the individual (4).[81]

3.1.1 Attributability

The CJEU already pointed out in the *Brasserie* case that the rules under which conduct is attributable to a state under international law for a breach of its international obligations must "apply *a fortiori* in the Community legal order".[82] The Member State is viewed as a single entity, irrespective of whether its executive, legislature or judiciary acted.[83] Hence, for all intends and purposes, EU law and international investment law run in parallel with respect to attributability.[84]

3.1.2 Conferral of Right to the Individual by EU law

Under the second condition, the EU rule in question must intend to confer a right to the individual. For the comparison to international investment law, two aspects are noteworthy. First, international investment law standards might find their way into national state liability proceedings as "EU law", and second, the condition of "conferral of rights" may be applied differently depending on the Member State's tort law tradition.

State liability under *Francovich* and *Brasserie* can arise, in principle, from the violation of any source of EU law. Typically, those concern primary or secondary law of the Union. However, international agreements concluded by the Union are also binding upon its institutions and the Member States (Art. 216(2) TFEU). Provisions of such agreements form an "integral part"[85] of the EU's legal order and take precedence over secondary Union law (and *a fortiori* also over Member States' law).[86] Hence, where the European Union itself is party to an international

---

[81] Joined cases C-46/93 and C-48/93 *Brasserie du pêcheur v Bundesrepublik Deutschland and The Queen / Secretary of State for Transport, ex parte Factortame and Others* (5 March 1996) ECLI: EU:C:1996:79, para 74.

[82] Joined cases C-46/93 and C-48/93 *Brasserie du pêcheur v Bundesrepublik Deutschland and The Queen / Secretary of State for Transport, ex parte Factortame and Others* (5 March 1996) ECLI: EU:C:1996:79, para 34.

[83] See also Case C-224/01 *Köbler* (30 September 2003) ECLI:EU:C:2003:513 on state liability for judicial decisions infringing upon EU law.

[84] Although coming to the same conclusion, Paparinskis (2016), 929–930 argues that EU law has not explicitly articulated attribution as a separate juridical category unlike international lsaw has done already some time ago.

[85] Case 181/73 *Haegemann v Belgian State* (30 April 1974) ECLI:EU:C:1974:41, para 5; C-386/08 Brita (25 February 2010) ECLI:EU:C:2010:91, para 39.

[86] Case C-61/94 *Commission v Germany* („International Fruit Company") (10 September 1996) ECLI:EU:C:1996:313, para 52; C-308/06 *Intertanko and Others* (3 June 2008) ECLI:EU: C:2008:312, para 42; see also Karpenstein and Sangi (2021), 3230–3231.

agreement with investment protection standards, the violation of those provisions by a Member State may constitute a violation of EU law as well.[87] However, an investor can only rely on the violation of such an international law provision if it has direct effect in the EU's legal order[88]—which the CJEU denies for many international agreements[89] and which the EU often excludes explicitly in its trade and investment agreements of the "new generation" (e.g. Art. 30.6 CETA,[90] Art. 8 EU-South Korea FTA,[91] Art. 23.5 EU-Japan FTA[92]).

In close proximity to the question of direct effect—however, not identical with—is the finding that national courts do not deal with the condition of "conferral of rights" uniformly. As *Granger* points out, despite this requirement forming part of the right for reparation under EU law, whether a rule of EU law confers rights to the individual has been interpreted differently depending on whether the Member State's national tort law tradition follows a subjective rights approach (e.g. "*Schutznormenlehre*") or an objective one.[93] Courts from diverging traditions have found the failure to transpose the very same EU Directive 91/676/EEC to incur state liability in one tradition but not the other.[94] Hence, investors may get treated differently in one Member State than in another, despite relying on the same EU law violation.

3.1.3 Sufficiently Serious Breach

Under the third condition, the breach of EU law must be sufficiently serious. As the CJEU held in *Brasserie*, "the decisive test for finding that a breach of Community law is sufficiently serious is whether the Member State or the Community institution concerned manifestly and gravely disregarded the limits on its discretion."[95] The factors which the national court may take into consideration include the clarity and precision of the rule breached, how much discretion it left to the authority applying it, the subjective intention to infringe upon the rule (or lack thereof), whether the error of law was excusable, and circumstances where an EU institution has

---

[87] Cf. Dimopoulos (2011), p. 296 et seq.

[88] Erlbacher (2019), Article 216 TFEU, p. 1649–1650.

[89] For an overview, ibid.

[90] Supra n 49.

[91] Free trade Agreement between the European Union and its Member States, of the one part, and the Republic of Korea, of the other part, OJ L 127, 14.5.2011, p 6–1344.

[92] Agreement between the European Union and Japan for an Economic Partnership, OJ L 330, 27.12.2018, p 3–899.

[93] Granger (2017), p. 113–114.

[94] ibid. 113.

[95] Joined cases C-46/93 and C-48/93 *Brasserie du pêcheur v Bundesrepublik Deutschland and The Queen / Secretary of State for Transport, ex parte Factortame and Others* (5 March 1996) ECLI: EU:C:1996:79, para 55.

contributed towards the erroneous understanding.[96] In cases where judicial decisions by a national court itself constitute the infringement of EU law in question, the CJEU interprets this condition even more restrictively: "only in the exceptional case where the court has manifestly infringed the applicable law."[97] And furthermore, national courts from different Member States interpret this condition in varying degrees of strictness, giving some Member States more leeway than others.[98] On the contrary, in international law, any conduct attributable to the state which constitutes a breach of an international obligation entails international responsibility (see Art. 1 and 2 (b) Articles on the Responsibility of States for Internationally Wrongful Acts).[99]

As a result, the requirement of a "sufficiently serious breach" is statistically the main obstacle for injured parties to claim compensation for state liability under EU law.[100]

3.1.4 Direct Causal Link

Lastly, there must be a direct causal link between the breach of law and the damage sustained by the individual. The CJEU does not give much indication on the conditions to establish causation under EU law, finding that it is for the national courts to determine causality.[101] Despite the justified fears over the wide margin of possible interpretations according to different tort law traditions,[102] there is little evidence that national courts have either significantly diverged in their interpretations or favoured state-friendly approaches.[103]

---

[96] Joined cases C-46/93 and C-48/93 *Brasserie du pêcheur v Bundesrepublik Deutschland and The Queen / Secretary of State for Transport, ex parte Factortame and Others* (5 March 1996) ECLI: EU:C:1996:79, para 56.

[97] Case C-224/01 *Köbler* (30 September 2003) ECLI:EU:C:2003:513, para 53; see also Demark (2020), p. 352.

[98] Granger (2007), p. 168–174.

[99] Within the realm of the Articles on State Responsibility, as pointed out by Paparinskis (2016), p. 932, an *argumentum a fortiori* can be drawn by reading its Part One Chap. III on obligations under peremptory norms of general international law. According to Art. 40(1) contained therein, this chapter shall only apply to a "serious breach" arising under such a peremptory norm. Art. 40(2) defines a breach as "serious if it involves a gross or systematic failure by the responsible State to fulfil the obligation." Hence, with only this chapter on peremptory norms laying down the threshold of a "serious breach", one can conclude that the international responsibility under the rest of the Articles, which do not contain the same wording, is not limited by the heightened threshold.

[100] Lock (2012), p. 1688–1689; Granger (2017), p. 114.

[101] Joined cases C-46/93 and C-48/93 *Brasserie du pêcheur v Bundesrepublik Deutschland and The Queen / Secretary of State for Transport, ex parte Factortame and Others* (5 March 1996) ECLI: EU:C:1996:79, para 65.

[102] Smith and Woods (1997), p. 925; Demark (2020), p. 369.

[103] On the contrary, most scholars agree that national courts generally interpret causation in clear opposition to their states trying to argue that their own wrongdoing has not directly caused the

3.1.5 Interim Conclusion

The *Francovich* and *Brasserie* conditions for claiming the right to reparation under EU law are in many ways comparable to those of investment claims. However, there are two caveats: First, all of the four conditions already leave significant room for interpretation up to the national courts and their diverging tort law traditions. Second, finding a state liable for its breach of a substantive legal protection standard only if that breach was "sufficiently serious" falls short of the protection under today's international investment law regime.

3.2 *National Rules on State Liability*

While the *Francovich* and *Brasserie* conditions should—at least in theory—provide for a uniform backdrop to state liability claims before national courts, they are not designed to be conclusive. Rather, the CJEU explicitly refers to the domestic rules on liability with respect to making reparation for the consequences of the loss and damage caused by the breach of Union law, provided they comply with the principles of equivalence and effectiveness.[104] This leaves the door open, in particular, for diverging treatment under national law with respect to rules on procedure and compensation.[105]

On the nature and extent of compensation, the CJEU has only given some indication as to what kind of compensation national courts ought to award. In *Brasserie*, it held that "[a]s for the various heads of damage [. . .], Community law imposes no specific criteria. It is for the national court to rule on those heads of damage in accordance with the domestic law which it applies".[106] In *Bonifaci*, the Court indirectly acknowledged that the Member State may award restitution in kind and not (only) monetary damages.[107] However, in cases of lost profits, the Court did not accept their total exclusion as a form of damage awarded in case of a breach of

---

infringement or the damage, see Granger (2017), p. 180; Paparinskis (2016), p. 934; Lock (2012), p. 1699.

[104] Joined cases C-46/93 and C-48/93 *Brasserie du pêcheur v Bundesrepublik Deutschland and The Queen / Secretary of State for Transport, ex parte Factortame and Others* (5 March 1996) ECLI: EU:C:1996:79, para 67; For this reason, Ossenbühl and Cornils (2013) p. 618 refer to the criteria as "*Rumpftatbestand*" (as in "criteria making up only the torso, not the whole body").

[105] ibid. 620.

[106] Joined cases C-46/93 and C-48/93 *Brasserie du pêcheur v Bundesrepublik Deutschland and The Queen / Secretary of State for Transport, ex parte Factortame and Others* (5 March 1996) ECLI: EU:C:1996:79, para 88.

[107] Ossenbühl and Cornils (2013), p. 624.

Community law, making an explicit reference to the special characteristics of economic and commercial litigation.[108]

Apart from the nature of the compensation awarded in state liability claims, the second question concerns its extent. Are the sums being awarded by an arbitral tribunal in an international investment law case equivalent to the same case being adjudicated by the national court? Comprehensive empirical analyses are lacking in this respect, and they would require making certain assumptions difficult to prove.[109] Without trying to compare apples with oranges, the Spanish judgment on the 2003 *CSD* case awarded EUR 26.4 million to the injured party and is considered to be exceptional with respect to the sum awarded in all EU state liability cases.[110] In contrast, according to the UNCTAD database of ISDS disputes, Spain has been ordered to pay more than that in 40 known ISDS awards alone (with EUR 290.6 million having been the largest sum awarded against Spain in the intra-EU case of *NextEra v. Spain*[111]).[112] So while it may be true that "*Francovich* is not only a dog that barks, but it can also, at times, bite",[113] it is at least plausible to assume that ISDS arbitration bites significantly stronger.[114]

4 Enforcement Deficits

Assuming that an investor suffers from a breach of an EU law protection standard for which all of the *Francovich* criteria are met, the investor must win its case against the Member State in that Member State's court and find a way to enforce the judgment in order to recieve effective protection in the end.

Pursuant to Art. 19(1) TEU, Member States shall provide remedies sufficient to ensure effective legal protection in the fields covered by Union law. Everyone has the right to an effective remedy before a tribunal in compliance with Art. 47 CFR, in particular an independent and impartial tribunal previously established by law. On questions regarding EU law, the Member States' courts must initiate preliminary reference procedures to the CJEU in accordance with Art. 267 TFEU. The European Commission argues that these normative guard rails provided by EU law offer an

[108] Joined cases C-46/93 and C-48/93 *Brasserie du pêcheur v Bundesrepublik Deutschland and The Queen / Secretary of State for Transport, ex parte Factortame and Others* (5 March 1996) ECLI: EU:C:1996:79, para 87.

[109] Paparinskis (2016), p. 940; see however on English and German courts, Lock (2012), pp. 1699 et seq.

[110] Paparinskis (2016), pp. 939–940.

[111] *NextEra Energy Global Holdings B.V. and NextEra Energy Spain Holdings B.V. v. Kingdom of Spain*, ICSID Case No ARB/14/11, Final Award (31 May 2019), para 37.

[112] UNCTAD, Investment Policy Hub. https://investmentpolicy.unctad.org/investment-dispute-settlement, database sorted by "amount awarded (or settled for)".

[113] Granger (2017), p. 125.

[114] Cf. Paparinskis (2016), p. 940.

effective and "complete system of judicial remedies at EU and Member State level" for the protection of investors' rights.[115] In contrast, arbitral tribunals are not considered as courts that can refer questions to the CJEU under Art. 267 TFEU[116] and which, therefore, "cannot properly apply EU law, in the absence of the indispensable judicial dialogue with the Court of Justice."[117]

However, the law in the books might not always align with the law in action. As statistics sourced from the Eurobarometer show, in 11 out of the 27 EU Member States, less than 50% of the questioned companies perceive the independence of courts and judges to be "very good" or "fairly good".[118] Poland suffers the most from lack of trust in their judicial independence, with circa 60% of companies perceiving it to be "fairly bad" or "very bad".[119] Both Poland and Hungary are facing intense scrutiny by the European Commission, the CJEU and scholars regarding the "rule of law crisis".[120,121] But there also exist concerns where national courts are independent from political interference. If the investor rests its claim for compensation on the erroneous application of EU law by the national court of last instance, the pursuant state liability claim might end up at the very same court of last instance, depending on that Member State's system of court hierarchy.[122] This is in stark contrast to an *independent* arbitral tribunal whose members typically make up one arbitrator appointed by each party to the dispute and the third arbitrator being chosen in agreement.[123]

That said, even for an independent judgment to be effective, investors must have confidence in being able to enforce it. The enforcement of foreign judgments presupposes their recognition.[124] At least in the state whose court has given the judgment, this is supposed to be straightforward—subject to the rules on state immunity, as alluded to above. However, one does not need to look at Poland to find Member States refusing to implement EU law after having been ordered to do so by (their own) courts. The CJEU even had to decide on whether members of government could be coercively detained for not setting up air quality plans in accordance with an EU directive.[125] With respect to enforcing outside the respective country, one of the key benefits associated with ISDS arbitration, in particular with ICSID awards, is the possibility to enforce the pecuniary obligations of an award in

---

[115] European Commission (2018), p. 20.

[116] Case C-284/16 *Achmea* (6 March 2018) ECLI:EU:C:2018:158, para 43.

[117] European Commission (2018), p. 2.

[118] European Commission (2022), p. 41.

[119] ibid.

[120] See among many Mickonytė (2019), p. 815; Kelemen and Pech (2019), p. 59; Jakub (2022).

[121] On the consequences of the rule of law concerns on investment protection under EU law, Wilske (2018); Andersen and Hindelang (2016), p. 990; Berger (2023), pp. 205–206.

[122] Demark (2020), p. 372 also citing Wattel (2004), p. 180.

[123] Dolzer et al. (2022), p. 401.

[124] Michaels (2009), para 4.

[125] Case C-752/18 *Deutsche Umwelthilfe* (19 December 2019) ECLI:EU:C:2019:1114.

all ICSID members (Art. 54 ICSID Convention). In contrast, it is fundamentally more difficult to enforce one state's judgment in another EU Member State. Within the EU, the regulations on the recognition and enforcement of judgments exempt state liability cases from their scope of application.[126] The exemption in the Brussels Ia Regulation—incidentally—goes back to a request by the Federal Republic of Germany which wanted to ensure that decisions on state liability for German war crimes could not be confirmed as European Enforcement Orders, following the international law cases of *Distomo* and *Kalavrita*.[127,128] And with no customary international law obligation to recognize foreign judgments in principle,[129] enforcing the state liability judgment might pose the most difficult obstacle for investment protection under EU law in practice.

5 Conclusion

In a sense, the protection of investments under international investment law and EU law can be described as "same same, but different". Their substantive protection standards often align, while in some instances international investment law goes beyond protection under EU law, and other times, EU law guarantees may go further than what protection BITs provide. However, investors are only protected satisfactorily if all national courts apply the *Francovich* and *Brasserie* conditions adequately and consistently, interpret the legal margins left for national rules on procedure and compensation strictly and if other Member States were to accept enforcement of the judgments. In practice, we witness discrepancies to this ideal. Investors must find their way around various different national state liability rules among national courts with sometimes questionable judicial independence which often interpret the same *Francovich* and *Brasserie* condition differently. If, in the end, the investor receives a

---

[126] See Art. 1(1) Regulation (EU) No 1215/2012 of the European Parliament and of the Council of 12 December 2012 on jurisdiction and the recognition and enforcement of judgments in civil and commercial matters ("Brussels Ia"), Art. 2(1) Regulation (EC) No 805/2004 of the European Parliament and of the Council of 21 April 2004 creating a European Enforcement Order for uncontested claims, Art. 2(1) Regulation (EC) No 1896/2006 of the European Parliament and of the Council of 12 December 2006 creating a European order for payment procedure, Art. 2-(1) Regulation (EC) No 861/2007 of the European Parliament and of the Council of 11 July 2007 establishing a European Small Claims Procedure, Art. 1(1) Regulation (EC) No 864/2007 of the European Parliament and of the Council of 11 July 2007 on the law applicable to non-contractual obligations ("Rome II"); technically, the exclusion of "the liability of the State for acts and omissions in the exercise of State authority (acta iure imperii)" is not a matter of the Regulations' scope of applicability but a matter of state immunity under public international law.

[127] *Jurisdictional Immunities of the State (Germany v. Italy; Greece intervening)*, Judgment, I.C.J. Reports 2012, p 99; see on the private internal law implications of the ICJ judgment, Boschiero (2013).

[128] Mankowski (2021), Artikel 1 Brüssel Ia-VO, para 70.

[129] Michaels (2009), para 11.

judgment by an independent national court in his or her favour, its recognition and enforcement in other Member States is anything but straightforward.

Hence, an alternative system to guarantee the adequate legal protection of investors' interests under EU law, in particular with respect to the issuance of judgments and their enforcements, is needed. In 2016, Austria, Finland, France, Germany and the Netherlands have presented a non-paper on intra-EU investment protection after the phasing out of existing intra-EU BITs.[130] Regarding the substantive protection, it proposes the codification of EU investor rights into a single framework (para 8). Procedurally, they acknowledge that most cases shall be heard by national courts (para 9), but—aside from an investor-state mediation scheme (para 10)—they also consider a binding and enforceable dispute settlement mechanism outside the national courts necessary (para 11). It goes beyond the scope of the present contribution to evaluate the non-paper's various proposals or to fully develop such a new separate mechanism itself. However, if, after having struck down intra-EU ISDS, EU law does not develop adequate protections for intra-EU investments which are enforceable *in lieu* of arbitral awards, this might incentivise investors wanting to invest in the EU to go "extra-EU" beforehand—awkwardly making post-Brexit UK a better destination for investing in the EU *than the EU*.[131]

References

Andersen TT, Hindelang S (2016) The day after: alternatives to intra-EU BITs. J World Invest Trade 17(6):984

Ankersmit L (2018) Achmea: the beginning of the end for ISDS in and with Europe? https://www.iisd.org/itn/en/2018/04/24/achmea-the-beginning-of-the-end-for-isds-in-and-with-europe-laurens-ankersmit/. Accessed 16 Mar 2023

Association of German Chambers of Industry and Commerce (DIHK e.V.) (2017) Feedback on the initiative 'Prevention and amicable resolution of investment disputes within the single market' (22 August 2017). https://ec.europa.eu/info/law/better-regulation/have-your-say/initiatives/1438-Prevention-and-amicable-resolution-of-investment-disputes-within-the-single-market/F6769_en. Accessed 17 Mar 2023

Basener N (2017) Investment protection in the European Union: considering EU law in investment arbitrations arising from intra-EU and extra-EU bilateral investment agreements. Nomos

Berger J (2023) International investment protection within Europe: the EU's assertion of control. In: Routledge research in international economic law. Routledge

Bjorklund AK (2009) State immunity and the enforcement of investor-state arbitral awards. In: Binder C et al (eds) International investment law for the 21st century: essays in honour of Christoph Schreuer. OUP

Börnsen N (2016) Nationales Recht in Investitionsschiedsverfahren. Mohr Siebeck

Boschiero N (2013) Jurisdictional immunities of the state and exequatur of foreign judgments: a private international law evaluation of the recent ICJ judgment in Germany v. Italy. In:

[130] 'Intra-EU Investment Treaties: Non-paper from Austria, Finland, France, Germany and the Netherlands' (7 April 2016) https://www.bmwk.de/Redaktion/EN/Downloads/intra-eu-investment-treaties.pdf?__blob=publicationFile&v=2.

[131] Wilske (2018), p. 334.

Boschiero N et al (eds) International courts and the development of international law: essays in honour of Tullio Treves. Asser Press
Breuer M (2011) Staatshaftung für judikatives Unrecht: Eine Untersuchung zum deutschen Recht, zum Europa- und Völkerrecht. Mohr Siebeck
Caro de Sousa P (2015) The European fundamental freedoms: a contextual approach. OUP
Demark A (2020) Contemporary issues regarding member state liability for infringements of EU Law by National Courts. EU Comp Law Iss Challeng Ser 4:352
Dietz S, Streinz T (2015) Das Marktzugangskriterium in der Dogmatik der Grundfreiheiten. Europarecht (EuR) 50(1):50
Dimopoulos A (2011) EU foreign investment law. OUP
Dolzer R, Kriebaum U, Schreuer C (2022) Principles of international investment law, 3rd edn. OUP
Erlbacher F (2019) Article 216 TFEU. In: Kellerbauer M, Klamert M, Tomkin J (eds) The EU treaties and the charter of fundamental rights. OUP
European Commission (2015) Commission asks Member States to terminate their intra-EU bilateral investment treaties (IP/15/5198 18 June 2015)
European Commission (2017) Inception impact assessment: prevention and amicable resolution of investment disputes within the single market: Ref.Ares(2017)3735364 (25 July 2017)
European Commission (2018) Protection of intra-EU investment, COM(2018) 547 final (19 July 2018)
European Commission (2022) The 2022 EU justice scoreboard: communication from the Commission to the European Parliament, the Council, the European Central Bank, the European Economic and Social Committee and the Committee of the Regions, COM(2022) 234
Fermeglia M, Mistura A (2020) Killing all birds with one stone: is this the end of Intra-EU BITs (as we know them). https://www.ejiltalk.org/killing-all-birds-with-one-stone-is-this-the-end-of-intra-eu-bits-as-we-know-them/. Accessed 16 Mar 2023
Georgaki K (2023) Conflict resolution between EU law and bilateral investment treaties of the EU member states in the aftermath of Achmea. Yearb Eur Law 1:374. https://doi.org/10.1093/yel/yeac012
Glinski C (2018) Achmea and its implications for investor dispute settlement. Z Eur Stud 21(1):47
Gonin E, O'Reilly R (2020) Intra-EU investment protection and the rule of law. In: Baltag C, Stanič A (eds) The future of investment treaty arbitration in the EU: intra-EU BITs, the energy charter treaty, and the multilateral investment court. Wolters Kluwer
Gött H (2023) Rules of the organization: Article 5 of the Vienna Convention on the Law of Treaties and the Relevance of European Union Law in Investment Arbitration. J World Invest Trade 24(1):37
Granger M-PF (2007) National applications of Francovich and the construction of a European administrative jus commune. Eur Law Rev 32:157
Granger M-PF (2017) Francovich liability before national courts: 25 years on, has anything changed? In: Giliker P (ed) Research handbook on EU tort law. Edward Elgar Publishing
Intra-EU Investment Treaties: Non-paper from Austria, Finland, France, Germany and the Netherlands (7 April 2016). https://www.bmwk.de/Redaktion/EN/Downloads/intra-eu-investment-treaties.pdf?__blob=publicationFile&v=2. Accessed 28 Mar 2023
Jakub A (2022) Three misconceptions about the EU rule of law crisis. https://verfassungsblog.de/misconceptions-rol/. Accessed 28 Mar 2023
Karpenstein U, Sangi R (2021) Investitionsschutz vor nationalen Gerichten – Zur Zukunft der Energiecharta. Neue Jurist Wochenschr 74(44):3228
Kelemen D, Pech L (2019) The uses and abuses of constitutional pluralism: undermining the rule of law in the name of constitutional identity in Hungary and Poland. Camb Yearb Eur Leg Stud 21:59
Kellerbauer M (2019) Article 340 TFEU. In: Kellerbauer M, Klamert M, Tomkin J (eds) The EU treaties and the charter of fundamental rights. OUP
Kleinheisterkamp J (2012) Investment protection and EU law: the intra- and extra-EU dimension of the energy charter treaty. J Int Econ Law 15(1):85

Kriebaum U (2007) Regulatory takings: balancing the interests of the investor and the state. J World Invest Trade 8(5):717

Kröll S (2015) Enforcement of awards. In: Bungenberg M, Griebel J, Hobe S (eds) International investment law: a handbook, 1st edn. Nomos; C.H. Beck; Hart Publishing

Kulick A (2013) Sneaking through the backdoor—reflections on public interest in international investment arbitration. Arbitr Int 29(3):435

Lavranos N, Lath A, Varma R (2023) The meltdown of the energy charter treaty (ECT): how the ECT was ruined by the EU and its member states. Zeitschrift für Schiedsverfahren 21(1):38

Levy I (2022) Green Power v. Spain: intra-EU game changer or an exception that confirms the rule? (20 July 2022). https://efilablog.org/2022/07/20/green-power-v-spain-intra-eu-game-changer-or-an-exception-that-confirms-the-rule/. Accessed 29 Mar 2023

Liebscher F (2022) Die "Modernisierung" des Energiechartervertrages. In: Beiträge zum Transnationalen Wirtschaftsrecht, vol 181

Lock T (2012) Is private enforcement of EU law through state liability a myth? An assessment of 20 years after Frankovich. Common Mark Law Rev 49:1675

Mankowski P (2021) Artikel 1 Brüssel Ia-VO. In: Rauscher T (ed) Europäisches Zivilprozess- und Kollisionsrecht EuZPR/EuIPR: Band I: Brüssel Ia-VO, 5th edn. Verlag Dr, Otto Schmidt

Mestral A d, Vanhonnaeker L (2022) Art. 8.4 - Market access. In: Bungenberg M, Reinisch A (eds) CETA investment law: article-by-article commentary. Nomos; C.H. Beck; Hart Publishing

Michaels R (2009) Recognition and enforcement of foreign judgments. In: Peters A (ed) MPEPIL

Mickonytė A (2019) Effects of the rule-of-law crisis in the EU: towards centralization of the EU system of judicial protection. Zeitschrift für ausländisches öffentliches Recht und Völkerrecht 79(4):815

Newman J (2023) Nobody expects the Spanish arbitration: playing dirty with clean energy subsidies. Financial Times (2 February 2023). https://www.ft.com/content/c7f12d55-2d54-4b87-ae28-65f080f63c29. Accessed 28 Mar 2023

Ossenbühl F, Cornils M (2013) Staatshaftungsrecht. C.H. Beck

Paparinskis M (2016) 'Investors' remedies under EU law and international investment law. J World Invest Trade 17(6):919

Reinisch A, Tropper J (2021) Introductory note: from the intra-EU objection to the reach of umbrella clauses and the limited scope of review in annulment proceedings—ICSID arbitration in 2019. In: Capaldo GZ (ed) The global community yearbook of international law and jurisprudence 2020. OUP

Rennert K (2007) Bestandskraft rechtswidriger Verwaltungsakte und Gemeinschaftsrecht. Deutsches Verwaltungsblatt 7:400

Salacuse JW (2010) The law of investment treaties, 1st edn. OUP

Sattorova M (2016) Investor rights under EU law and international investment law. J World Invest Trade 17(6):895

Scheu J (2020) Note on intra-EU BITS not covered by the termination agreement. https://iilcc.uni-koeln.de/sites/iilcc/user_upload/IILCC_Note_on_Intra-EU_BITs_NOT_Covered_by_the_Termination_Agreement_05_2020.pdf. Accessed 16 Mar 2023

Schreuer C (2010) Investment disputes. In: Peters A (ed) MPEPIL

Schreuer C (n.d.) Investments, international protection. In: Peters A (ed) MPEPIL

Smith F, Woods L (1997) Causation in Francovich: the neglected problem. Int Comp Law Q 46(4): 925

Stanič A (2020) Enforcement of awards and other implications of Achmea. In: Baltag C, Stanič A (eds) The future of investment treaty arbitration in the EU: intra-EU BITs, the energy charter treaty, and the multilateral investment court. Wolters Kluwer

Streinz R (2002) 3. Bericht von Prof. Dr. Rudolf Streinz, Bayreuth: Zweiter Beratungsgegenstand: Primär- und Sekundärrechtsschutz im Öffentlichen Recht. In: Alexy R et al. (eds) Verfassungsrecht und einfaches Recht - Verfassungsgerichtsbarkeit und Fachgerichtsbarkeit. Primär- und Sekundärrechtsschutz im Öffentlichen Recht: Berichte und Diskussionen auf der

Tagung der Vereinigung der Deutschen Staatsrechtslehrer in Würzburg vom 3. bis 6. Oktober 2001. de Gruyter

Sullivan J, Ingle D (2021) Arbitration under the energy charter treaty: the relevance of EU law. In: Dona JRM, Lavranos N (eds) International arbitration and EU law. Edward Elgar Publishing

UNCTAD (2018) Fact sheet on intra-European Union Investor-State Arbitration Cases. https://unctad.org/system/files/official-document/diaepcb2018d7_en.pdf. Accessed 16 Mar 2023

van Aaken A (2010) Primary and secondary remedies in international investment law and national state liability: a functional and comparative view. In: Schill SW (ed) International investment law and comparative public law, 1st edn. OUP

van der Beck M (2022) Intra-EU investment protection in the energy sector – The Komstroy decision of the ECJ. Zeitschrift für Internationales Wirtschaftsrecht 7(6):260

van Harten G (2010) Investment treaty arbitration, procedural fairness, and the rule of law. In: Schill SW (ed) International investment law and comparative public law, 1st edn. OUP

van Harten G, Loughlin M (2006) Investment treaty arbitration as a species of global administrative law. Eur J Int Law 17(1):121

Voon T, Merriman D (2022) Incoming: how international investment law constrains foreign investment screening. J World Invest Trade 24(1):75

Wälde TW (2007) The specific nature of investment arbitration. In: Kahn P, Wälde TW (eds) New aspects of international investment law. Nijhoff

Wattel PJ (2004) Köbler, CILFIT and Welthgrove: We can't go on meeting like this. Common Mark Law Rev 41(1):177

Wiedmann T (2018) Investitionsschutzabkommen zwischen EU-Staaten als unionsrechtswidriges Relikt? Die Antworten des EuGH in den Urteilen vom 6. März 2018, Achmea und SEGRO. In: Ludwigs M, Remien O (eds) Investitionsschutz. Schiedsgerichtsbarkeit und Rechtsstaat in der EU, Nomos

Wilske S (2018) Investitionsschiedsgerichtsbarkeit und Rechtsstaatlichkeit: Die andere Seite der Medaille – Einige unbequeme Wahrheiten? In: Ludwigs M, Remien O (eds) Investitionsschutz. Schiedsgerichtsbarkeit und Rechtsstaat in der EU, Nomos

Zasheva D, Lentner G (2021) ECJ in PL Holdings: ad hoc arbitration agreement between EU investor and Member State not compatible with EU law. https://europeanlawblog.eu/2021/11/08/ecj-in-pl-holdings-ad-hoc-arbitration-agreement-between-eu-investor-and-member-state-not-compatible-with-eu-law/. Accessed 16 Mar 2023

Completing the Woodcut: On the Feasibility of an Intra-EU Investment Court

Check for updates

Nicolaj Kuplewatzky

Contents

Abstract In theory, the ECJ's judgment in C-284/16 *Slovak Republic v. Achmea BV* marked the end to intra-EU investment arbitration under bilateral or multilateral investment treaties. In practice, the underlying grievances remain. That need for a workable post-*Achmea* dispute settlement system for intra-EU investment disputes was highlighted once more by the Commission's 2020 Inception Impact Assessment on an Investment Protection and Facilitation Framework, which showed a clear preference for an institutionalised path for resolving such disputes. This working paper accordingly seeks to discuss the policy proposals voiced to-date. It assesses respectively the legal feasibility of conferring jurisdiction to the Court of Justice of the European Union and treating intra-EU investment disputes through a specialized chamber or a specialized investment tribunal attached to that institution; a self-standing intra-EU investment court modelled on the Unified Patent Court; as well

I am indebted to Ana Bobić, Dominik Moskvan, and Dano Brossmann for their helpful comments on an earlier draft. The opinions herein are entirely my own.

N. Kuplewatzky (✉)
Court of Justice of the European Union, Luxembourg, Luxembourg
e-mail: nicolaj.kuplewatzky@curia.europa.eu

M. Bungenberg, A. Reinisch (eds.), *New Frontiers for EU Investment Policy*, Special Issue, https://doi.org/10.1007/978-3-031-41977-5_8

as the idea of 'docking' intra-EU investment disputes to a third body standing 'outside' the system of judicial remedies of the EU legal order. Of those options, the working paper concludes that a self-standing intra-EU investment court appears a (legally) feasible and an institutionally attractive option, both for investors and the Member States, for the future of intra-EU investment disputes.

1 Introduction

Albrecht Dürer's woodcut of an Indian rhinoceros in not an accurate representation of the real animal. It is thought that he never saw a rhinoceros in the flesh. And yet, his is a surprisingly precise depiction of the 'beast' which arrived as a present from Goa to Portugal for King Manuel I.

In 2015, the delegations of a number of capital-exporting Member States sat together at an 'informal technical meeting' in the Council to discuss the day after the termination of intra-EU bilateral investment treaties ('BITs'). The thoughts exchanged at that meeting resulted, in 2016, in the distribution of a Non-Paper on the future of intra-EU investment treaties to the Council's Trade Policy Committee ('2016 Non-Paper').[1] That paper inter alia floats three options for a binding and enforceable investment dispute settlement mechanism after the 'phasing out' of intra-EU BITs. First, it proposes to rely upon Article 273 TFEU to confer jurisdiction in intra-EU investment disputes to the ECJ. Second, the 2016 Non-Paper introduces the idea of a self-standing specialised court with access to the preliminary ruling procedure, modelled on the Unified Patent Court ('UPC'). Third, the Member States considered it possible to enter into a 'compromis', within the meaning of the 1907 Hague Convention for the Pacific Settlement of International Disputes to assign intra-EU investment disputes to an existing dispute settlement body outside the EU judicial system.[2]

Fast forward a few years, and the judgments in *Achmea*,[3] *Komstroy*,[4] *PL Holdings*,[5] and *Commission v European Food*[6] have made a discussion of those proposals an inevitability. In its 2020 Inception Impact Assessment on an Investment

[1]General Secretariat of the Council of the European Union (2016), p. 2, highlighting the need for 'an appropriate level of substantive and procedural protection for EU-Investors so that the phasing-out of intra-EU BITs do not result in any gaps in the protection of cross-border investment within the internal market'.

[2]Ibid.

[3]ECJ, case C-284/16, *Slovak Republic v. Achmea BV*, ECLI:EU:C:2018:158 ('*Achmea*').

[4]ECJ, case C-741/19, *Republic of Moldova v. Komstroy LLC*, ECLI:EU:C:2021:655 ('*Komstroy*').

[5]ECJ, case C-109/20, *Republiken Polen v. PL Holdings Sàrl*, ECLI:EU:C:2021:875 ('*PL Holdings*').

[6]ECJ, case C-638/19 P, *European Commission v. European Food SA and Others*, ECLI:EU:C:2022:50 ('*Commission v European Food*').

Protection and Facilitation Framework ('Inception Impact Assessment'),[7] the Commission takes on some of the 2016 Non-Paper ideas. It adds suggestions of its own (such the development of an 'Ombudsman-like EU administrative body' or a specialized SOLVIT database).[8] There have also been voices suggesting a specialized chamber at the European Court of Justice ('ECJ') or the General Court ('GC'), or even a specialized tribunal attached to the GC.[9]

Alas, like Dürer's woodcut, all of those proposals are short of detail on the legal feasibility of the respective policy options. In this contribution, I will accordingly seek to make that assessment with a view to recommending a workable post-*Achmea* dispute settlement system for intra-EU investment disputes. That discussion is subject to a few asterisks. First, the below analysis will be limited to the normative requirements for a court or tribunal tasked with resolving intra-EU investment disputes. Second, it is assumed that there is no political appetite for Treaty change. Third, given the reality of engaging the international responsibility of States and the thusly needed de-politicisation of disputes, it is also assumed that the involvement of specialized hybrid court branches at the level of the national judiciaries is not a viable alternative.[10] Fourth, in the light of the need for the actual resolution of disputes, it appears inapposite to discuss the non-binding dispute resolution alternatives proposed in the Inception Impact Assessment.

This contribution is structured as follows. First, I shall consider the possibility of resolving intra-EU disputes 'in-house', that is to say by the Court of Justice of the European Union ('CJEU') (part 2). That discussion will consider, first, the conferral option by means of Article 273 TFEU, as proposed by the Member States in their 2016 Non-Paper (2.1); second, the possibility for a specialized chamber at either the ECJ or the GC (2.2); as well as, third, the idea of establishing a separate investment

[7] European Commission (2020).

[8] Ibid, p. 4 (suggesting both options as an alternative to seeking resolution through a national or EU level court-like system).

[9] See Moskvan (2022), p. 211; Paschalidis (2020).

[10] Although, as Moskvan (2022) notes, such specialized national courts are a third alternative. Moreover, sight need not be lost of the many possibilities for a melange between national court branches specialized in investment arbitration and enabling such courts to fit the existing system within the framework of Article 267 TFEU. While that would not address the distrust in national judicial systems, there remains always the possibility for recourse to a 'super-charged' *juge d'appui*; that is to say a national judge designated by the procedural law of a Member State competent to act as interlocutor/review-mechanism between questions on the interpretation/application of EU law and the on-going work of the arbitration tribunal. See, by analogy, Rozas (2001), p. 130 (noting that this type of intervention, 'utilisée avec modération, ne peut que favoriser l'arbitrage' and that, as regards the interpretation of EU law, 'rien ne s'oppose à ce que l'arbitre demande l'aide du juge pour l'interprétation d'une règle qui exige la présentation d'une question préjudicielle'). However, for that to work, the national judge needs to be equipped with full powers of review under national law of all elements of analysis of the arbitration tribunal. See, in this regard, ECJ, case C-741/19, *Republic of Moldova v. Komstroy LLC*, ECLI:EU:C:2021:655, paras. 57 and 58 (requiring full powers of review by a competent Member State court so that the fundamental provisions of EU law can be examined in the course of that review and thus, if necessary, be brought to the ECJ for a preliminary ruling).

tribunal attached to the GC (2.3). I will conclude that section with some interim reflections (2.4). Thereafter, the discussion will turn to the 'outside' options for such a dispute settlement system. In this regard, I will consider the proposal for a self-standing intra-EU investment court modelled on the UPC (part 3). That section shall take account of both substance requirements (3.1) as well as a possible legal basis (3.2). Finally, I shall discuss the possibility of assigning jurisdiction to a 'third' body, by means of a 'compromis' between the Member States (part 4). I shall conclude that the legally most defendable solution would be a self-standing investment court modelled on the UPC. However, under the current state of the case-law, it even appears that a 'docking' to a third body may be possible, so long as the 'commonality' requirement arising from *Parfums Christian Dior*[11] (as repeated in Opinion 1/09 (*Agreement creating a Unified Patent Litigation System*))[12] is satisfied (part 5).

2 Jurisdiction of Investment Disputes by the Court of Justice of the European Union

2.1 Getting There

Under Article 19(1), first subparagraph, TEU, the CJEU ensures that, in the interpretation and application of the Treaties, EU law is observed. It exercises its powers in respect of disputes which come within the scope of the provisions of the Treaties. Once modest, that scope now encompasses not just disputes falling within the *Kompetenzkatalog* of the Union, but an ever-increasing area of law.[13] The protection of investments within the territory of the Treaties falls within the scope of EU law.[14] As such, the CJEU would naturally have jurisdiction to decide on disputes between

[11] ECJ, case C-337/95, *Parfums Christian Dior SA and Parfums Christian Dior BV v. Evora BV*, ECLI:EU:C:1997:517.

[12] ECJ, Opinion 1/09, *Agreement creating a Unified Patent Litigation System*, ECLI:EU:C:2011:123.

[13] On the broad mapping and development of the material scope of EU law, see Ćapeta (2016), pp. 268–270.

[14] See, to that effect, ECJ, case C-284/16, *Slovak Republic v. Achmea BV*, ECLI:EU:C:2018:158, para. 42 (finding that such a link is inter alia reflected in the provisions on the fundamental freedoms, including the freedom of establishment and the free movement of capital). See also, as regards the protection afforded by the latter right in cases of (indirect) expropriation, ECJ, joined cases C-52/16 and C-113/16, *'SEGRO' Kft. v. Vas Megyei Kormányhivatal Sárvári Járási Földhivatala* and *Günther Horváth v. Vas Megyei Kormányhivatal*, ECLI:EU:C:2018:157, para. 129 (relating to the EU-law compatible nature of legislation bringing about the extinction of rights of usufruct acquired by contract over agricultural land). Consider further that the Commission takes the position that 'EU law protects all forms of EU cross-border investments throughout their entire life cycle.' See General Secretariat of the Council of the European Union (2016), p. 3. See finally the impressive analysis by Moskvan (2022), pp. 6–23, who, as regards the personal and material scope of protection of EU law concludes that 'intra-EU protection pursuant to EU law may still offer

natural and legal persons and the Member States relating to intra-EU investments (in whatever form). That would include raising claims based on EU law which derive, originally, from the Union's membership to international agreements, such as the Energy Charter Treaty (to the extent that those provisions can be invoked and are directly effective).[15] However, accessing that jurisdiction is the real elephant in the room. Given the multilevel judiciary of the EU legal order, access to the ECJ by natural or legal persons is primarily dependent on preliminary references from the national courts. Direct actions are procedurally restricted,[16] for even where an EU measure would lead to the interference with the right to enjoy an investment, the conditions of standing are notoriously difficult to meet.[17] In other words, there are two natural avenues by which (investor) disputes could reach the CJEU to decide on the compatibility, with EU law, of certain Member State or Union measures, such that their disputes could then be assigned either to a specialized chamber or a specialized tribunal. However, as DG FISMA of the Commission itself has previously noted: 'the added value [of that idea] is limited as investors could not have legal standing to bring claims directly to the CJEU even in a specialised chamber'[18] (while not further explained, the argument of DG FISMA appears to be that the General Court would not be competent to review the EU law-compatibility of those measures, given that said measures do not directly result from acts from the EU

functionally equivalent or perhaps even more (or less) extensive protection in some cases.'; ibid., p. 200.

[15] There are two important asterisks that should follow this argument: first, in *Komstroy*, the Court did not exclude the intra-EU applicability of the substantive provisions of the Energy Charter Treaty and, second, that the Energy Charter Treaty as a whole, or substantive provisions thereof, can actually be directly invoked (since, by virtue of Article 2 of the Energy Charter Treaty, that agreement sought to establish 'mutual benefits' among signatories, thus raising the familiar 'asymmetry' argumentation that closed the door to the direct effect of the WTO Agreements; see ECJ, case C-149/96, *Portugal v. Council*, ECLI:EU:C:1999:574, paragraph 42).

[16] Needless to say, there are also substantive restrictions to bring cases directly before the CJEU under the second paragraph of Article 340 TFEU, given that non-contractual liability of the Union can only be established where a set of conditions is satisfied; see, for example, joined cases T-546/13, T-108/14 and T-109/14, *Šumelj and Others v Commission*, ECLI:EU:T:2016:107, paragraph 79 (dismissing a claim for non-contractual liability of the Union arising from the commitment, entered into by Croatia in view of its accession to the Union, to repeal certain legislation pertaining to public bailiffs, which allegedly led to harm of persons previously appointed as public bailiffs).

[17] Consider, however, the promising development arising from ECJ, case C-348/20 P, *Nord Stream 2 AG v. European Parliament and Council of the European Union*, ECLI:EU:C:2022:548, para. 67 (finding direct concern, on the part of a legal person, to challenge an amendment to an EU directive, by placing 'substance' over 'form', in a scenario where said amendment extended the scope of the rules of Directive (EU) 2019/692, OJ L 117 of 17.04.2019, p. 1 to situations and addressees, such as the applicant, which were not previously caught by those rules).

[18] European Commission, Minutes of the ninth Meeting of the Member States' Expert Group on intra-EU investment environment, pp. 1 and 2, available at: https://ec.europa.eu/transparency/expert-groups-register/screen/meetings/consult?lang=en&meetingId=22373&fromExpertGroups=true.

institutions or of bodies, offices or agencies of the EU within the meaning of Article 263 TFEU).

What then are the prospects of a third avenue of offering (systematised) direct access, at least to the ECJ? Pursuant to Article 273 TFEU, the ECJ can be conferred jurisdiction in any dispute between the Member States which relates to the subject-matter of the Treaties. Assignment may happen by means of a general dispute settlement provision in an agreement between (a limited group of) the Member States.[19] Thereby, an entire 'class' of disputes could be assigned to the ECJ,[20] at least so long as the resulting dispute has an objectively identifiable link with the subject-matter of the Treaties.[21] However, the confines of that idea arguably lie in the limitation of Article 273 TFEU to disputes 'between the Member States'. In *Pringle*, the ECJ appeared open to extend that wording also to the European Stability Mechanism ('ESM') as party, that is to say a body established by the ESM Treaty, which is not a Member State, and thus a 'third party' to the ESM Treaty.[22] That logic would assume the possibility of 'assignment', by means of an agreement between the Member States, of possible parties to a dispute brought under Article 273 TFEU. In that way, jurisdiction could be granted to the ECJ through the 'standing offer to arbitrate' logic.[23]

However, does Article 273 TFEU really allow for assignment of such an unspecified class of applicants? That is questionable. It appears that the reason given by the ECJ in *Pringle* as to the presence of the ESM in disputes under the ESM Treaty was linked to the ESM's mandate arising from a treaty to which only the Member State could be signatories. That is quite different from extending jurisdiction to subjects of a Member State's legal order (apart from the fact that such a type

[19] See, by analogy, ECJ, case C-370/12, *Thomas Pringle v. Government of Ireland and Others*, ECLI:EU:C:2012:756, para. 172 (finding that the reference to 'special agreement', in Article 273 TFEU, does not prevent the Member States from designating the ECJ as arbiter of disputes by means of a dispute settlement provision in an international agreement).

[20] See to that effect, ibid. para. 172 (finding that an advance agreement 'with reference to a whole class of pre-defined disputes' satisfies the Article 273 TFEU standard).

[21] See ECJ, case C-648/15, *Republic of Austria v. Federal Republic of Germany*, ECLI:EU:C:2017:664, para. 25 (explaining that '[t]he condition laid down in Article 273 TFEU that the dispute should be related to the subject matter of the treaties is therefore satisfied when it is established that the dispute brought before the Court has an objectively identifiable link with the subject matter of the Treaties.')

[22] See ECJ, case C-370/12, *Thomas Pringle v. Government of Ireland and Others*, ECLI:EU:C:2012:756, para. 175 (holding that 'since the membership of the ESM consists solely of Member States, a dispute to which the ESM is party may be considered to be a dispute between Member States within the meaning of Article 273 TFEU').

[23] See, in this regard, Opinion of Advocate General Wathelet in ECJ, case C-284/16, *Slovak Republic v. Achmea BV*, ECLI:EU:C:2017:699, point 154 (explaining that 'the investor is not exercising a right of his own but a right which that BIT confers on his State of origin'). See also, more generally, Paulsson (1995), pp. 232–257.

of assignment assumes the presence of intra-EU investment agreements to which the Member States are signatories).

Moreover, the ECJ's position on standing offers to arbitrate appears unresolved. On the one hand, in the judgment in *Commission v European Food and Others*,[24] the ECJ explained that standing consent by a Member State to BIT dispute settlement 'does not originate in a specific agreement reflecting the freely expressed wishes of the parties concerned'.[25] On the other hand, in Opinion 2/15 (*EU-Singapore Free Trade Agreement*), despite expressing no opinion on the compatibility of the content of that agreement, and although relating to an entirely different question of law, the ECJ appeared less preoccupied with the EU-Singapore Free Trade Agreement's standing offer to arbitrate than with the possibility of removing jurisdiction of such disputes from national courts.[26] Provided either of those precedents can be extended to assignments by means of standing offers to arbitrate at the international law plane, the *Commission v European Food and Others* reasoning would bar recourse to Article 273 TFEU as insufficiently direct, whereas the Opinion 2/15 (*EU-Singapore Free Trade Agreement*) reasoning implicitly appears content with that possibility. And yet, the question remains why that distinction did not really enter the discussion in *Pringle*. One clue may lie in the View of Advocate General Kokott in *Pringle*, who noted that 'a dispute between an ESM Member and the ESM is in fact, or at least can be assimilated to, a dispute between the ESM Member and the other ESM Members, who within the ESM have adopted a majority decision be followed.'[27] That logic certainly appears transposable to other scenarios. Thus, if sufficiently clear at the outset, there could be some merit in arguing that a dispute settlement provision, in an agreement between two Member States, assigning standing jurisdiction to a restricted class, or a restricted type of cases, to the ECJ should be compatible with the Article 273 TFEU logic of *Pringle*. In other words, a sort of individualising measure within a separate agreement between the Member States. Where, in turn, the required clarity would be lacking, such as, for instance, where the offer to arbitrate is too general or insufficiently precise so as to identify a clearly-demarked group of potential claimants, jurisdiction would then be precluded.

Whichever way an investment dispute reaches the CJEU, how could it be dealt with?

[24] ECJ, case C-638/19 P, *European Commission v European Food SA and Others*, ECLI:EU:C:2022:50.

[25] Ibid, para. 144.

[26] Opinion 2/15 of the Court, *EU-Singapore Free Trade Agreement*, ECLI:EU:C:2017:376, paras. 288–292 (specifically referring to a prior paragraph highlighting the purely competence-related nature of the opinion before it, but then, when explaining the outlines of the envisaged dispute settlement system, including the standing offer to arbitrate, inserting a sentence on said regime 'remov[ing] disputes from the jurisdiction of the courts of the Member States').

[27] View of Advocate General Kokott in ECJ, case C-370/12, *Thomas Pringle v Government of Ireland and Others*, ECLI:EU:C:2012:675, point 189.

2.2 A Specialised Chamber at the European Court of Justice or the General Court

The specialisation of chambers, be that at the GC or the ECJ, is an evergreen topic.[28] With specialisation comes synergy, and thus expertise, on the side of the bench, as well as legal certainty, on the side of litigants. Despite those benefits,[29] specialisation at the ECJ never quite took off.[30] That said, since 2019, the GC is operating a (limited) system of specialised chambers for civil service and intellectual property cases.[31] Even at the ECJ, it has been observed that the system of '*connexité*' already now functions as a cautious means of specialisation among the Judges-Rapporteur and the Advocates-General.[32]

Legally, one (or more) specialised investment chamber(s) could be set up in accordance with Article 25(1) of the Rules of Procedure of the GC. That would also alleviate the role of the Vice-President of the GC, which, so far, was tasked with the role of ensuring legal coherence among judgments. Specialisation of chambers could similarly act as a catalyst to appoint an Advocate General at GC level, which is possible under Article 30 of the same rules of procedure, potentially also specialized on investment matters, to provide a thorough (independent and thus third) opinion on the dispute before the chamber. Similar considerations apply for a specialized chamber at the ECJ level, set up in accordance with Article 60(1) of the latter's rules of procedure.

There is one immediate drawback of a specialized chamber within an established institution. The first is the composition of any specialized chamber. Said chamber would be composed of judges of the GC or the ECJ. For the purposes of their mandate, those judges are EU law generalists (even if they may hold a particular interest, or prior specialization, in a specific area of law). That type of composition,

---

[28] See, for instance, Öberg et al. (2017), p. 212, who argue that '[s]pecialisation could contribute to fulfil the General Court's founding promise of improving the judicial protection of individual interests, in particular in proceedings requiring a close examination of complex facts, and maintaining quality and effectiveness of judicial review in the EU legal order'. See also, more generally, Montag and Hoseinian (2012).

[29] In 1988, the Commission pleaded for specialisation in its guidelines concerning the establishment of the Court of First Instance, suggesting the creation of two specialised chambers (for administrative and economic law cases), and for the recruitment of judges specialised in these areas. See European Commission (1988), pp. 2 and 3.

[30] Although, as Judge Forwood confirmed to the House of Lords European Union Committee in 1999, 'when trade mark law was a new area of work for the [General Court], in order to achieve consistency of judgment in the evolving case law, all trade mark cases were remitted to a particular chamber of the Court'. See House of Lords (2011), para. 120. See also Öberg et al. (2017), p. 220 (explaining further that 'two specialised chambers for intellectual property cases were operational between 1998 and 2003 and a specialised *chambre des pourvois* was created to deal with appeals against decisions of the Civil Services Tribunal').

[31] Court of Justice of the European Union (2019), p. 1.

[32] See, for instance, Dehousse (2016), pp. 60–61 (referring to that attribution key as a 'nascent form of specialisation').

in turn, does not address the criticism of lack of expert knowledge of arbitration and/or (international) investment law. In reality, there is little lasting engagement with arbitration in general.[33] In response, as is done in a number of national systems,[34] a specialized chamber could be composed of both, EU judges and lay experts (in arbitration/investment/international law).[35] Those ‘non-permanent judges’ could be appointed on an ‘ad hoc’ basis, from a previously drawn-up roster of eligible candidates.[36]

2.3 A Specialized Tribunal Attached to the General Court

In many Member States, there are specialized tribunals on which expert judges are empanelled for areas of law that are complex or exhibit other special features.[37] At the level of EU law, recourse to such a type of tribunal also reaches back as far as 1978.[38] Akin to creating trial courts at the EU ‘federal’ level, there was even

[33] Which has led to the (hasty) reputation among arbitration practitioners that the CJEU is averse to arbitration. Take the example of the often-criticised ‘West Tankers’ judgment. That judgment must be viewed through the prism of the arbitration exception of Regulation (EC) No. 44/2001, OJ L 12 of 22/12/2000, p. 1: merely because jurisdiction before the ordinary courts is contested on the basis of an agreement to arbitration makes that regulation’s rules no less applicable to the dispute; see ECJ, case C-185/07, *Allianz SpA and Generali Assicurazioni Generali SpA v. West Tankers Inc.*, ECLI:EU:C:2009:69, para. 24 in particular. The question of whether arbitration should be exempted from the scope of Regulation (EC) No 44/2001 (or its successor) is then an entirely different one, which is not for the ECJ to decide. See, for instance, ECJ, joined cases C-106/19 and C-232/19, *Italian Republic and Comune di Milano v. Council of the European Union and European Parliament*, ECLI:EU:C:2022:568, para. 146 (and the case-law cited). The principle of institutional balance implies that it is for the EU legislature alone to decide the content of a measure.

[34] For instance, in the area of competition law, in Austria, the Supreme Cartel Court (16th panel of the Supreme Court) acts as specialized chamber competent to hear appeals from the Cartel Court on points of law ((§ 58 II KartG). It is composed of three professional judges and two lay experts. Similarly, the Court of Appeal of Brussels is competent to hear cases concerning the public-law control of national competition authority decisions at first instance. It has two specialised chambers (one in Flemish and one in French), each sitting with three judges.

[35] Such a combination of profiles is already proposed for the UPC; see Article 15 UPCA, which explains that ‘the Court shall comprise both legally qualified judges and technically qualified judges.’

[36] See, for instance, the pool of individuals eligible for appointment as arbitrators and trade and sustainable development experts in bilateral disputes under trade agreements with third countries; European Commission (2022a). See also, in that regard, Article 16 UPCA, which explains that the Advisory Committee sets up a similar roster for suitable candidates to be appointed as judges of the UPC Court.

[37] On that account, Jacobs et al. (2019), p. 1221 (alleging that such specialisation would be the only way to ensure that judgment of sufficient quality are issued within a short period of time).

[38] See Naômé (2018), point. 1.06 (explaining that, in 1978, H. Kutscher, President of the ECJ at the time, suggested by means of memorandum that a court of first instance be created with jurisdiction to hear staff cases).

discussion of multiple first instance courts of subject-matter specialisation.[39] However, recourse to the possibility for a specialised tribunal was made only once, and then solely in relation to disputes within the civil service of the EU.[40] The resulting Civil Service Tribunal, which commenced its work in 2005, ceased operations in 2016.[41]

Article 19(1) TEU specifically speaks of specialized courts as part of the CJEU architecture. The rules for the establishment of those courts are set out in Article 257 TFEU. That provision clarifies that said specialized courts are 'attached to the GC', and thus not self-standing (or external to the CJEU). Moreover, the first subparagraph of Article 257 TFEU also explains that such courts would hear and determine classes or actions of cases, at first instance, 'in specific areas'. That latter concept is not further elaborated in the Treaties. It must thus be assumed that it falls to the EU legislator, in line with the attribution of competences to the Union, to decide which areas should be covered by the jurisdiction of a specialized tribunal. Once that decision is made, the discretion of actually establishing said court by means of regulation is left, in line with the first and third subparagraphs of Article 257 TFEU, to the European Parliament and the Council (subject to the initiative of the Commission or the ECJ, and the requirement for consultation of the respective other institution).

Although not required by Article 257 TFEU, some link to EU law would be required to establish a dedicated tribunal for the purpose of resolving disputes involving EU investors and the Member States. That arises not least from the mandate of the CJEU, such that there will be a need to make stipulation for the applicable law in a particular dispute.

Organisationally, there is little doubt that a specialized investment tribunal could hierarchically fit well within the existing judicial structure of the CJEU. Article 257(5) TFEU requires said tribunal to set up its own rules of procedure. That would allow for the adoption of arbitration-specific rules, or the possibility to simply adopt progressive model rules of existing arbitration institutions. The latter would likely be preferred by the arbitration community, and would arguably also add to the

[39] See, for instance, the idea of a customs and social security court, in Brown and Kennedy (1994), p. 366.

[40] Although certainly (then) Court of First Instance President Jaeger floated the idea of a specialised court for intellectual property litigation (in particular EU trademark cases, which continue to occupy a large part of the work of the General Court). See General Court of the European Union (2009). See also CJEU (2014): 'the plenary meeting of the General Court stated its preference for the establishment of a specialised trade mark court and for the status quo to be maintained as regards the [Civil Service Tribunal]'.

[41] See Regulation (EU, Euratom) 2015/2422 of the European Parliament and of the Council of 16 December 2015 amending Protocol No 3 on the Statute of the Court of Justice of the European Union, OJ L 341 of 24/12/2015, p. 14, recital 9 (explaining that, at the request of the ECJ, jurisdiction was transferred to the General Court to assist with the backlog of pending cases).

legitimacy of the specialised tribunal. Furthermore, the investment tribunal could make use of the GC's existing institutional structure, including that of its registry.[42]

Article 256(2) TFEU designates the GC as the competent jurisdiction for appeals from specialized tribunals. Article 257(3) TFEU then leaves the discretion on the scope of such appeals to the ordinary legislator. These may concern appeals on law only, or also on matters of fact. While there may be a certain danger of extending the appeal process, given the lack of administrative fact-finding prior to an investment dispute, there is likely to be a preference to extend appeals to challenges in law and fact.[43] That way, the GC would be given the (unenviable) task of reviewing factual as well as substantive and procedural issues (such as relating to interlocutory decisions or decisions on leave to appeal). Article 256(2), second subparagraph, TFEU assumes a role for the ECJ at the hierarchical apex, and allows any further appeals on specific (constitutional) issues of law only. Such an arrangement would make efficient use of the existing 'leave to appeal' system (already in place for a number of areas on appeal from the GC),[44] pursuant to which only 'issues significant with respect to the unity, consistency and development of EU law' could make their way to the ECJ.[45] That way, a third layer of review would ensure the uniformity (and legitimacy) of all legal questions of a horizontally-important nature.

So as to further preserve subject-matter recognition, the composition of any specialised investment tribunal could be mixed, or 'ad hoc' even (potentially drawing from a roster of candidates drawn up previously[46]). Consider also that there is precedent in amending the Statute of the CJEU to allow for the possibility to attach temporary judges to the specialized tribunals created under Article 257(1) TFEU.[47]

At the same time, it would be foolish to disregard the CJEU's opposition, during the reform process of the GC, of the creation of specialised courts of subject-matters falling within the horizontal competence of the latter, given that that institution must

[42] Although, for instance, the Civil Service Tribunal had its own registry and secretariat.

[43] Note that this differs from the procedure applicable, at the time, to the Civil Service Tribunal. See Article 11(1) of Annex I to the Statute, which limited appeals to the General Court in law only.

[44] Regulation (EU, Euratom) 2019/629 of the European Parliament and of the Council of 17 April 2019 amending Protocol No 3 on the Statute of the Court of Justice of the European Union, OJ L 111 of 25/04/2019, p. 1, Article 1(2) (detailing that cases already having gone through two instances of appeals should not proceed further 'unless the Court of Justice first decides that it should be allowed to do so').

[45] Since the introduction of the 'leave to appeal system', the ECJ has only once deemed a case to satisfy that threshold; see ECJ order, Case C-382/21 P, *European Union Intellectual Property Office (EUIPO) v The KaiKai Company Jaeger Wichmann GbR*, ECLI:EU:C:2021:1050, para. 34.

[46] See text at footnote 36 above.

[47] Regulation (EU, Euratom) No. 741/2012 of the European Parliament and of the Council of 11 August 2012 amending the Protocol on the Statute of the Court of Justice of the European Union and Annex I thereto, OJ L 228 of 23/8/2012, p. 1, Article 1 (relating, however, solely to the possibility to cover the absence of judges who are prevented from participating in the disposal of cases for a lengthy period of time).

be consulted as part of any legislative process under Article 257(1) TFEU.[48] Generally speaking, it should also be observed that a specialized tribunal under the auspices of the GC would add a subject-specific discipline that, realistically, would be of little use to the jurisdiction as a whole,[49] particularly if the case-load is time-limited or if investors chose to restructure their intra-EU investments through third countries (thereby removing themselves from the (likely) scope of jurisdiction of any (intra-EU) investment tribunal).[50]

2.4 *Interim Reflection*

There appears to be little legal difficulty to either of the above two approaches. Naturally, there will be questions surrounding the composition of such a chamber/tribunal; the law it may resort to; as well as technical and logistical issues. However, those issues appear secondary against the larger benefits of resolving intra-EU investment disputes within an existing institutional framework.

A further benefit derived from resorting to the full-time judiciary of the CJEU is that its judges do not 'double-hat', as some arbitrators occasionally do. If limited to intra-EU disputes, the 'domestic court bias' argument would also not be credible. The CJEU itself is a multilateral court, and thus stands as third party to disputes before it. Granted, under the judicial system of the Treaties, the Member States are deemed privileged applicants, attached to which are a number of procedural benefits.[51] However, that does not make the CJEU judiciary biased in favour of the Member States. In fact, there may be a certain benefit to interventions by multiple

[48] See, Schima (2019), Article 257 TFEU, p. 1771 (explaining that the CJEU based itself on the likely lack of long-term effectiveness of the proposed solution to create a specialised court in the field of intellectual property; the urgency of the situation; the flexibility of the measure envisaged; as well as the need to ensure the consistency of EU law).

[49] On the opposing view, see generally Vandersanden (2015), p. 88 (complimenting the work of the Civil Service Tribunal, which was subject to similar criticism, as a 'high-quality jurisdiction that gave new and enriching impulse to European civil service case law'; as well as Union syndicale fédérale des Services publics européens et internationaux (2015).

[50] Which is precisely why the Commission brought its infringement action against the United Kingdom in case C-516/22, *European Commission v. United Kingdom of Great Britain and Northern Ireland* (pending), given that it feared that such jurisprudence could, in a post-Brexit world, 'circumvent and undermine the Commission's efforts to ensure the effective implementation of judgments reiterating the primacy of EU law over arbitral awards in the context of intra-EU investment disputes.' See European Commission (2022b).

[51] One of which is the possibility to intervene in any pending action without the need for evidencing 'interest' in the outcome of proceedings. See, for instance, the first, second, and third paragraphs of Article 40 of the Statute of the Court of Justice of the European Union, which grants intervention rights to Member States and EU institutions, but attaches the same right to conditions in the case of 'non-privileged' applicants (like natural or legal persons).

Member States, such as in case of similar measures across the Union,[52] or even the EU institutions, where a measure has a horizontal EU policy nexus.[53] Moreover, the (admittedly important) issue of like access, by means of intervention, by 'other' interested parties, such as environmental organisations, could be addressed through a change in the Statute of the CJEU.[54] Finally, and equally going to the question of accessibility of the ensuing system, a specialized chamber and/or tribunal would satisfy the right of access to an independent tribunal, also for individuals and small and medium-size companies.[55]

3 A Permanent Intra-EU Investment Court

3.1 Structural Features and Requirements

Under Article 344 TFEU, the Member States undertake not to submit a dispute concerning the interpretation or application of EU law to any method of settlement not embedded within the judicial architecture of the Union.[56] That provision thus complements Article 19(1) TEU, according to which the CJEU alone, as apex court in the judicial architecture of the Treaties, holds the jurisdiction to ultimately ensure

[52] Such as the many arbitration cases challenging Member States' decisions to amend pre-existing incentive regimes applicable to subsidies renewable energy projects. See, for instance, Award of 15 June 2018, *Antin Infastructure Services Luxembourg Luxembourg S.à.r.l. and Antin Energia Termosolar B.V.* (ICSID Case No. ARB/13/31) and Award of 2 May 2018, *Antaris and Göde v. Czech Republic* (PCA Case No. 2014-01).

[53] See, for instance, Award of 26 July 2018, *Marfin Investment Group Holdings S.A., Alexandros Bakatselos and Others v Cyprus* (ICSID Case No. ARB/13/27) or Award of 8 January 2019, *Cyprus Popular Bank v Hellenic Republic* (ICSID Case No. ARB/14/16 (relating to claims brought by investors in response to the forced restructuring of Greek Government bonds).

[54] Currently, interventions are limited to any person 'which can establish an interest in the result of a case submitted to the Court'. See Article 40 of the Statute of the CJEU. That requirement for an interest has been interpreted as covering solely the legal (and not economic) interest of parties. See, in this regard, order of the Vice-President of the Court, case C 12/18 P(I), *United States of America v Apple Sales International and Others*, ECLI:EU:C:2018:330, paras. 8 and 23. See, in this regard, Award of 14 October 2016 *Pac Rim Cayman LLC v. Republic of El Salvador* (ICSID Case No. ARB/09/12) (where an investment tribunal admitted a third party submission by a number of civil society groups supporting the host State's decision to deny a mining concession given the potential risks for the local population and the environment).

[55] See, in this regard, Opinion 1/17 of the Court, EU-Canada CET Agreement, ECLI:EU:C:2019: 341 paras. 217, 218 and 21 (finding that, so as to ensure, in practice, accessibility of the CETA Tribunal not only by investors who have available to them significant financial resources, the approval of the CETA by the Union would be dependent on a commitment, by the Union, to guarantee access of small and medium-sized enterprises and private individuals through, for instance, a co-financing mechanism).

[56] See, in this regard, ECJ, case C-284/16, *Slovak Republic v. Achmea BV*, ECLI:EU:C:2018:158, paragraph 17.

the interpretation and application of EU law. Such exclusivity is not a unique feature of EU law.[57] But it is an essential feature of that legal order, as it ensures that the allocation of powers fixed by the Treaties are preserved.[58] Any (potential) threat to the integrity of (even part of) that system is automatically viewed as putting in jeopardy the entire autonomy of EU legal order.[59]

The baseline established by those outlines of the case-law implies, in essence, that any system of dispute settlement between the Union and its Member States which is external to the CJEU cannot circumvent the EU judicial architecture, but must be squarely placed within it. At its heart, that is the message delivered by *Achmea*, *Komstroy*, *PL Holdings*, and *Commission v European Food*.

The difficulty of squaring that circle with regard to intra-EU investment dispute settlement is substantially reminiscent of that relating to the compatibility of the Agreement on a Unified Patent Court ('AUPC').[60] The draft version of that agreement, put to the ECJ in Opinion 1/09 (*Agreement creating a Unified Patent Litigation System*),[61] envisaged the creation of a pan-European patent organisation, established by means of international agreement, whose decisions would be subject, in large measure, to judicial control only by the (thusly-created) Unified Patent Court

---

[57] For instance, Article III Section 2 of the United States Constitution vests original (and exclusive) jurisdiction in the United States Supreme Court over 'controversies between two or more States'. See also Article 131 of the Constitution of India, which assigns exclusive original jurisdiction to the Indian Supreme Court in all cases between the Government of India and the States of India, or between States themselves. In addition, Article 32 of the Constitution of India grants original jurisdiction to the Indian Supreme Court on all cases involving the enforcement of fundamental rights of citizens

[58] See, to that effect, Opinion 2/13 of the court, Accession of the European Union to the ECHR, ECLI:EU:C:2014:2454, para. 201 (explaining that an international agreement cannot affect the allocation of powers fixed by the Treaties or, consequently, the autonomy of the EU legal system).

[59] To that effect, ECJ, case C-284/16, *Slovak Republic v. Achmea BV*, ECLI:EU:C:2018:158, para. 56 (finding that the mere possibility of interpretation and application of EU law is sufficient to undermine the autonomy of EU law); ECJ, case C-741/19, *République de Moldavie v. Komstroy LLC*, ECLI:EU:C:2021:655, paras. 59 and 60 (highlighting that the mere 'possibility' of undermining the effectiveness of EU law is sufficient to render an 'outside' dispute settlement system incompatible with the Treaties); ECJ, case C-109/20, *Republiken Polen v. PL Holdings Sàrl*, ECLI:EU:C:2021:875, paras. 46 and 47 (explaining that an '*ad hoc*' dispute settlement system arising from an arbitration clause is 'capable' of calling into question not only the principle of mutual trust but also the preservation of the 'particular nature' of EU law is incompatible with the judicial structure established by the Treaties); and ECJ, case C-638/19 P, *European Commission v. European Food SA and Others*, ECLI:EU:C:2022:50, paras. 141 and 145 (finding that the consent, by Romania, to an arbitral tribunal 'which does not form part of the EU judicial system within the second subparagraph of Article 19(1) TEU ... lacked any force' from that Member States' accession to the Union).

[60] Agreement on a Unified Patent Court, OJ C 175 of 20/6/2013, p. 1.

[61] Opinion 1/09 of the court, Agreement creating a Unified Patent Litigation System, ECLI:EU:C:2011:123.

('UPC'), an international and decentralized[62] court system set up under said agreement, and thus external to the judicial structure of the Treaties. The ECJ deemed such a system incompatible with the autonomy of the EU legal order.[63] The system, as proposed, would 'alter the essential character' of the structure of EU law.[64] Indeed, the draft AUPC's most characteristic feature was to give exclusive competence to the UPC to apply EU law in the field of patents, all the while divesting jurisdiction from the national courts of the Member State signatories of that competence. That, the ECJ found, was not compatible with the judicial structure of Article 267 TFEU, as that provision envisages the cooperation of the national courts on matters of EU law.[65] Moreover, damages arising from decisions of the UPC in breach of EU law would not be attributable to the Member States (so-called '*Köbler* liability'), so that a failure, by the UPC, to make a reference to the ECJ, or a failure, by the UPC, to abide by EU law generally would remain without remedy.[66]

From those considerations arise two essential pointers for the creation of a (self-standing) intra-EU investment court.

The first is the requirement for 'internalisation' of that body. The draft UPCA, as it was presented to the ECJ, described a court system which was outside the EU's institutional and judicial framework, and to which even non-Member States could adhere. In creating such a system, the ECJ explained, the national courts would be divested of their ordinary powers as '*juges de droit commun du droit de l'Union*'[67] at the national level to interpret, in particular, (what is now) the Unitary Patent Regulation[68] and other secondary EU law, since these retain only those powers which are not subject to the exclusive jurisdiction of the UPC.[69] That focus on the

[62] A solution which led Dehousse to term the UPC 'the most dis-unified international court'; see Dehousse (2013), p. 26.

[63] Opinion 1/09 of the court, Agreement creating a Unified Patent Litigation System, ECLI:EU:C:2011:123, para. 89 (finding that the national courts would be deprived of their powers in relation to the interpretation and application of EU law, and the ECJ of its power to reply).

[64] Ibid.

[65] Ibid, paras. 84 and 85 (explaining that the 'tasks attributed to the national courts and to the [ECJ] respectively are indispensable to the preservation of the very nature of the law established by the Treaties').

[66] Ibid, paras. 86 to 88 (explaining that '[i]t is clear that if a decision of the PC were to be in breach of [EU law], that decision could not be the subject of infringement proceedings nor could it give rise to any financial liability on the part of one or more Member States').

[67] Often clumsily translated into English as 'EU law judges'; that is to say national judges of the Member States which, under the system established by Article 19(1) TEU, interpret and apply EU law.

[68] Regulation (EU) No 1257/2012 of the European Parliament and of the Council of 17 December 2012 implementing enhanced cooperation in the area of the creation of unitary patent protection, OJ L 361 of 31/12/2012, p. 1.

[69] Opinion 1/09 of the court, Agreement creating a Unified Patent Litigation System, ECLI:EU:C:2011:123, paras. 72 and 73 (explaining the exclusive jurisdiction of the UPC and its role to supplant the national courts of the signatory parties, including those of the Member States, 'of the main part of the jurisdiction *ratione materiae* held, normally, by the national courts').

role of Member States' national courts within the judicial architecture of the Union is the most innovative element of Opinion 1/09 (*Agreement creating a Unified Patent Litigation System*), since it recognises the inherent 'tilt', in the 'division of labour', of the system established by the Treaties, 'in the direction of national courts'.[70] Thus, it would not just be sufficient to allow, by means of a preliminary reference procedure, for a dialogue between the ECJ and the 'external' court common to the Member States (whose jurisdiction is exclusive for certain types of disputes), if that means that the national courts are divested of EU law jurisdiction in favour of a court outside the EU judicial architecture.

The resulting system of the now-ratified AUPC follows the ECJ's directions. Following Opinion 1/09 (*Agreement creating a Unified Patent Litigation System*), the Commission redesigned the legal status of the system with the Benelux Court of Justice in mind. In its Opinion, the ECJ had specifically mentioned that that court, common to Belgium, the Netherlands and Luxembourg, and tasked with ensuring uniformity among the rules common to those Member States, would be compatible with the judicial structure of Article 19(1) TEU.[71] The UPCA takes up that hint and now specifically proclaims that its court is a 'court common to the Contracting Member States and thus part of their judicial system'.[72]

Those changes matter for the creation of any intra-EU investment court. Given the directions arising from Opinion 1/09 (*Agreement creating a Unified Patent Litigation System*), it is clear that that system of dispute settlement must be 'common' to the Member States, or at least to a number of them.

However, what does that requirement for 'commonality' entail?

It is clear that limiting access *ratione personae* to an intra-EU investment court to EU investors and the Member States only is one piece to the larger puzzle. It also appears that what is needed are certain national law characteristics beyond express assignment through an international agreement.[73] Thus, while, in *Achmea*, Advocate General Wathelet deemed an arbitral tribunal arising from a dispute settlement provision of a bilateral investment treaty between two Member States as 'common' to those Member States, the ECJ considered that type of assignment too loose, and thereby not featuring 'any links with the judicial systems of the Member States'.[74] That certainly entails that the mere ratification, by a Member State, of an international agreement assigning jurisdiction to a dispute settlement mechanism not forming part of the domestic courts of that Member States creates an insufficiently-close link to its national system, and thus the system of dispute

[70] To use the language of Rosas (2017), p. 67.

[71] Ibid, para. 82 (explaining that 'the Benelux Court is a court common to a number of Member States, situated, consequently, within the judicial system of the European Union, [so that] its decisions are subject to mechanisms capable of ensuring the full effectiveness of the rules of the European Union.')

[72] UPCA, recital 7.

[73] Such as is present in the UPCA, Articles 1(2) and 21.

[74] ECJ, case C-284/16, *Slovak Republic v. Achmea BV*, ECLI:EU:C:2018:158, para. 48.

settlement established by Article 19(1) TEU.[75] And yet, the precise 'qualitative' contours beyond ratification would be required of a 'common' court remain elusive. In *Parfums Christian Dior*, the ECJ's decision to recognise the Benelux Court as 'common' to the judicial system of the Member States was based on the consideration that proceedings before the Benelux Court were but a 'step in the proceedings before the national courts leading to a definitive interpretation of common Benelux rules'.[76] That singular observation, while far from conclusive, appears to point to two elements of organisation of a 'common' court between the Member States. The first is its domestic law organisation: the Court's emphasis, in *Parfums Christian Dior*, on proceedings before the Benelux Court constituting a 'step' within the national procedural organisation of the Belgian judicial architecture implies that there must be specific rules within Belgian law laying down the organisational integration of that court among the ordinary judicial system of that Member State. That is to say that there must be clear rules on who can call upon the 'common' court, at what time, and how proceedings before that court relate to national proceedings. Part of that organisation would thus be rules at national procedural level to assign sole and mandatory jurisdiction in the realm of intra-EU investment disputes to the 'common' intra-EU investment court.[77] The second element of organisation naturally flows from the first and constitutes the 'other side of the same coin': if what is required is the positive integration of the 'common' court within the respective national systems, then that must mean that a mere declaration or affirmation—solely at international law level—by means of a treaty would be insufficient to satisfy the *Parfums Christian Dior* threshold. How that is affected at national level is naturally left to the respective constitutional requirements of the (participating) Member States.

However, does that entail that national courts *must* be part of the conversation, such as through a system of internal preliminary references (as is the case with the Benelux Court and the national courts of Belgium, Netherlands, and Luxembourg)? Or can those national courts be absolved of their ordinary competence in favour of a 'one-stop-shop' dispute resolution mechanism before that 'common' court? The answer to this does not arise from the case-law. On the one hand, the ECJ previously considered the Complaints Board of the European Schools not to constitute a 'court or tribunal', for the purposes of Article 267 TFEU, because it lacked a procedural

[75] To that effect also Opinion of Advocate General Szpunar in ECJ, case C-741/19, *République de Moldavie v. Komstroy LLC*, ECLI:EU:C:2021:655, point 77 (opining that a tribunal established under Article 26 ECT 'is not a part of the judicial system of the Member States ... [n]or does it constitute a court or tribunal common to several Member States, since it has no connection with the judicial systems of the Member States').

[76] ECJ, case C-337/95, *Parfums Christian Dior SA and Parfums Christian Dior BV v. Evora BV*, ECLI:EU:C:1997:517, para. 22.

[77] As was the case in the Order of the Court, case C-555/13, *Merck Canada Inc. v Accord Healthcare Ltd and Others*, ECLI:EU:C:2014:92, paras. 19 and 20, where the ECJ found the assignment of exclusive jurisdiction of certain types of disputes to an arbitral body, as satisfying the conditions of Article 267 TFEU.

connection to the national courts, and thus was not deemed 'common' enough.[78] Similarly, in *Komstroy*, the ECJ was clear that the national courts must hold full review of 'fundamental provisions of EU law' for a system of arbitration proceedings outside the judicial structure of the Member State to be compatible with EU law.[79] Those judgments could thus be interpreted as requiring a role for the national courts, in some shape or form. On the other hand, there is certainly an argument that removing exclusive jurisdiction from the otherwise-competent national courts to a 'common internal' body does not divest the former type of courts (holding the task of ensuring the interpretation and application of EU law, under Article 19(1) TEU), of their jurisdiction, if the Member States, in their national law, also stipulate that the 'common' court must, forthwith, be considered as the (sole) court competent for those disputes.[80] In effect, such a transfer of competences merely moves jurisdiction from one 'internal' court to another 'internal' court (even if the latter is common to a number of Member States), while the ECJ remains at the apex of that system.[81] In theory, that type of re-organisation of the national judiciary ought to fall within the national procedural autonomy of the Member States, given that it does not otherwise appear to affect the allocation of competences of the Treaty (that is to say the system of 'dual vigilance').[82]

It has moreover been argued that the situation of the Benelux Court is special since its existence is sanctioned by primary law, namely Article 350 TFEU.[83] Under that provision, the Treaties 'shall not preclude the existence or completion of regional unions' between the Benelux countries, 'in so far as that region union is

[78] ECJ, case C-196/09, *Paul Miles and Others v. Écoles européennes*, ECLI:EU:C:2011:388, para. 41 (distinguishing the Complaints Board from the Benelux Court, since the former 'does not have any such links with the judicial systems of the Member States').

[79] ECJ, case C-741/19, *République de Moldavie v. Komstroy LLC*, ECLI:EU:C:2021:655, paras. 57 to 62 (essentially requiring full powers of review by a court of a Member State of an arbitral award decided outside the system of judicial review constituted by Article 19(1) TEU).

[80] See, for instance, ECJ, case C-54/96, *Dorsch Consult Ingenieurgesellschaft mbH v Bundesbaugesellschaft Berlin mbH*, ECLI:EU:C:1997:413, para. 38 (deeming a supervisory board, as the only body competent to review the legality of determinations made by national bodies responsible for reviewing public procurement awards, a 'court and tribunal', despite its organizational placement within the Bundeskartellamt, which is itself subject to supervision by the German Ministry for Economic Affairs.) See also Order of the Court, case C-555/13, *Merck Canada Inc. v Accord Healthcare Ltd and Others*, ECLI:EU:C:2014:92, paras. 19 and 20.

[81] See, to that effect, ECJ, case C-337/95, *Parfums Christian Dior SA and Parfums Christian Dior BV v. Evora BV*, ECLI:EU:C:1997:517, paras. 22 and 23) (explaining that the Benelux Court, 'faced with the task of interpreting Community rules in the performance of its function, . . . follow [s] the procedure provided for by [Article 267 TFEU] . . . [and] therefore serve[s] the purpose of that provision, which is to ensure the uniform interpretation of Community law').

[82] See Lenaerts and Gutierrez-Fons (2018), p. 105 (explaining that the judicial protection of EU rights is based on a system of 'dual vigilance' because 'in addition to the supervision carried out by the European Commission and the Member States, individuals are entitled to rely on their EU rights in the national courts').

[83] See Jaeger (2012), p. 290 (arguing that the 'existence of the Benelux court is specifically recognized by the Treaties').

further advanced than the internal market'.[84] The argument thus goes that such specific primary law authorization is required for a court to be considered 'common' to be Member States. That position is unconvincing. The Benelux Court certainly appears to have a 'hook', in primary law, to enable its existence. However, in none of its case-law relating to the Benelux Court has the ECJ referred to Article 350 TFEU (or its predecessors) as a reason to sanction that 'common' court's existence. Quite the contrary, when referring to its compatibility with EU law, the ECJ has consistently highlighted the Benelux Court's integration into the judicial system of the Benelux countries, in such a way that the resulting dispute resolution mechanism features the same qualitative criteria as a national court or tribunal, within the meaning of Article 267 TFEU.[85] In other words, even a dispute mechanism that does not copy in full the Benelux Court system could be sanctioned as an EU law-compatible type of integration.[86]

However, structural internalisation of an intra-EU investment court is not the end of the line. Possibly *the* defining feature of a 'common' court tasked with resolving investment disputes is its role of reviewing national and EU measures allegedly undermining or exhausting the value of investments within the territory of the Member State or the Union. That mandate is directly linked to the review of national laws and administrative and judicial acts and measures. Therefore, the jurisdiction of an intra-EU investment court would entail, fundamentally, the interpretation and application of national law, and thereby also EU law (since the latter forms part of the former).[87] Add to that the possibility of an additional link to EU law, either through a provision on applicable law,[88] or the seat of the arbitration,[89] and a hook to EU law jurisdiction (and its required respect for the judicial architecture of the Treaties) would be established either way.[90] That is what distinguishes the idea of

[84] Which is how the ECJ in judgment of 14 July 2016, case C-230/15, *Brite Strike Technologies Inc. v. Brite Strike Technologies SA*, ECLI:EU:C:2016:560, para. 57, explained the limits to Article 350 TFEU.

[85] See text at footnote 65 above.

[86] Along the same line of argument, Tilmann and Passmann (2018), p. 470 (arguing that although the remodelled PC 'is integrated into the judicial systems of the Member States in a different way compared with the Benelux Court of Justice, it is a "court common to the Member States"').

[87] See, by analogy, ECJ, case C-741/19, *République de Moldavie v. Komstroy LLC*, ECLI:EU:C:2021:655, para. 33) (explaining that 'EU law forms part of the law in force in every Member State').

[88] Article 24(1)(a) UPCA expressly stipulates EU law as a source of law of the PC.

[89] See, by analogy, ECJ, case C-741/19, *République de Moldavie v. Komstroy LLC*, ECLI:EU:C:2021:655, para. 33) (finding the mere presence of a French 'lexi fori' in the arbitration agreement a sufficient hook to the potential applicability of EU law).

[90] In other words, even if no applicable law provision would be contained in the agreement establishing an Intra-EU Investment Court (a presumption, which, albeit unlikely, must be entertained), that court will apply EU law. On the potentiality of such application being enough to trigger the requirements of Article 19(1) TEU, see the case-law at footnote 57 above as well as ECJ, case C-64/16, *Associação Sindical dos Juízes Portugueses v. Tribunal de Contas*, ECLI:EU:C:2018:117, para. 40 (finding the mere possibility that the Portuguese Court of Auditors may apply

an intra-EU investment court from the CETA Tribunal, which famously not only stands outside the EU and Canadian judicial systems, but whose jurisdiction is also additionally limited to the provisions of the CETA.[91] In other words, the (direct or even tangential) use of EU law is the flipside of the 'internalisation coin' requiring placement of the intra-EU investment court squarely within the EU judicial architecture. Those considerations apply '*mutatis mutantis*' even if the intra-EU investment court would be designed to act as a 'fork-in-the-road' institution (alongside the United States District Court model), whereby EU investors would be given the choice of either staying under national court jurisdiction or removing their dispute to the intra-EU investment court.[92]

The second pointer for the envisaged type of dispute system flows from the first and concerns the level of safeguards to ensure the full application of EU law. That entails a measure of review, by the ECJ, through the preliminary ruling procedure, and means of accountability in case of breach of EU law. By virtue of the removal of jurisdiction from national courts in favour of an 'external' dispute settlement system, the draft agreement at issue in Opinion 1/09 (*Agreement creating a Unified Patent Litigation System*) fell short of those requirements. First, while it contained a preliminary ruling procedure, that procedure was reserved to the UPC, without the national courts holding any ancillary competence to refer such questions.[93] Second, there was no means of holding the signatory Member States accountable if the UPC did not comply with EU law, nor of attributing financial liability to the former.[94]

In response, the UPCA contains a plethora of commitments by the Member States. Thus, the UPC 'shall apply Union law in its entirety and respect its primacy' (Article 20 thereof) (Article 24(1)) of the same agreement specifying EU law as an

---

EU law a sufficient link to require the satisfaction of the requirement for effective judicial protection, as flowing from Article 19(1) TEU). Along the same lines, ECJ, joined cases C-585/18, C-624/18 and C-625/18, *A.K. and Others v Sąd Najwyższy, CP v. Sąd Najwyższy and DO v. Sąd Najwyższy*, ECLI:EU:C:2019:982, para. 83.

[91] Opinion 1/17 of the Court, EU-Canada CET Agreement, ECLI:EU:C:2019:341, para. 134 (noting that the ECJ's involvement is not necessary if the powers of interpretation of the CETA Tribunal and Appellate Tribunal are confined to the provisions of the CETA).

[92] Such 'fork-in-the-road' types of settlement have been upheld by the ECJ to satisfy the principles of Article 267 TFEU (see, for instance, ECJ, case 109/88, *Handels- og Kontorfunktionærernes Forbund i Danmark*, ECLI:EU:C:1989:383, para. 7 (relating to proceedings between the parties to collective agreements and their employers before an industrial arbitration board, whose jurisdiction was established by law); and ECJ, case C-203/14, *Consorci Sanitari del Maresme v. Corporació de Salut del Maresme i la Selva*, ECLI:EU:C:2015:664, paras. 22 to 25 and the case-law cited (finding recourse to the administrative courts at second instance sufficient to ensure that EU public procurement law is observed).

[93] Opinion 1/09 of the court, Agreement creating a Unified Patent Litigation System, ECLI:EU:C:2011:123, para. 79 (explaining that the draft PC 'takes the place of national courts and tribunals . . . [and] deprives, therefore, those courts and tribunals of the power to request preliminary rulings from the Court in that field').

[94] Ibid, paras. 86 to 88 (observing that, under EU law, the Member States must make good damage caused as a result of breaches thereof by their national courts, and even hold them financially liable; however, neither of those safeguards would exist under the draft agreement).

express source of law); the UPC must 'cooperate' with the CJEU, as if it were a national court, 'in accordance with Article 267 TFEU in particular'; and that decisions of the CJEU be binding upon it (Article 21); and any damage resulting from an infringement of Union law by its Court of Appeal is not only attributable to the signatory Member States individually and collectively (for the purposes of Articles 258–260 TFEU) (Article 23 of the UPCA), but the Member States also assume joint and several liability any resulting damage (Article 22 of that agreement). Without it being necessary to enter into further discussion of those requirements, it suffices to say that a proposal for an intra-EU investment court, if established within the judicial structure of the Member States and tasked with (partial or exclusive) jurisdiction over intra-EU investment disputes, would have to satisfy those requirements in like measure.

Besides those pointers, there are two additional factors, not explored in Opinion 1/09 (*Agreement creating a Unified Patent Litigation System*) given the type of dispute settlement system created by the UPCA, which will flow into the assessment of the creation of an intra-EU investment court.

The first additional element is that of accessibility of the entire system. In its current design, investor-State dispute settlement is expensive.[95] Therefore, depending on the institutional, staffing, and funding structure of an intra-EU investment court, as well as cost and damages arrangements for ensuring proceedings, the right to an effective remedy enshrined in Article 47 of the Charter may require certain arrangements to enable natural persons or a small and medium-sized enterprise to bring proceedings. When discussing that issue in Opinion 1/17 (*EU-Canada CET Agreement*), the ECJ noted that, indeed, the 'extent of the financial risk undertaken by bringing proceedings' may act as a deterrence to bring a case for such parties,[96] and thereby also undermine the guarantee of accessibility of a court or tribunal under the right to an effective remedy.[97] Accordingly, and again subject to the institutional and procedural structure of the resulting court, it would appear necessary, pursuant to the overall requirement to ensure the full application of EU law, to take guidance of the commitment, by the Union, of guaranteeing access to the CETA Tribunal, once it is established in the flesh.[98]

[95] Recall, for instance, that a 2021 empirical study by the British Institute of International and Comparative Law and Allen & Overy (2021), p. 4, found that, for 'respondent States, the mean costs incurred in an ISDS proceeding are around US$4.7 million . . . [while] [t]he median figure is US$2.6 m', whereas '[f]or investors, the mean costs exceed US$6.4 m . . . [while] [t]he median figure is US$3.8 m.'

[96] Opinion 1/17 of the Court, EU-Canada CET Agreement, ECLI:EU:C:2019:341, para. 211 (explaining that the design of the CETA Tribunal is such that the claimant investor may have to carry the fees and expenses of the Member of the Tribunal, so that, in particular for natural and small and medium-sized legal persons, there may be an inherent deterrence in filing investment claims).

[97] Ibid, para. 201 (referring to the guarantee of accessibility as 'the very essence of the right of access to such a tribunal', although that right may involve proportionate restrictions).

[98] Ibid, para. 221 (referring to the commitment, further outline in Statement No 36 by the Commission and the Council, that 'the Commission is committed to further review, without delay, of the

The second additional element is that of independence. In the general framework of its task of judging, independent decision-making is one of the core elements of a 'court or tribunal'.[99] It gains particular importance where a system of dispute settlement is set up to function as the sole and exclusive venue for a particular type of cases.[100] Independence has both 'internal' and 'external' aspects.[101] The former aspect is linked to impartiality and the appearance of independence.[102] The latter aspect of independence protects the autonomous exercise of the functions of a court or tribunal, requiring the lack of any hierarchical control by, or subordination to, any internal or external source.[103] As the ECJ in Opinion 1/17 (*EU-Canada CET Agreement*) explained, those guarantees 'require rules, particularly as regards the composition of the body and the appointment, length of service and grounds for abstention, rejection and dismissal of its members, in order to dispel any reasonable doubt in the minds of individuals as to the imperviousness of that body to external factors and its neutrality with respect to the interests before it.'[104]

---

dispute settlement mechanism . . . allowing sufficient time so that Member States can consider it in their ratification processes'). That statement is included in Statements to be entered in the Council minutes (OJ L 11 of 14/01/2017, p. 20).

[99] See, in particular, ECJ, joined cases C-585/18, C-624/18 and C-625/18, *A.K. and Others v Sąd Najwyższy, CP v. Sąd Najwyższy and DO v. Sąd Najwyższy*, ECLI:EU:C:2019:982, paras. 127 and 153 and the case-law cited (referring to the 'appearance of independence' as a relevant standard under Article 6(1) ECHR and referring to the possibility of doubts 'in the minds of the subjects of the law' as to the imperviousness of a court or tribunal as being the relevant standard under Article 267 TFEU).

[100] See, in particular, ECJ, joined cases C-357/19, C-379/19, C-547/19, C-811/19 and C-840/19, *Euro Box Promotion and Others*, ECLI:EU:C:2021:1034, para. 224 (explaining that requires that the court concerned exercise its functions wholly autonomously, without being subject to any hierarchical constraint or subordinated to any other body and without taking orders or instructions from any source whatsoever, thus being protected against external interventions or pressure liable to impair the independent judgment of its members and to influence their decisions').

[101] See, in particular, ECJ, case C-506/04, *Graham J. Wilson v. Ordre des avocats du barreau de Luxembourg*, ECLI:EU:C:2006:587, paras. 49 to 52 (recognising for the first time that the concept of independence, which is inherent in the task of adjudication, has three distinct aspects: that the body must stand as a third party to the dispute; that it is 'externally' independent; and that it is 'internally' independent).

[102] See, for instance, ECJ, case C-192/18, *European Commission v. Republic of Poland*, ECLI:EU:C:2019:924, para. 110 and the case-law cited (explaining that the aspect of impartiality, 'seeks to ensure that an equal distance is maintained from the parties to the proceedings and their respective interests with regard to the subject matter of those proceedings. That aspect requires objectivity and the absence of any interest in the outcome of the proceedings apart from the strict application of the rule of law').

[103] See, to that effect, Opinion 1/17 of the Court, EU-Canada CET Agreement, ECLI:EU:C:2019:341, para. 90 (finding that because the 'CETA Tribunal is not a court that has compulsory jurisdiction, since an investor may submit a dispute either before an ordinary court or before that Tribunal. It follows that the requirement of independence does not apply to that Tribunal in the same way as it does to an ordinary court or tribunal').

[104] Ibid, para. 204.

To the extent that an intra-EU investment court would be designed to fit within the EU judicial structure, as a court 'common' to the Member States, be that with sole and exclusive or shared jurisdiction, the importance of the criterion of independence of a court or tribunal arises essentially from three (separate yet analogous) angles. The first angle, subsumed within Article 19(1) TEU, concerns the systemic and structural design of the system of dispute settlement intended to apply EU law.[105] The second angle takes an individual rights-centred approach and is protected from the perspective of Article 47 of the Charter.[106] The third angle links specifically to the preliminary reference procedure under Article 267 TFEU, and relates to the question of admissibility of a question referred to the ECJ ('can I talk to this body at all?').[107] While the conditions for independence overlap for all of those angles,[108] given that Articles 19(1) TEU, 47 Charter and 267 TFEU all tackle different aspects of the EU judicial architecture, all three of those angles will have to be satisfied for the resulting system of dispute settlement to be a 'mechanism [] capable of ensuring the full effectiveness of the rules of the European Union.'[109]

3.2 *Legal Basis*

Supposing the above framework would be acceptable for the design of an intra-EU investment court, the next question to turn to is the legal basis for that arrangement.

---

[105] See, in particular, the wording in the second subparagraph of Article 19(1) TEU, referring to the obligation on Member States to 'provide remedies sufficient to ensure effective legal protection in the fields covered by EU law.'

[106] See, in this regard, the language of Article 47 of the Charter, which protects the right to an effective remedy and a fair trial, and which refers to the entitlement to a fair and public hearing 'by an independent and impartial tribunal previously established by law.'

[107] The text of Article 267 TFEU does not specifically refer to the concept of independence of a 'court or tribunal'. However, that connection was established already in the early case-law of the ECJ in case 61/65, *G. Vaassen-Göbbels (a widow) v Management of the Beambtenfonds voor het Mijnbedrijf*, ECLI:EU:C:1966:39, p. 273 (introducing the essential characteristics of what can be considered a 'court or tribunal' of (what is now) Article 267 TFEU).

[108] See Opinion of Advocate General Bobek in Joined Cases C-748/19 to C-754/19, *Prokuratura Rejonowa w Mińsku Mazowieckim and Others*, ECLI:EU:C:2021:403, point 161 et seq (arguing that there is only one EU law principle of independence, which is addressed from different angles). That being said, the ECJ appears to have taken a softer approach as regards Article 267 TFEU; see, for instance, ECJ, case C-103/97, *Josef Köllensperger GmbH & Co. KG and Atzwanger AG v Gemeindeverband Bezirkskrankenhaus Schwaz*, ECLI:EU:C:1999:52, paras. 19 to 24 (finding that even though the condition of external independence appears not satisfied, jurisdiction under Article 267 TFEU can nonetheless be asserted, since it is 'not for the Court to infer that such a provision [of national law] is applied in a manner contrary to the Austria's constitution and the principles of a State governed by the rule of law').

[109] See Opinion 1/09 of the court, Agreement creating a Unified Patent Litigation System, ECLI: EU:C:2011:123, para. 82 (explaining that a system of dispute settlement common to the Member States must ensure 'the full effectiveness' of EU law).

In contrast with the UPCA, no singular legal basis of the Treaties provides for a hook as neatly designed as Article 118 TFEU. That provision specifically explains that, '[i]n the context of the establishment and functioning of the internal market, . . . [the EU legislator] shall establish measures for the creation of European intellectual property rights to provide uniform protection . . . [thereof] throughout the Union and for the setting up of centralised Union-wide authorisation, coordination and supervision arrangements.' However, although foreign direct investment falls within Article 207 TFEU, and thus the common commercial policy,[110] the free movement of capital falls within the Internal Market arena.[111]

That implies recourse to two possibilities. If remaining within the Treaty framework, the EU legislator could resort to like integration through the fall-back legal basis contained in Article 114 TFEU. Alternatively, a limited number of Member States could resort to 'enhanced cooperation', as laid down in Article 20 TEU, particularly where there appears that no uniform line can be reached. Naturally, a detailed discussion of the limits of either procedure escapes the scope of this contribution. However, for the purposes of completeness, both options will be discussed briefly.

First, on Article 114 TFEU. That provision appears the most likely legal basis for a self-standing intra-EU investment court given that it acts to achieve the aim expressed by Article 26 TFEU: a functioning internal market, including in the free movement of capital. It thus is in particular aimed at removing divergences between the laws of the Member States.[112] In its 2020 Inception Impact Assessment, the Commission appears to hint precisely at that issue, and thus the likely use of Article 114 TFEU, when it explains that '[d]iverging levels of investment protection in the different Member States may have a negative impact on the free movement of capital and investment flows in the internal market' and that therefore '[m]easures taken at EU level can ensure more consistent protection across Member States, thereby improving the functioning of the internal market[.]'[113] While those explanations, in themselves, may not satisfy the burden for proving a need for recourse to Article 114 TFEU, for all effects and purposes, it appears feasible that that provision could

[110] See, in this regard, Opinion 2/15 of the Court, EU-Singapore Free Trade Agreement, ECLI:EU:C:2017:376, paras. 80, 81, 109 and 110 (defining (foreign) direct investment as 'investments of any kind made by natural or legal persons which serve to establish or maintain lasting and direct links between the persons providing the capital and the undertakings to which that capital is made available in order to carry out an economic activity', and thus finding the Union competent to approve that part of the EU-Singapore agreement itself).

[111] See Article 26(2) TFEU (listing the free movement of capital among those elements which constitute the Internal Market). The free movement of capital is then contained in Articles 63 *et seq.* TFEU.

[112] See, for instance, ECJ, case C-300/89, *Commission of the European Communities v. Council of the European Communities*, ECLI:EU:C:1991:244, paras. 15 and 23 (explaining that Article 114 TFEU can be used to harmonize measures to 'deal with disparities between the laws of the Member States', and thereby may distort competition within the Internal Market).

[113] European Commission (2020), p. 3.

act as a legal basis for any EU law measure establishing an intra-EU investment court.

Second, 'enhanced cooperation', within the meaning of Article 20 TEU. That procedure is essentially a way of advancing the interest and integration of the Union where the objectives of such integration cannot be attained by the Union itself. That may be necessary especially in areas where diverging views on the direction or content of a Union initiative would otherwise not be bridged in the foreseeable future.[114] The UPCA is one example of such enhanced cooperation. There, recourse to Article 20 TEU was made given that there remained 'insurmountable difficulties' as regards translation arrangements for that agreement.[115] However, the conditions for enhanced cooperation are strict and thus not a 'carte blanche' to use the EU legal and institutional framework to push integration in one or more directions. Above all, the Council must conclude 'that the objectives of such cooperation cannot be attained within a reasonable period by the Union as a whole'.[116] In response, it must grant a sufficiently clear and specific authorisation regarding the radius of action.[117] The implementation of said authorization is then subject to a number of conditions.[118]

---

[114] See, for instance, Council Decision 2013/52/EU of 22 January 2013 authorising enhanced cooperation in the area of financial transaction tax, OJ L 22 of 25/01/2013, p. 11, recital 5 (explaining that the 'persistent and essential differences in opinion as regards the need to establish a common system of [financial transaction tax] at the Union level . . . will not receive unanimous support within the Council in the foreseeable future').

[115] See Council Decision 2011/167/EU of 10 March 2011 authorising enhanced cooperation in the area of the creation of unitary patent protection, OJ 2011 L 76, p. 53, recital 4 (explaining that, at a Council meeting, 'it was recorded that there was no unanimity to go ahead with the proposed Regulation on the translation arrangements' and that thus 'insurmountable difficulties existed, making unanimity impossible at the time and in the foreseeable future').

[116] Article 20(2) TEU.

[117] The latter requirement does not arise from the Treaties but is mentioned by Kellerbauer as one of the defining features of such an authorization. See, in this regard, Kellerbauer (2019), Article 20 TEU, p. 193. Note also that, in the decision granting said authorization, the Council need not provide further information with regard to the possible content of the system by the participants in the enhanced cooperation in question; see ECJ, joined cases C-274/11 and C-295/11, *Kingdom of Spain and Italian Republic v. Council of the European Union*, ECLI:EU:C:2013:240, para. 92.

[118] Those are as follows. First, that the cooperation remains within the scope of the authorization (see, to that effect, Article 329(1) TFEU); second, that it stays within the Union's non-exclusive competence (see Article 20(1), first subparagraph, TEU); third, that it 'aim[s] to further the objectives of the Union, protect its interests and reinforce the integration process' (Article 20(1), second subparagraph, TEU); fourth, that it complies with EU law (see the first paragraph of Article 326 TFEU); fifth, that it does not 'damage . . . the internal market and discriminat[e] and distort[] . . . competition' (see ECJ, joined cases C-274/11 and C-295/11, *Kingdom of Spain and Italian Republic v. Council of the European Union*, ECLI:EU:C:2013:240, para. 76) subscribing the more lengthy wording of the second paragraph contained in the second paragraph of Article 326 TFEU; sixth, that it respects 'the competences, rights and obligations of non-participating Member States' (see Article 327 TFEU); and seventh, that it remains open to all Member States (see Article 328(1) TFEU).

For the purposes of the present discussion, it is neither necessary nor feasible to enter into all of those requirements. There are simply too many variables under the enhanced cooperation procedure. However, it appears as if one of the foundational pillars for recourse to that procedure is satisfied: the presence of a competence shared between the Member States and the Union, the objective of which could be advanced through further integration by means of a common system dispute settlement. Putting aside for now the fact that, at the external plane, the ECJ has deemed investor-State dispute settlement a shared competence,[119] it is only logical that if the Union and the Member States share the competence to regulate the substantive parts of free movement of capital, then it must follow that the *means* of achieving that objective are likewise covered by the same competence. After all, the latter is merely accessory in the achievement of the former.[120] Furthermore, as the Commission explained in its Inception Impact Assessment, intra-EU 'investors . . . can be confronted with difficulties in enforcing their rights and obtaining a remedy'.[121] As such, an intra-EU investment court, aimed at improving the enforcement of investment rules would assist in deeper integration of the Capital Markets Union, and thus satisfy the overall objective of resorting to enhanced cooperation in the first place.

4 A 'Compromis' to Confer Jurisdiction on a 'Third' Body

The second 'outside' possibility of regulating dispute settlement in the intra-EU sphere would be to resort to a 'compromis'[122] between the Member States to 'dock' the resolution of intra-EU investment disputes to a body or institution that does not form part of the Treaties. That policy idea, too, was raised in the 2016 Non-Paper. Thusly, the Member States would provisionally decide, by means of an international agreement, on a 'compromis' dedicated to intra-EU investment disputes, allocating those disputes to a particular forum.[123] In the 2016 Non-Paper, the Permanent Court of Arbitration ('PCA'), as established intergovernmental organization that provides

---

[119] See, in this regard, Opinion 2/15 of the Court, EU-Singapore Free Trade Agreement, ECLI:EU:C:2017:376, paras. 276 and 292 to 293) (finding an investor-State dispute settlement system in an EU agreement of such a nature as to require joint conclusion).

[120] See, by analogy, Opinion 2/15 of the Court, EU-Singapore Free Trade Agreement, ECLI:EU:C:2017:376, para. 505 and the case-law cited) (explaining that where the Union holds the competence as regards the substantive provisions of an international agreement that it also enjoys the competence as regards its dispute settlement).

[121] European Commission (2020), p. 2.

[122] Within the meaning of Article 52 of the 1907 Convention for the Pacific Settlement of International Disputes (UKTS 6 (1971) Cmnd. 4575).

[123] See, in particular, General Secretariat of the Council of the European Union (2016), point 13, which explains that '[t]he Delegations are however of the view that a permanent court system, either through the ECJ or a specific mechanism modeled on the Unified Patent Court, would in principle be more in line with the EU's new trade policy on investor-to-State dispute settlement and should therefore be envisaged as a longer term perspective. Accordingly, the "Compromis" relying

services to arbitral tribunals for the settlement of international disputes, was considered the most appropriate addressee of such a 'compromis'.[124] That institution (or one more closely akin to that of an established dispute resolution body) would then be tasked with the resolution of those disputes as well as to 'directly address requests for preliminary rulings to the ECJ'.[125]

The compatibility of that approach is easily discarded. Generally speaking, Article 344 TFEU prevents the Member States from agreeing to a method of dispute settlement 'other than those provided for' in the Treaties.[126] That includes assignments by means of ad hoc or standing 'compromis' (the most famous of the latter type of assignment being the Dispute Settlement Understanding of the WTO Agreement), if the area of dispute settlement falls within the scope of the Treaties.[127] For that 'Article 344 TFEU prohibition' to be triggered, what is required is that 'a significant part' of the dispute relates to the interpretation or application of EU law.[128] That being said, in the light of the case-law in *Achmea*, it could even be argued that the mere *potential* of a 'significant part' of the dispute relating to EU law could trigger Article 344 TFEU.[129] A low bar, in other words. Given that the resolution of intra-EU investment claims almost certainly raises questions of EU law,[130] it would appear that Article 344 TFEU prevents any assignment, by means of 'compromis', of intra-EU investment disputes for exclusive resolution by the PCA.

---

on the PCA, as envisaged above, could be a provisional scheme that would be subsequently replaced by a permanent solution for investment disputes within the internal market.'

[124] For completeness, it should be added that the PCA is not an ideal choice of example as, first, it is strictly speaking not an established court or tribunal (but rather, for want of a better description, a 'secretariat with a tribunal service attached to it'), and, second, its membership is also open to third States.

[125] 2016 Non-Paper, point 14.

[126] Although there is disagreement on whether an assignment of disputes not directly concerning the interpretation and application of the Treaties (which is the language of Article 344 TFEU), but merely relating to their 'subject matter' (referred to as the baseline for Article 273 TFEU to apply) is compatible with that general prohibition of Article 344 TFEU. To that effect, see Opinion of Advocate General Mengozzi in case C-648/15, *Republic of Austria v. Federal Republic of Germany*, ECLI:EU:C:2017:311, points 41 to 42 (arguing that Article 273 TFEU permits, 'on the basis of a special agreement, the extension of the Court's jurisdiction to disputes which relate not to EU law . . . but to international law, provided that the area of international law in question relates to the subject matter of the Treaties').

[127] In fact, it appears that the ECJ has gone so far as finding that, upon accession to the Union, the Member States parted with their international law competence to agree to a 'compromis' incompatible with the judicial framework of Article 19(1) TEU. See, by analogy, ECJ, case C-638/19 P, *European Commission v. European Food SA and Others*, ECLI:EU:C:2022:50, para. 139 (finding that 'with effect from Romania's accession to the European Union, the system of judicial remedies provided for by the EU and FEU Treaties replaced that arbitration procedure, the consent given to that effect by Romania, from that time onwards, lacked any force').

[128] ECJ, case C-459/03, *Commission of the European Communities v. Ireland*, ECLI:EU:C:2006:345, para. 135.

[129] See the references in footnote 57 above.

[130] See text after footnote 86 above.

Need that be the end of the line? Possibly not. What if one were to return to the possibility of designating said dispute resolution body as a specialized (and 'common') court tasked by (some of) the Member States with the resolution of intra-EU investment disputes? It is at least arguable that such a consideration would paint a more favourable picture. Thus, the Member States could simply enter into a 'compromis', with the added twist that they designate, at the same time, under that agreement and their national laws, the dispute settlement body at issue as 'common' between them for the purposes of a specific class of classes (i.e. intra-EU investment disputes). Legally, that approach would not be much different than that adopted for the remodelled UPC, supposing that it complies with the other conditions for a 'court or tribunal' under Article 267 TFEU and has its membership limited to the Member States.[131] Thereby, the chosen dispute settlement body would become the exclusive (or parallel) jurisdiction for intra-EU investment disputes. Granted, the conditions discussed in this contribution[132] would also have to be satisfied for that type of system to fit neatly into the EU judicial system. In other words, one returns to the discussion surrounding the qualitative conditions for commonality, and their limits. As discussed, those are yet to be further explored in the case-law of the Court, even if can be argued that the Member States should hold quite some discretion in the design of such a system. The bottom line, however, is that, legally, the 'docking' of intra-EU investment disputes to the PCA does not appear precluded if that court is sufficiently 'common' between the (participating) Member States. And yet, whether that idea represents a politically-feasible alternative in the first place is an entirely different question, possibly to be resolved during those famous late night meetings at Council level.

5 Conclusion

In theory, *Achmea* marked the end to the dubious temples of intra-EU investment arbitration. In practice, the underlying grievances remain.[133] The resulting silence on how to resolve that impasse is deafening, not least given that national time limits may, on the face of it, appear to preclude access to national courts, even if investors sought protection otherwise.[134] What to do then? In line with the mantra '*est maître*

[131] See text at footnote 60 et seq. above.

[132] See text from footnote 66 to 121 above.

[133] As is also evidenced by the sheer number of arbitral tribunals which declined to accept the intra-EU objection lodged by the Commission and (most) 'home' Member States of the EU investor at issue. See, *ex multis*, the recent decision of 19 August 2022 on Spain's second request for reconsideration of the 'intra-EU objection' in *Infracapital F1 S.à r.l. and Infracapital Solar B.V v. Kingdom of Spain* (ICSID Case No. ARB/16/18).

[134] Although, as is clear from the case-law of the ECJ, national procedural provisions must give way to the principle of effectiveness of EU law, and thus access to effective judicial protection. See, by analogy, ECJ, case C-869/19, *L v. Unicaja Banco SA*, ECLI:EU:C:2022:397, paras. 37 to

des lieux celui qui les organise', the Communication on the protection of intra-EU investment[135] and the Intra-EU Termination Agreement,[136] both issued in the wake of *Achmea,* certainly gaze at the functional continuity of (intra-EU) investment disputes under the umbrella of an EU law-compatible system of dispute settlement. However, how such continuity could be achieved remains essentially unexplored.

This contribution has sought to show that there is little reason why that should remain the case. Like Dürer's woodcut, the 2016 Non-Paper stands as a strong preliminary outline of how the institutional future of intra-EU investment could look like. Of those options, a self-standing intra-EU investment court, akin to that pursued by the UPCA appears a (legally) feasible and an institutionally attractive option, both for investors and the Member States, for the future of intra-EU investment disputes.[137] However, as has also been explained, under the current state of the case-law, it even appears possible that such a self-standing dispute settlement body may be established by 'docking' intra-EU investment disputes onto an existing institution outside the EU judicial system, if the conditions of 'commonality' of such a court (arising originally from *Parfums Christian Dior*) and the related conditions under Article 267 TFEU are satisfied. The resulting system would also address (real or presumed) concerns of 'domestic court bias'. It would equally lay to rest those voices that deem the case-law of the CJEU too rigid to allow for 'new' modes of dispute settlement.

One loose end remains. After the above discussion, the reader will be curious to know what happened to the rhinoceros, which Dürer famously depicted. In 1515, King Manuel I of Portugal graciously decided to send it on as a gift to Pope Leo X. The animal drowned when the boat it was travelling in sunk en route.

---

39 (finding that, even where a consumer did not bring proceedings in time against an unfair contractual term, barring such claims later on by reason of national time limits render the protection of EU-law-based rights impossible or excessively difficult, and thereby undermine the principle of effectiveness). See also Agreement for the termination of Bilateral Investment Treaties between the Member States of the European Union, OJ L 169 of 29/05/2020, p. 1 ('Intra-EU Termination Agreement'), Article 10, where the same principle is specified.

[135] European Commission (2018), p. 28: 'The Commission strives to increase the effectiveness of the enforcement system in the EU, including actions to support administrative capacity building or to strengthen justice systems, and to tackle breaches of EU law by national authorities.'

[136] Intra-EU Termination Agreement (referring, inter alia, to the ECOFIN Council conclusions of 11 July 2017, and the need to 'intensify discussions without undue delay with the aim of better ensuring complete, strong and effective protection of investments within the European Union … [including] the assessment of existing processes and mechanisms of dispute resolution as well as the need and, if the need is ascertained, the means to create new or improve relevant existing tools and mechanisms under Union law').

[137] And yet, as Austria, Finland, France, Germany and the Netherlands themselves conclude in relation to such a court, 'this option, while providing for the technically most well-rounded solution, would however most probably not be reached within a reasonable timeframe.' See, General Secretariat of the Council of the European Union (2016), point 12.

References

British Institute of International and Comparative Law, Allen & Overy (2021) Costs, damages and duration in investor-state arbitration, 02/06/2021. https://www.allenovery.com/en-gb/global/news-and-insights/publications/costs-damages-and-duration-in-investor-state-arbitration

Brown LN, Kennedy T (1994) The Court of Justice of the European Union, 4th edn. Sweet & Maxwell, London

Ćapeta T (2016) EU judiciary in need of reform? In: Łazowski A, Blockmans S (eds) Research handbook on EU institutional law. Edward Elgar, Cheltenham, pp 263–288

Council of the European Union (2016) General Secretariat, Trade Policy Committee (Services and Investment), Intra-EU Investment Treaties Non-paper from Austria, Finland, France, Germany and the Netherlands (7 April 2016)

Court of Justice of the European Union (2014) Response to the invitation from the Italian Presidency of the Council to present new proposals in order to facilitate the task of securing agreement within the Council on the procedures for increasing the number of judges at the General Court, 13/10/2014. Available at: https://curia.europa.eu/jcms/upload/docs/application/pdf/2015-05/8-en-reponse-274.pdf

Court of Justice of the European Union (2019) The General Court of the European Union prepares to welcome additional Judges, Press release No 111/19, 19/09/2019. Available at: https://curia.europa.eu/jcms/upload/docs/application/pdf/2019-09/cp190111en.pdf

Dehousse F (2013) The unified court on patents: the new oxymoron of European Law. Egmont Paper No. 60, 10/2013. Available at: https://www.egmontinstitute.be/app/uploads/2013/10/ep60.pdf?type=pdf

Dehousse F (2016) The reform of the EU Courts (II): abandoning the management approach by doubling the general court, Egmont Paper 83, 03/2016. Available at: https://www.egmontinstitute.be/app/uploads/2016/03/ep83.pdf.pdf?type=pdf

European Commission (1988) Establishment of a Court of First Instance, Preliminary guidelines adopted by the Commission for the preparation of an opinion on the proposal put forward by the Court of Justice for a Council Decision establishing a Court of First Instance (CFI) and amending the Statutes of the Court of Justice (SEC (88) 366 final)

European Commission (2018) Communication from the Commission to the European Parliament and the Council, Protection of Intra-EU investment (COM/2018/547 final)

European Commission (2020) Inception impact assessment, regulation establishing a framework for intra-EU investment protection, facilitation and dispute resolution (ARES(2020)2716046)

European Commission (2022a) Stepping up trade agreements enforcement: the European Commission publishes pool of individuals eligible for appointment as arbitrators and TSD experts, 23/06/2022. Available at: https://policy.trade.ec.europa.eu/news/stepping-trade-agreements-enforcement-european-commission-publishes-pool-individuals-eligible-2022-06-23_en

European Commission (2022b) Sincere cooperation and primacy of EU law: commission refers UK to EU Court of Justice over a UK Judgment allowing enforcement of an arbitral award granting illegal State aid, 09/02/2022. Available at: https://ec.europa.eu/commission/presscorner/detail/en/IP_22_802

General Court of the European Union (2009) President of the Court of First Instance Marc Jaeger, Is it time for reform? The Court of First Instance of the European Communities is celebrating its 20th anniversary, 09/2009. Available at: https://curia.europa.eu/jcms/jcms/P_52392

House of Lords (2011) European Union Committee, The Workload of the Court of Justice of the European Union, 29/03/2011. Available at: https://publications.parliament.uk/pa/ld201011/ldselect/ldeucom/128/12810.htm#a38

Jacobs M, Münder M, Richter B (2019) Subject matter specialization of European Union Jurisdiction in the preliminary rulings procedure. Ger Law J 20(8):1214–1231

Jaeger T (2012) All back to square one? - An assessment of the latest proposals for a patent and court for the internal market and possible alternatives. Int Rev Intellect Prop Compet Law 43(3): 286–308

Kellerbauer M (2019) Article 20 TEU. In: Kellerbauer M, Klamert M, Tomkin J (eds) The EU treaties and the charter of fundamental rights: a commentary. Oxford University Press, Oxford, pp 192–196

Lenaerts K, Gutierrez-Fons J (2018) The European Union: a constitutional perspective. In: Schütze R, Tridimas T (eds) Oxford principles of European Union Law - Volume I: The European Union Legal Order. Oxford University Press, Oxford, pp 103–141

Montag F, Hoseinian F (2012) The forthcoming reform of the General Court of the European Union - potential specialisation within the General Court. In: Hawk BE (ed) International antitrust law & policy: Fordham competition law 2012. Juris, New York, pp 83–89

Moskvan D (2022) Protection of foreign investments in an intra-EU context. Edward Elgar, Cheltenham

Naômé C (2018) Appeals before the Court of Justice of the European Union. Oxford University Press, Oxford, p 2018

Öberg U, Ali M, Sabouret P (2017) On specialisation of chambers at the General Court. In: Derlén M, Lindholm J (eds) The Court of Justice of the European Union: multidisciplinary perspectives. Hart, London, pp 211–224

Paschalidis P (2020) The pressing need for a European investment court, 10/02/2020. Available at: https://globalarbitrationreview.com/the-pressing-need-european-investment-court

Paulsson J (1995) Arbitration without privity. ICSID Rev For Invest Law J 10(2):232–257

Rosas A (2017) Court Procedures for cooperation between the Court of Justice of the European Union and national courts - contribution by Mr. Allan Rosas. Court of Justice of the European Union, European Justice Network, A guarantee of high-quality justice: proceedings of the meeting held on the occasion of the 60th anniversary of the treaties of Rome, 27/03/2017. Available at: https://op.europa.eu/en/publication-detail/-/publication/1fe5352d-cb4b-11e7-a5d5-01aa75ed71a1/language-en

Rozas JCF (2001) Le rôle des juridictions étatiques devant l'arbitrage commercial international. Académie de Droit International de la Haye/Hague Academy of International Law Recueil des cours, Collected Courses, vol 290

Schima B (2019) Article 257 TFEU. In: Kellerbauer M, Klamert M, Tomkin J (eds) The EU treaties and the charter of fundamental rights: a commentary. Oxford University Press, Oxford, pp 1770–1772

Tilmann W, Passmann C (2018) Article 24 sources of law. In: Winfried T, Passmann C (eds) Oxford University Press, Oxford. pp 467–577

Union Syndicale Fédérale des Services Publics Européens et Internationaux (2015) Resolution on the recasting of the EU's judicial framework and the planned abolition of the Civil Service Tribunal, 01/05/2015. Available at: https://unionsyndicale.eu/wp-content/uploads/2021/05/Resolution-TFP-EN.pdf

Vandersanden G (2015) The real test–how to contribute to a better justice: the experience of the civil service tribunal. In: Bobek M (ed) Selecting Europe's Judges: a critical review of the appointment procedures to the European Courts. Oxford University Press, Oxford, pp 86–94

Nicolaj Kuplewatzky is a legal secretary (référendaire) in the chambers of Advocate General Ćapeta at the Court of Justice of the European Union and a lecturer (Dozent) at the University of Cologne. Prior to joining the Court, he served as a member of the Legal Service of the European Commission with a special focus on EU economic law, including intra-EU investment arbitration. Nicolaj completed his studies at the universities of Buckingham, Tsinghua, Hong Kong and Columbia and is a member of the editorial and review boards of the Global Trade and Customs Journal and the Revista General de Derecho Europeo. He is admitted as an attorney-at-law in New York State.

Intra-EU Investor State Contracts After PL Holdings

Patricia Nacimiento

Contents

P. Nacimiento (✉)
Herbert Smith Freehills LLP, Frankfurt, Germany
e-mail: patricia.nacimiento@hsf.com

M. Bungenberg, A. Reinisch (eds.), *New Frontiers for EU Investment Policy*, Special Issue, https://doi.org/10.1007/978-3-031-41977-5_9

1 Introduction

The decision in *Republic of Poland v. PL Holdings*[1] ("PL Holdings") marks another considerable milestone in the Court of Justice of the European Union's ("CJEU") backlash against investment law disputes between an investor of an EU Member State and another EU Member State ("intra-EU dispute").

The decision has—apart from the academic discussion on the underlying issues—considerable implications for investment law practice within the EU. The aim of this assessment is to shed light on the new challenges regarding intra-EU investments and investment disputes from the viewpoint of a practitioner.

The decision in *PL Holdings* reflects the current status of a longer development marked by certain milestones, dealing first with Bilateral Investment Treaties ("BIT") and subsequently the Energy Charter Treaty ("ECT"). Delving into this topic requires some context. It is inevitable to look into the past so as to see how we got here and where we may go from here.

In the beginning, it is always an important exercise to step back and look at the full picture, in particular at broader interests and the reasons behind the current developments. Often, when dealing with complex issues, it is crucial to remember the very basics. In this context, the very basic question goes back to the beginning of investment protection: In the 1950s, the need and wish of certain States to attract foreign investments led to the need and wish of other States to protect their nationals investing in foreign States. This led to the development of BITs and sometimes even Multilateral Investment Treaties, such as the ECT.[2] Meaningful protection was needed and this led to the inclusion of an extraordinary remedy into such Treaties, namely the right of an investor to sue the host State. This in turn led to further developments both in terms of the substantive and procedural protection afforded. It created a body of case law and a full system of protection.[3]

In the past, any company in an EU Member State, which felt that its investment in another EU Member State had been impaired, could invoke a BIT or the ECT. These treaties regularly include arbitration clauses, to allow for investor-state dispute settlement ("ISDS") before arbitral tribunals. From a practitioner's point of view, this constituted an adequate system of protection, raising the dispute to an international level and placing it in the hands of tribunals chosen by the parties. Whether the CJEU has or has not successfully incapacitated this system of protection will be explored over the course of this assessment. For this reason, the focus will remain on the *PL Holdings* decision and Intra-EU Investor State Contracts, i.e. contracts with arbitration clauses that have been individually concluded between the investor and the host State, instead of relying on a standing offer to arbitrate in investment treaties.

---

[1] Republic of Poland v. PL Holdings Sàrl, Judgment of the Court (Grand Chamber) (26 October 2021) Case C-109/20.

[2] Dolzer and Schreuer (2012), p. 5.

[3] Dolzer and Schreuer (2012), pp. 8 et. seq.

2 Milestones

A number of milestones led to the latest development and will be briefly described below.

2.1 *Achmea*

The ISDS system was significantly changed by the CJEU's decision in the case of *Slovak Republic v. Achmea B.V.*[4] ("Achmea"). Simply put, the effect of the CJEU's decision in *Achmea* is essentially a finding that the investor-state arbitration provisions of approximately 200 intra-EU BITs are incompatible with EU law. It is important to note that the judgment refers to provisions found in "*international agreement[s] concluded between Member States*", and thus did not touch the validity of arbitration clauses in BITs between EU Member States and non-Member States.

2.2 *The Aftermath of Achmea*

The *Achmea* decision invoked a wide variety of reactions, ranging from immediate declarations that the ISDS system was abolished, to total denial of any implications outside the Dutch-Slovakian-BIT. It is fair to say that tribunals have largely continued to find that the CJEU limited its ruling to BITs concluded between EU Member States, and left it open for investors to initiate arbitral proceedings under other international instruments that were not solely intra-EU BITs, such as the ECT.[5]

On 5 May 2020, a multilateral treaty to terminate intra-EU BITs was concluded by a majority (23) of the Member States of the EU ("Termination Agreement") (non-signatories include: Austria, Finland, Ireland and Sweden).[6] The Termination Agreement entered into force on 29 August 2020, following its ratification by Denmark and Hungary. ISDS arbitration provisions of the terminated intra-EU BITs could no longer serve as a legal basis for new investor-state arbitration proceedings. The Termination Agreement contains transitional measures that address pending intra-EU investor-state disputes. However, the Termination Agreement

---

[4] Slovak Republic v. Achmea B.V., Judgment of the Court (Grand Chamber) (6 March 2018) Case C-284/16.

[5] See for example, Sun Reserve Luxco Holdings Sàrl, Sun Reserve Luxco Holdings II Sàrl and Sun Reserve Luxco Holdings III Sàrl v. Italy, Final Award (25 March 2020) SCC Case No. 132/2016, para. 428 et seq.

[6] Agreement for the Termination of Bilateral Investment Treaties between the Member States of the European Union (29 May 2020) EU L 169/1.

does not concern the ECT. In its preamble it states that the issue of intra-EU investor-state arbitration under the ECT will be addressed "*at a later stage*".

2.3 *Komstroy*

Again, this changed with the decision in *Republic of Moldova v. Komstroy* ("Komstroy"). On 2 September 2021, the CJEU found that, under EU law, Article 26 ECT is not applicable to intra-EU investment disputes, effectively agreeing with the opinion of the Advocate General.[7] This meant that *inter alia* investors' participation in the so-called "solar claims" against Spain, Italy, the Czech Republic, and other Member States, lost an important line of argument. Previously, investors regularly argued that the *Achmea* jurisprudence could not be applied to claims brought under the ECT as it was a multilateral treaty with extra-EU Member States.

3 Reactions of Courts and Arbitral Tribunals

The jurisprudence of the CJEU did not only force arbitral tribunals to cope with the Court's findings, also domestic courts had to consider the leading case law of the CJEU.

3.1 *Arbitral Tribunals*

Shortly after the CJEU's decision, a number of arbitral tribunals were faced with renewed intra-EU objections on the basis of *Komstroy*. Petitions by EU States asking tribunals to reconsider previous jurisdictional rulings have been largely unsuccessful with one exception:

- In November 2021, the tribunal in *Landesbank Baden-Württemberg and others v Kingdom of Spain*[8] declined to amend an earlier decision, finding that it was not hindered by EU law to hear an intra-EU claim under the ECT. The tribunal had formed the view that its decision was now *res judicata* and its finding that it had jurisdiction would not have been altered by the CJEU's decision in *Komstroy*.
- The tribunal in *Mathias Kruck and others v. Kingdom of Spain*[9] dismissed the Respondents Request for Reconsideration of the Tribunal Decision, rejecting the

[7] Republic of Moldova v Komstroy, Judgment of the CJEU (Grand Chamber) (2 September 2021) Case C-741/19.

[8] Landesbank Baden-Württemberg and others v Kingdom of Spain, ICSID Case No. ARB/15/45.

[9] Mathias Kruck and others v. Kingdom of Spain, ICSID Case No ARB/15/23.

finding of the CJEU because of the discriminatory structure. The tribunal recognises a clash of *Grundnormen*, because the CJEU made itself clear that ECT arbitration tribunals are not part of the EU legal order, but their role and authority is established by an international treaty. The tribunal concluded that the solution lies in the hands of the Contracting Parties of the ECT.

- In December 2021 the tribunal in *Rockhopper v. Italian Republic*[10] joined this growing trend of ECT tribunals dismissing requests for reconsideration of the respondents' intra-EU objections following *Komstroy*.
- Drawing the same conclusion, the tribunal in *Cavalum v. Spain*[11] applied its initial reasoning to the *Komstroy* Decision, emphasizing that Spain had given unconditional consent to arbitration, that the new decision did not affect its jurisdiction under international law and the fact that EU law is at least in part international law does not change this conclusion.
- The same goes for the Respondent's Request for Reconsideration in the recent case of *Infracapital v. Kingdom of Spain* [12] where the tribunal explicitly rejected the separate and different treatment for intra-EU disputes and non-intra-EU disputes. It found that "*nothing in the ECT gives an ECT tribunal the authority to disregard or modify the explicit provisions of the ECT and decline jurisdiction on the basis of a Contracting Party's status or its obligations under a different legal order*". All in all, the tribunal deemed the *Komstroy* judgement irrelevant to its rulings on jurisdiction and on liability.
- The only exception was in *Green Power v. Spain.*[13] In this case, the tribunal considered that, in assessing its jurisdiction, Article 26(6) of the ECT and rules of international and domestic law (including EU law) were relevant irrespective of the characterisation of EU law as international or national law (e.g. given references in the ECT to Regional Economic Integration Organisation, declarations post ECT such as the termination of intra-EU arbitration agreements of 2019, and systematic integration of EU law pursuant to Article 31(3)(c) Vienna Convention on the Law of Treaties ("VCLT")). By resorting to EU law, including the *Achmea* and *Komstroy* decisions, the tribunal considered Spain's unilateral offer to arbitrate as invalid. Accordingly, the tribunal concluded that it lacked jurisdiction *ratione voluntatis*.
- The tribunals in *RWE v. the Netherlands*[14] and *Uniper v. the Netherlands*[15] both issued provisional measures orders, declining to order the Netherlands to pursue

[10] Rockhopper Italia S.p.A., Rockhopper Mediterranean Ltd., and Rockhopper Exploration Plc v. Italian Republic, ICSID Case No. ARB/17/14.

[11] Cavalum v. Spain, ICSID Case No. ARB/15/34.

[12] Infracapital v. Kingdom of Spain, ICSID Case No. ARB/16/18.

[13] Green Power Partners K/S, SCE Solar Don Benito APS v Kingdom of Spain, Award (16 June 2022) SCC Case No. 2016/135.

[14] RWE AG and RWE Eemshaven Holding II BV v. Kingdom of the Netherlands, ICSID Case No. ARB/21/4.

[15] Uniper SE, Uniper Benelux Holding B.V. and Uniper Benelux N.V. v. Kingdom of the Netherlands, ICSID Case No. ARB/21/22.

their challenge of the arbitral tribunal before the Higher District Court of Cologne due to the lack of a valid arbitration agreement. Although the tribunals declined the request on the merits, they have *prima facie* jurisdiction over the dispute and the claimants had a "prima facie right to pursue arbitration".

3.2 Courts

Domestic courts appear divided in two categories: courts of the EU Member States, on the one hand, and courts of non-EU Member States on the other hand. Given the applicability of EU law to the first group, it is safe to assume that those courts would likely be cautious and set aside or refuse to enforce awards based on intra-EU investment arbitration agreements.

- In France, the Paris Court of Appeal set aside the award in Slot Group a.s. v. Republic of Poland[16] and the award in Strabag SE, Raiffeisen Centrobank AG and Syrena Immobilien Holding AG v. Republic of Poland[17] because they were based on intra-EU investment arbitration clauses.
- In Germany, the Federal Supreme Court set aside the award in Achmea following the CJEU's preliminary ruling.[18] It also confirmed a lower court decision holding that an intra-EU arbitration (based on a bilateral investment treaty and not the ECT) was inadmissible. [19]
- In Sweden, the Nacka District Court in Stockholm refused to enforce the award rendered in Micula v. Romania, given the EU principle of sincere cooperation with respect to the EU Commission's decision on State Aid, should the award be paid.[20]
- Also in Micula, the Court of Cassation of Luxembourg overturned the appeal court ruling and decided that the award could not be enforced, given that the

[16] Judgment of the Paris Court of Appeal (19 April 2022) Case 49/2022, regarding the decision rendered in Slot Group a.s. v. Republic of Poland, Award (3 February 2020) PCA Case No. 2017-10.

[17] Judgment of the Paris Court of Appeal (19 April 2022) Case 49/2022, regarding the decision rendered in Strabag SE, Raiffeisen Centrobank AG and Syrena Immobilien Holding AG v. Republic of Poland, Partial Award (4 March 2020) ICSID Case No. ADHOC/15/1.

[18] Decision of the Federal Court of Justice of Germany (31 October 2018) Case No. I ZB 2/15, regarding the decision rendered in Achmea B.V. (formerly Eureko B.V.) v. The Slovak Republic, Award, (7 December 2012), PCA Case No. 2008-13.

[19] Decision of the Federal Court of Justice (17 November 2021) Case No. I ZB 16/21, regarding the competence of the tribunal in Raiffeisen Bank International AG and Raiffeisen Bank Austria d.d. v. Croatia, PCA Case No. 2020-15.

[20] Decision of the Nacka District Court in Stockholm (23 Jan 2019) Ä 2550-17, regarding the decision rendered in Ioan Micula, Viorel Micula and others v. Romania (I), Final Award (11 December 2013) ICSID Case No. ARB/05/20.

arbitration clause under the treaty was nullified by Romania's accession to the EU.[21]

- However, courts outside the EU do not always pay deference to the intra-EU objection. For instance, the Supreme Court of the United Kingdom lifted a stay on enforcement considering that the EU principle of sincere cooperation did not apply as the UK had a prior obligation under the ICSID Convention to enforce the award issued in the Micula case.[22]
- Similarly, the United States Court of Appeals for the District of Columbia Circuit confirmed the lower court's decision on allowing enforcement on the Micula case.[23]

German Courts, in general, have been quick to adapt to the jurisprudence of the CJEU, as can be seen by the decisions of the Federal Supreme Court. The jurisdiction of German Courts regarding the question of whether the arbitration agreement is valid derives from Sect. 1032(2) of the German Code of Civil Procedure ("ZPO").[24] This application to the courts must be done before the tribunal is established. The provision has no equivalent in the UNCITRAL Model Law, which has been the basis for the specific arbitration chapter of the ZPO. However, the provision seeks to clarify any issues regarding the constitution or competence of the tribunal to prevent the parties from having to undergo potentially futile arbitration proceedings.

German Courts may also assume jurisdiction for the challenge of an arbitral tribunal under Sect. 1040(3) Sentence 2 ZPO.[25] Under the provision of Sect. 1040 ZPO, the arbitral tribunal may decide its jurisdiction. However, the decision of the tribunal can be challenged before a German court within a month. During the scrutiny period, the arbitral tribunal is not allowed to render an award.

The latest decision was rendered by the Higher Regional Court of Cologne, which held in its decision of 1 September 2022 that "*[f]rom the findings of the CJEU [. . .], it also follows that the arbitration clause in Art. 26 para. 2 c) in conjunction with para. (3) and (4) ECT for intra-EU disputes, i.e. a dispute between a Member State*

[21] Decision of the Court of Cassation of Luxembourg (14 July 2022) Case No. 45337, regarding the decision rendered in Ioan Micula, Viorel Micula and others v. Romania (I), Final Award (11 December 2013) ICSID Case No. ARB/05/20.

[22] Judgment of the Supreme Court of the United Kingdom (19 Feb 2020) Case No. [2020] UKSC 5, regarding the decision rendered in Ioan Micula, Viorel Micula and others v. Romania (I), Final Award (11 December 2013) ICSID Case No. ARB/05/20.

[23] Judgment of the United States Court of Appeals for the District of Columbia Circuit (19 May 2020) 17-cv-02332-APM, regarding the decision rendered in Ioan Micula, Viorel Micula and others v. Romania (I), Final Award (11 December 2013) ICSID Case No. ARB/05/20.

[24] Official English translation: "(2) Until the arbitral tribunal has been formed, a request may be filed with the court to have it determine the admissibility or inadmissibility of arbitral proceedings".

[25] Official English translation: "(3) Where the arbitral tribunal considers that it has jurisdiction, its decision on an objection raised pursuant to subsection (2) generally takes the form of an interlocutory decision. In this case, either party may request a court decision within 1 month of having received the written notice of the interlocutory decision. While such a request is pending, the arbitral tribunal may continue the arbitral proceedings and may make an award".

and an investor from another Member State, is incompatible with EU law and thus cannot be an effective legal basis for an arbitration obligation based on this provision."[26]

4 Pl Holdings

The decision in *PL Holdings* now deals with Investor State Contracts.

4.1 *Investor State Contracts and the Underlying Arbitration and Court Proceedings*

Whereas the *Achmea* and *Komstroy* decisions of the CJEU regarded the validity of standing arbitration offers in bi- and multilateral investment agreements involving EU Member States, the decision in *PL Holdings* dealt with a different angle and new arguments. The case turned on the validity of *ad hoc* arbitration clauses and whether they would allow—after *Achmea*—to continue an arbitration which was initiated on the basis of an arbitration clause in a BIT. This then leads to the wider issue of the validity of arbitration agreements in Investor State Contracts.

4.1.1 The Underlying Arbitration

Initially, a few words on the underlying arbitration:

PL Holdings is a Luxembourg company. Between 2010 and 2013 it acquired shares in two Polish banks. After these merged in 2013, PL Holdings held 99% of the shares of the new bank. In the same year, the Polish Financial Regulatory Commission withdrew the voting rights of PL Holdings and decided to sell the shares.

PL Holdings initiated arbitration proceedings under the rules of the Stockholm Chamber of Commerce ("SCC") on the basis of Article 9 of the BIT between Poland and the Belgian-Luxembourg Economic Union ("BLEU").

Poland objected to the jurisdiction of the tribunal on the basis that it violated EU law, however this was not raised by Poland in its first round of submissions in November 2011, but only in May 2016.

The tribunal found that it had jurisdiction and that Poland had violated the BIT by expropriating the investor's stake in a local bank.[27]

[26] Decision of the Higher Regional Court Cologne (1 September 2022), 19 SchH 14/21, para 44.

[27] PL Holdings Sàrl v. Republic of Poland, Final Award (28 August 2017) SCC Case No. V 2014/163.

The tribunal was seated in Stockholm and the Swedish courts became involved.

4.1.2 The Underlying Court Proceedings

Poland sought to set aside the award; however the Svea Court of Appeal rejected the request in 2019.[28] The Svea Court of Appeal sided with the arguments of the investor in relation to the underlying arbitration clause:

The investor argued that even if the clause in the BIT was invalid under the *Achmea* case law, Poland would have concluded an *ad hoc* arbitration clause with the same contents by actively participating in the arbitration without objecting to the jurisdiction of the tribunal until May 2016. Hence, the investor maintained that an *ad hoc* arbitration agreement was concluded between the parties to the dispute in the main proceedings, in accordance with Swedish law and the principles of commercial arbitration, having regard to the conduct of those parties. By making a request for arbitration, *PL Holdings* submitted an "*offer of arbitration*" in accordance with the same conditions as those laid down in the (invalid) arbitration clause of the respective BIT, and the Republic of Poland tacitly accepted that offer by refraining from validly and timely challenging the jurisdiction of the arbitral tribunal on the basis of that agreement.[29]

Particularly, the court found that although the *Achmea* decision may have been relevant to the dispute, Poland did not raise any intra-EU objections in time, thereby consenting to arbitrate the dispute on an *ad hoc* basis.

On appeal, the Swedish Supreme Court decided to refer the dispute to the CJEU for a preliminary ruling on whether an *ad hoc* arbitration clause would be incompatible with EU law.

4.2 The Decision by the CJEU

On 26 October 2021, the CJEU rendered its preliminary ruling.[30] The CJEU considered that "*by concluding an ad hoc arbitration agreement with the same content as that clause, would in fact entail a circumvention of the obligations arising for that Member State under the Treaties and, specifically, under Article 4(3) TEU and Articles 267 and 344 TFEU, as interpreted in the judgment of 6 March 2018, Achmea*".[31]

[28] Republic of Poland v. PL Holdings Sàrl, Judgment of Svea Court of Appeal on Set-Aside Application (22 February 2019) Case No. T 8538-17 and T 12033-17.

[29] Republic of Poland v. PL Holdings Sàrl, Judgment of Svea Court of Appeal on Set-Aside Application (22 February 2019) Case No. T 8538-17 and T 12033-17, Section 3.2.3.

[30] Republic of Poland v. PL Holdings Sàrl, Judgment of the Court (Grand Chamber) (26 October 2021) Case C-109/20.

[31] Ibid, para 47.

The CJEU reaches this conclusion on the assumption that Poland had failed to object to the jurisdiction of the tribunal on the basis of the *Achmea* case law in time. It further assumed that Poland had entered into an ad hoc arbitration clause by tacitly agreeing and that the ad hoc clause would be identical with the clause in the BIT.[32]

Against this background, the CJEU concludes that this results in a circumvention of the *Achmea* principles. The main reason is that the purpose of such an *ad hoc* clause is precisely to replace the invalid arbitration clause in the BIT so as to maintain its effect despite the invalidity of the BIT clause.[33]

The CJEU further held that the situation in *PL Holdings* is not just an individual case. Rather, a similar approach could be adopted in other situations where the application and interpretation of EU law is at stake.[34]

In addition, the CJEU held that the validity of a title could not depend on the behaviour of each individual party (i.e. failure to raise an intra-EU objection). Accordingly, this creates legal uncertainty for investment contracts, which might contain investment arbitration clauses and eventually could be categorised as "ad hoc" arbitration agreements.[35]

In this regard, the CJEU followed the opinion of Advocate General Kokott, who distinguished commercial contractual arbitration agreements between private parties, and those between investors and states. In the view of the Advocate General, commercial parties enter into contractual arbitration agreements out of their own autonomy and freely expressed wishes, operating on equal footing. In such disputes, it is not only the arbitration agreement but also the disputed legal relationship itself that is based on the autonomous will of the parties.[36]

However, this is not the case in Investor State Contracts. If a private party is subjected to a sovereign measure there can be no question of free will, at least for that party. For that reason alone, the Advocate General considered it unlikely that a Member State would subsequently enter into an arbitration agreement with the private party in relation to such a measure of its own free will. Even if the parties did so, Member States may not remove disputes relating to the sovereign application of EU law from the EU judicial system.[37]

The CJEU, however, did not follow another proposal of the Advocate General, namely, to declare arbitration clauses as compatible with EU law, if courts of the Member States could fully assess the arbitral award in relation to its compliance with EU law.

---

[32] Ibid, para 38, 50.

[33] Ibid, paras 47–49.

[34] Ibid, para 53.

[35] Ibid, para 51.

[36] Republic of Poland v. PL Holdings Sàrl, Opinion of Advocate General Kokott (22 April 2021) Case C-109/20, para 52.

[37] Republic of Poland v. PL Holdings Sàrl, Opinion of Advocate General Kokott (22 April 2021) Case C-109/20, para 54.

Rather, the CJEU found that such a constellation always leads to a circumvention of the *Achmea* principles since the purpose of ad hoc clauses is to replace an invalid ISDS clause in an Intra EU BIT.[38]

5 What Now?

So what follows from the findings of the CJEU in *PL Holdings*.

The CJEU found that an ad hoc clause replacing the invalid clause in the BIT is a circumvention of the *Achmea* principles and is therefore also invalid.

However, the broader question is: does this finding extend generally to Investor State Contracts containing an arbitration clause?

5.1 What are Investor State Contracts?

Investor State Contracts are, in contrast to bi- or multilateral investment treaties, not agreed between States but rather between an investor and the State, forming a contractual agreement which could also have been formed among commercial parties.[39] While such contracts can set out the rules for an investment endorsed by the State, it may also contain an arbitration agreement.

These are usually voluminous contracts which are entered into in advance of a certain investments. The arbitration clause, if contained, is usually tailored to the specific contract and situation. However, this constitutes the main difference between Investor State Contracts and arbitration clauses in investment treaties: It is not a general offer for a number of potential investors, but it is a very specific offer for one specific investor.

Another difference is that there is no arbitration initiated before and relying on an arbitration clause in an Intra EU BIT.

5.2 Interim Conclusion

To assess the current status of ISDS, it must be pointed out that the circumstances in *PL Holdings* were very specific and the CJEU does not generally deal with Investor State Contracts. Additionally, there is no specific clarification from the CJEU.

---

[38] Republic of Poland v. PL Holdings Sàrl, Judgment of the Court (Grand Chamber) (26 October 2021) Case C-109/20, para 54.

[39] UNCTAD (2004).

In the current situation, it seems that everyone expects to hear certain statements from the CJEU and so practitioners and scholars start taking it as granted that arbitration clauses in intra-EU Investor State Contracts generally have to be viewed as invalid.

However, given the facts and circumstances presented so far, this conclusion cannot be easily reached. As of now, the milestones leading to today's situation have been addressed as well as the reactions of courts and tribunals to illustrate the reality.

Gaining an understanding of the milestones and the reactions is crucial to assess how the developments in the CJEU's jurisprudence to close all gaps have evolved. But it also goes to show the current situation in intra-EU ISDS, which is one of confusion, lack of certainty and riddled with inconsistencies.

The damage for established investors resulting from this status of legal uncertainty is significant: an award in favor of investors may be set aside by courts of the EU Member States, which would result in having to bear the extensive costs of arbitration, even in case of success.

Even if no dispute has arisen so far from an investment, the CJEU's backlash also creates a significant lack of protection for established as well as new investors.

These assessed "milestones" are more than just that. They represent years of arbitration, litigation and economic uncertainty for investors. They represent millions of Euros of expenditure for investors and states on legal proceedings. And most of all, each milestone caused further legal uncertainty for established and new investors.

6 Alternative Means Of Protection?

Given the retrograde developments in traditional intra-EU ISDS, the question must be raised concerning which additional means of protection investors can resort to.

6.1 Investment Planning

Some investors may be in the advantaged position to maximize their investment protections, and their ability to enforce arbitral awards rendered against an EU Member State, by selectively choosing a nationality that is not affected by the decisions regarding intra-EU arbitration proceedings.

The line between legitimate investment planning and forum shopping, or even abuse of rights, is not always clear. Nationality planning requires that one or more subsidiaries of an investor are based outside of the EU in their investment structure.[40] This could grant access to the protection of one or more BITs signed between

[40] Dolzer and Schreuer (2012), pp. 53, 54.

the subsidiary's State of incorporation, being a non-EU State, and the EU Member State ("extra-EU BITs"). The jurisdiction of arbitral tribunals under extra-EU BITs, and the enforcement of awards rendered under them, are not expressly affected by the CJEU's jurisprudence.

Nonetheless, such a strategy is still not risk-free, as neither the Commission nor the EU Courts have directly addressed the issue of compatibility with EU law in this scenario. Additionally, EU Member States could still refuse to enforce any awards which averted the CJEU jurisprudence on the grounds of an *ordre public* violation.

Ideally, such review is done at the time of investment planning, at which point an investor can consider the potential tax, foreign investment protection, and other consequences of various proposed structures. However, notwithstanding that no strategy is risk-free, EU investors who have already invested in EU Member States may still be able to mitigate risk by restructuring their investments in an attempt to rely on the protection of one or more extra-EU BITs. This approach, however, requires that the facts or circumstances giving rise to a dispute have not arisen or become foreseeable at the time of the restructuring.

6.2 Multilateral Investment Court

The crucial idea behind a Multilateral Investment Court ("MIC"), or an Intra-EU-Investment Court for that matter, is to create a central forum in which investors can exercise their rights granted by any applicable investment treaty. In case of an MIC, this forum would be established by states within a newly developed and self-standing international court system, such as the European Court of Human Rights ("ECtHR") or the CJEU itself.[41] While the European Commission is one of the major critics of ISDS, it does not intend to abolish investment protection within the EU. The Commission is a driving force behind the modernization process of the ECT and in particular its alignment with the Paris Agreement on sustainability goals.

However, it may suffice to say that such a court system as envisaged is an aliud to the system of investment protection as we know from the past and outside of the EU. It would require immense effort and broad agreement between states to develop such a court system, both financially as well as politically. In particular, a new enforcement system would have to be developed, as court decisions cannot be enforced in reliance on the New York Convention or ICSID Convention.[42]

Thus, as of now, ISDS in the form of an MIC is a vague idea rather than a concrete concept appearing on the horizon.

[41] Scheu (2022), p. 28.

[42] Müller (2022), pp. 254 et. seq.

6.3 *National Courts*

The main criticism of the CJEU is that arbitral tribunals may have to decide on EU law without having any means to ask the CJEU for a preliminary ruling, as they are no "court or tribunal of a Member State" per the meaning of Article 267 of the Treaty on the Functioning of the European Union ("TFEU"). This raises the question whether domestic courts may offer a suitable forum to solve investor-state-disputes.

The CJEU's decision in *PL Holdings* demonstrates the conviction that investors within the EU should resort to domestic courts to resolve their investment disputes. The CJEU will then act as the guardian angel of due process and ensure the outcome is compatible me with EU law.

This is (only) a viable option, amongst others, if the investment standards and their substantive and procedural protection are equal or at least comparable.

6.3.1 Substantive Protection

A side-by-side comparison of investment law and EU law shows that both regimes have a different mode of operation to promote the flow of investment between states. Traditional international investment law contains various standards of protection for foreign investors.

In contrast, there is no comprehensive EU policy specifically devoted to 'investment' within the understanding of the term in international investment law. The investment-related rules of EU law are diffused within the legal framework of the internal market. These rules are spread among primary and secondary EU law, the European Charter of Fundamental Rights ("CFR"), national law and the European Convention on Human Rights ("ECHR").[43] In sum, these rules are supposed to create a "Comprehensive system of economic freedom". However, EU law not only liberalizes investments, but also regulates them in many instances.

Some examples:

Expropriation

Concerning expropriation, there is a difference between EU law and investment law with regard to the concept of ownership, which is narrower in EU law than in in investment law.[44] Further differences are the scope of the concept of ownership and the hurdles for establishing indirect expropriation.[45] Overall, the protection of property under investment law goes slightly further than its EU law counterpart. This is particularly true in connection with indirect expropriation.

---

[43] Cf. Taton and Croisant (2019), pp. 79–80.

[44] Cf. Taton and Croisant 2019), pp. 89–94.

[45] Taton and Croisant (2019), p. 92.

Fair and Equitable Treatment

The Fair and Equitable Treatment Standard ("FET") encompasses fundamental values of the rule of law, which are also recognized, albeit only partially codified, in EU law. Particularly relevant are the case groups of the right to a fair trial, an effective judicial hearing and the protection of the investor's legitimate expectations.

The exact extent of the FET standard will, however, strongly depend on the provision of the respective treaty. If the FET provision is understood in such a way that it does not go much beyond the minimum standard required by international law, one will probably conclude that the protection afforded by EU law goes further than that provided for in investment law.[46] Many FET provisions, however, have not been interpreted as narrowly. In a broader understanding of FET, the concept in investment protection treaties is probably to be considered as broader than the comparable principles in EU law.

Umbrella Clauses

Umbrella clauses do not find a counterpart under EU law, neither do provisions providing for the standard of Full Protection and Security ("FPS"). However, EU Member States must prevent any type of action which constitute a barrier for the free flow of goods, even if conducted by private parties.[47] Thus, at least for the FPS Standard, EU law may even offer a higher standard of protection.

6.3.2 Procedural Protection

The procedural protection offered by arbitral tribunals is the body of accepted case law which established a system of "soft precedent". While domestic courts would be obliged to follow the jurisprudence of the CJEU regarding EU law, they are not required to follow the decision of a court of another Member State.[48] Hence, consistency can only be reached if an investor fought through multiple national instances and awaited a preliminary ruling by the CJEU, which is associated with an excessive burden both in terms of time and money.

In addition, choosing the arbitral tribunal is an expression of the equal footing investors and states have in arbitration. The voice of both investors and states in this choice is part of the procedural protection. Before national courts, or even before an MIC, the investors' case is heard by a body selected and paid for by the State.

[46] Cf. Taton and Croisant (2019), pp. 99–107.

[47] Cf. Judgment of the Court (9 December 1997) Case C-265/95; also cf. Taton and Croisant (2019), p. 87.

[48] They can only be compelled through reason, cf. Schreuer (1974), pp. 681–708.

With this in mind, one may arrive at a single, striking conclusion: Identical protection through domestic courts is a fiction. This is not just in the case of violations of the rule of law. Arbitration is an aliud to domestic court proceedings and not interchangeable without losing many of its benefits.

7 Conclusions

To conclude this assessment, it is important to recall where ISDS once started: There was a reason for bilateral- and multilateral investment treaties. There was a reason for including arbitration clauses and taking disputes out of the national and into the international dimension. And there was a reason for according to the investor an extraordinary right, namely to sue a State in an arbitration.

However, regardless of the object and purpose of ISDS, the CJEU's backlash cannot be disregarded. This overview given has shown that there is no effective way to circumvent current court jurisprudence. Additionally, the Termination Agreement demonstrates that the EU Commission and the Member States are actively moving away from traditional ISDS within the EU. Without the political will of the EU Member States to preserve intra-EU arbitration, it is very likely that the CJEU's and Commission's position will prevail.

Nonetheless, this is time to build and not just tear down. It is important to remember why investment protection developed as it did and the need for investment protection as we knew it. Abolishing investment protection in the Intra-EU domain will be a hurdle for future investments.

Investments are needed, now more than ever. We are living in times of disruption and transition. This is not just the energy sector but all global problems. Global problems need a global approach and a global solution.

It is not by coincidence that human rights, climate change and significant issues in the energy sector have been debated at the level of investment protection and have actually received a push they would not have on a local level.

Moreover, the world as we know it is shaken and our beliefs are shaken alongside. This does not mean that we should simply abandon the benefits and the thinking behind investment protection and the use of Public International Law.

In the current situation, Public International Law is more important than ever. Investments, protection of investments, and a globally connected world still have to be considered as the cornerstone of peace.

References

Dolzer R, Schreuer C (2012) Principles of international investment law, 2nd edn. OUP, Oxford

Scheu J (2022) The idea of a multilateral investment court. In: Scheu J (ed) Creation and implementation of a multilateral investment court. Nomos, Baden-Baden, p 28 ff

Müller C (2022) Recognition and enforcement of MIC decisions. In: Scheu J (ed) Creation and implementation of a multilateral investment court. Nomos, Baden-Baden, p 254 ff

Taton X, Croisant G (2019) Judicial protection of investors in the European Union: the remedies offered by investment arbitration. The European Convention on Human Rights and EU Law. IJAL 7(2):9–80

Schreuer C (1974) The authority of international judicial practice in domestic courts. ICLQ 23(4): 681–708

UNCTAD (2004) State contracts. In: UNCTAD series on issues in international investment agreements. United Nations Publication, New York, Geneva. Available at https://unctad.org/system/files/official-document/iteiit200411_en.pdf

Intra-EU Investment Mediation as an Alternative?

Catherine Kessedjian

Contents

Abstract There are many impediments to the use of mediation in investment matters. However, none are unsurmountable. The increased use of mediation would necessitate reforms internal to the host state. UNCITRAL texts adopted in the summer of 2023, hopefully, will help.

1 Introduction

The journey I am proposing you to join, at the end of this conference, resembles a visit one pays to a gallery or a museum: when you enter a room full of paintings, first you have a bird's view to grasp the extent to which you will have to stay in the room, the coherence of what is shown, the empty spaces when a painting is on loan or being restored (and the frustration you feel when you discover this is your favorite painting). Then you approach each piece one by one, and compare it with its neighbors. Finally, you decide which one you prefer and which one you will come back to see.

What is the big picture on mediation in Europe? What about investment mediation? What are the missing pieces? Is mediation really an alternative as suggested by

C. Kessedjian (✉)
University Paris-Panthéon-Assas, Paris, France
e-mail: catherine.kessedjian@u-paris2.fr

M. Bungenberg, A. Reinisch (eds.), *New Frontiers for EU Investment Policy*, Special Issue, https://doi.org/10.1007/978-3-031-41977-5_10

the title of this presentation? Here are the four questions that I will cover for you today.

2 What Is the Big Picture on Mediation in Europe?

In comparison with Asia, Africa and North America, for different reasons in each case, Europe has embraced mediation fairly late. Without diving deep into history, the concept of access to justice in Europe as conceived in the middle of the twentieth century, with the European Convention on Human Rights, did not include mediation. And when the Founding Fathers of the European Economic Community thought of what would be needed to enhance legal certainty for the free circulation in the common/single market, they had in mind judgments and awards but nothing else. This is not to say that mediation or conciliation was unknown at all, but it was simply not considered as a proper mechanism at least for economic disputes.

Later in the history of the European Community and then the European Union, mediation was considered as falling outside the EU competence and there was nothing the Union could do to favor recourse to mediation since the Member States were sovereign on that issue.

At the turn of the twenty-first century, there was a shift in European policy and ADR was finally on the radar of the Commission and the Parliament. That led to the adoption, among others, of the mediation directive in 2008.[1] This is a text "a minima" i.e. only providing encouragements to the Member States and specifying a very small number of uniform provisions, the most important of them being the suspension of the statute of limitations when a mediation is commenced (article 8). The directive is limited to civil and commercial matters in transborder cases.[2] However, its philosophy may be of help in other cases, *mutatis mutandis*.

The use of mediation does not impair the right of the parties to access justice.[3] Therefore, it can be used not only at the outset of the dispute, but also and probably more usefully, later when the dispute has sufficiently matured to allow the parties to have a better knowledge of the strength and weaknesses of their case and conduct a proper "reality check".

It is probably fair to say that the use of mediation is now strongly encouraged by European authorities, at least for civil and commercial matters. A question remains

[1] Directive 2008/52/EC of the European Parliament and of the Council of 21 May 2008 on certain aspects of mediation in civil and commercial matters, *OJ L 136, 24.5.2008, pp. 3–8.*

[2] We should not forget that UNCITRAL did work on conciliation in early days and more recently on mediation. The recents texts adopted under UNCITRAL auspices have preferred mediation over conciliation. See 2018 UNCITRAL Model Law on International Commercial Mediation and International Settlement Agreements Resulting from Mediation and the United Nations Convention on International Settlement Agreements Resulting from Mediation (New York, 2018) (the "Singapore Convention on Mediation").

[3] This is an important element to remember when we will address the last question.

as to the regulation policy concerning mediation. Should it be more regulated than it is at present? I am not convinced it should. If it is, I would plead for a fairly light regulation, because the beauty of mediation is its flexibility. Parties and mediators should be imaginative and think out of the box. It is a process and not a procedure; as such it is not as rigid as court or arbitration. Apart from public policy there is nothing that prevents parties to agree on innovative solutions. The only role of the mediator is getting the parties to say "yes". Some mediators are more hands on than others (some do propose solutions) although this is not usually the role of a mediator but more that of a conciliator.

Having said that, let's turn now to investment mediation.

3 What Is the Picture of Investment Mediation?

Investment mediation faces some specific hurdles that legislation or regulation may not alleviate.

The research conducted for the paper prepared for the Academic Forum[4] showed that several obstacles may hinder the use of mediation in investment disputes. Among them, the recurring identified difficulty was, on the part of the State (defendant) a perceived advantage of arbitration. Indeed, it seems easier for a State to pay X amount of money by virtue of a binding award, than to voluntarily pay the same amount out of negotiation. Refining this general identified difficulty, we found out that it has many causes:

(a) The civil servants in charge of the negotiation are not often at the highest level of the hierarchy in the State although this is always what mediators want to have in order to facilitate the power to say yes.
(b) It is rare to have around the negotiating table the persons representing the State who have the power to settle. The ones negotiating have to constantly refer to their hierarchy. This takes time. The message gets lost in the way up the hierarchy.
(c) The ones negotiating fear being held liable for what could be considered as poor results of the negotiation.
(d) The administrative structure of the State may oblige several agencies to deal with the negotiations and the coordination of them can reveal to be problematic. But there is nothing that international law can do about all of this. Perhaps the Advisory Center that is now discussed in the UNCITRAL, if it is ever created, could help States in structuring their administration in a manner that would help the recourse to mediation.

[4] Academic Forum on ISDS (2020), Concept Paper 2020/16, 24 Feb. 2020 available on the Forum website. Also published 12 July 2022, in *Journal of International Dispute Settlement,* see Kessedjian et al. (2022).

(e) Politically, the State may have difficulties explaining why it preferred to negotiate instead of going to arbitration or court.
(f) Legally speaking the heightened level of confidentiality in mediation may be another obstacle. However, this is easier to answer since confidentiality may be organized to allow the State to conduct public consultation or consultation of the Parliament (or any other entity) if its political system obliges the State to do so. At UNCITRAL, the possibility to have a transparency rule in the text on mediation was discussed. That would be indispensable if one considers the strict confidentiality requirements that usually applies to mediation as is exemplified by the European Directive of 2008.[5]
(g) Finally, there are always doubts as to potential corruption that lures around when negotiation is concerned.

As I said before, these are obstacles that, apart from confidentiality, are not easy to answer from the point of view of international law. I am not entirely certain that the mediation rules and guidelines that were discussed at UNCITRAL would actually fulfill the function of facilitating the use of mediation. In my view, adding more cumbersome procedural rules is not what we need. We need a strong political will from the part of States. We need to strengthen the Rule of Law with a view to respect the right of constituencies to know what the government does, the stake of the negotiations and what consequences may ensue. This is why, what we need is more capacity building for States (whatever the size) to put in place the proper political, administrative, legal environment that will support the recourse to mediation, facilitate the negotiation and, if successful, facilitate the application of the settlement.

4 What Are the Missing Pieces?

The big missing piece in Europe is the accession of the EU (and/or its Members States) to the Singapore Convention.[6] Not that I am an unconditional fan of the Convention. It is not an ideal text, but it has the merit to exist and to fulfill at least the goal to facilitate, hopefully, the enforcement of settlement agreements. I say "hopefully" because the Convention includes too many ways for a disgruntled party to oppose enforcement.[7] Therefore, the real positive impact of the Convention will occur only if courts or authorities charged to decide on oppositions to the enforcement of the settlement will exercise self-restraint.

[5] See also Rule 10.2 of ICSID Mediation Rules.

[6] The United Nations Convention on International Settlement Agreements resulting from Mediation was adopted in December 2018 under the auspices of UNCITRAL. It entered into force on 12 September 2020. As of the first of December 2022, it was signed by 55 countries and ratified by 10. None of the European Union Member States have signed it.

[7] See Article 5 which includes 8 main reasons to oppose the enforcement.

Until now, none of the Western World has signed the Convention, including none of the European Union Member States. Why is it that the European Union (and its Member States) are so reluctant to access to the Convention? It is very difficult to say in the absence of any official statement from the EU authorities. The fact that it may be a mixed agreement (one that needs both the Union and its Members States action) is not the answer. There is perhaps some distrust of the mediation process. It is true that it is a private means of dispute resolution, but so is arbitration. Consequently, this should not be the reason. It is also true that there is no scrutiny or control of who acts as a mediator. However, this is also true for arbitrators with far more stringent consequences since an award is a binding document whether or not the party who loses agrees with the result. To the contrary, mediation is much safer since none of the parties is obliged to sign the settlement agreement and without signature, no agreement exists. Party autonomy is a very strong component of mediation as it is in international commerce. Therefore, there should not be so much distrust.

There is a final aspect of mediation which should not be overlooked: that is the fact that using mediation has a cost to the development of the law. Indeed, nothing can be drawn in terms of rules, policies and regulation from settlements. I am ready to recognize that this may be an impediment to use mediation in a field that is still developing as investment law is. However, States have the power to develop that body of law either in their internal legislation or via new BITs or multilateral agreements. Thus, mediation should not be a major impediment in this respect.

The second missing piece is in the BITs. Most BITs say nothing about mediation, even those which provide a cooling off period.[8] The future texts to be adopted at UNCITRAL may be used to fill that gap. Indeed, if the agreements negotiated by the EU with third countries such as Canada (CETA) are to be considered as a good precedent,[9] the section on mediation is quite strong and may lead the way to a better understanding of its value in investment matters. Of course, there is no need to duplicate what already exists and future BITs or equivalent agreements could provide a reference to existing rules.[10] However, international agreements must make clear to the parties that mediation is an important step in the resolution of investment disputes and that the political will is clearly in favor of increasing and encouraging its use.

It is time to turn to the last question announced at the outset of this contribution.

5 Is Mediation Really an Alternative as Suggested by the Title of This Presentation?

At present, the simple answer is "no", but it should become the favorite means of dispute resolution also in investment matters, particularly in all the recent cases where an award has been annulled because of the *Achmea* decision and its progeny.

---

[8] This was another finding of the Academic Forum Concept Paper mentioned above.

[9] We realize that this may be of no help for internal EU purposes.

[10] See Article 4 of the Draft UNCITRAL Mediation Rules.

Investors should certainly seize that opportunity so that they do not embark again in a lengthy and extremely onerous litigation.

What is needed to make mediation the preferred mean of dispute resolution in the field?

First, we should remember that mediation is an additional mean of dispute resolution, not an alternative or a substitute. It is complementary to the more traditional ways of access to justice whether by way of arbitration or courts.

Second, mediation is available at all times:[11]

(a) before the dispute crystalizes,
(b) at an early stage before the proceedings are commenced,
(c) during the proceedings (arbitrators and judges must be alert to mediation windows),
(d) after the proceedings to organize the enforcement of the judgment or the award.

Parties and adjudicators alike must be alert to mediation so that they use it in the best manner possible within other means of dispute resolution. Mediation may also be used as a preventive tool. This is particularly important in investment matters because there are large interests at stake. Both investors and States should be aware from the outset that investments must be monitored carefully in order to avoid disputes to escalate. Mediation tools are very useful also in that respect.

Third, if mediation is commenced before a court or arbitral tribunal is seized of the matter, applicable limitation periods must be stopped so that parties do not feel compelled to rush to court or arbitration.

Fourth, if mediation is commenced while a court case or an arbitral proceeding is ongoing, parties should be entitled to a suspension, for a reasonable amount of time, so that they could concentrate on the mediation process in order to give it its best chance.

Fifth, there was a long discussion (*again*) at UNCITRAL on whether the recourse to mediation should be left entirely to the will of the parties or whether it should be mandatory.[12] To me, this is a non-issue because all mediators will tell you that even if mandatory, the only obligation to the parties is to go to the first meeting and do nothing more. The real issue is whether the parties are willing to negotiate in good faith or not. If they do, whether mediation is mandatory or not will have no impact. If they don't, whether mediation is mandatory or not will have no impact either because the parties have an inherent right to leave the mediation process at any point in time without having to justify their walkout.

[11] The time has ended when mediation was considered only before access to court or arbitration. Escalation clauses in contracts or treaties must be drafted differently to allow the use of mediation at any point in time when it is useful. Each case is special and will require careful analysis of the exact timing when mediation will be at its best.

[12] However, the latest status of the discussion shows that there is a preference for a non-mandatory process.

Sixth, it is often said that mediation is quicker and less expensive than court proceedings or arbitration.[13] Although true, this argument should not be the main reason for the parties to choose mediation. If that is the motivation, and parties are not ready to assess anew their actions and propose changes in the management and enforcement of the investment, mediation will be a failure.

Seventh, mediation needs a different mindset than court or arbitration. This is the reason why mediation is not proper for all cases and all parties. There are cases in which it would be a loss of time and effort to try mediation. It is not a panacea for a failed court or arbitration system. However, with the proper mindset and an imaginative mediator, the process may work marvels.

Eighth, confidentiality should be adapted to the specificities of investment mediation. Mediation is often more confidential than arbitration. However, because investment often concerns public or general interest, and because public money will be used to pay out a settlement when agreed, a certain degree of transparency should be provided for. The right balance between confidentiality and transparency is not a new controversy but in investment matters it is taking a certain amount of priority. This is probably the trickiest issue in the field, one that must be discussed much more than it is presently. The Mauritius Convention must be analyzed carefully in order to see whether it is adaptable to mediation. If it is not, it is certainly a worthy exercise to negotiate a Mauritius Convention bis just for mediation.

Ninth, mediation fulfills different goals than court and arbitration proceedings fulfill. Mediation allows for a more peaceful solution to a dispute than court or arbitration can. When successful, mediation allows parties to continue working together, by, for example, rearranging their working methods, planning new goals. In fact, the future relation of the parties is an integral part of the solutions crafted by a settlement agreement. Mediation is future oriented. It is not so much about repairing the past than planning and preparing the future.

Reference

Kessedjian C, van Aaken A, Lie R, Mistelis L, Reis JM (2022) Mediation in future investor-state dispute settlement. J Int Dispute Sett 14(2):192–212. https://doi.org/10.1093/jnlids/idac015

[13] This is the main argument put forward by a number of documents on mediation such as the ICSID Rules or the draft rules prepared by UNCITRAL.